Treasure in
Earthen Vessels

THE UNIVERSITY OF QUEENSLAND PRESS
SCHOLARS' LIBRARY

Treasure in Earthen Vessels

Protestant Christianity in New South Wales Society 1900~1914

Richard Broome

University of Queensland Press

© University of Queensland Press, St Lucia, Queensland 1980

Typeset by University of Queensland Press
Printed and bound by Silex Enterprise & Printing Co., Hong Kong

Distributed in the United Kingdom, Europe, the Middle East, Africa, and the Caribbean by Prentice-Hall International, International Book Distributors Ltd, 66 Wood Lane End, Hemel Hempstead, Herts., England.

Published with the assistance of the Publications Committee at La Trobe University, Melbourne.

National Library of Australia
Cataloguing-in-Publication data

Broome, Richard Laurence, 1948-
    Treasure in earthen vessels.

    Index
    Bibliography
    ISBN 0 7022 1525 2

    1. Church and social problems - New South Wales - Protestant church. 2. New South Wales - Social life and customs. I. Title.

261.1'09944

Contents

Publisher's Note

As the costs of labor-intensive book production have risen astronomically over the past few years, it has become increasingly difficult to produce short print run scholarly books at a reasonable price. This book is the first in a series designed by the University of Queensland Press to make available such reference and specialist works.

Books in the series will be set on an IBM Electronic Composer and of necessity certain refinements, such as superscript footnote numbers and costly jackets, will be replaced by cheaper substitutes. Ordinarily they will not be stocked by booksellers and may be obtained by writing directly to the publisher.

The University of Queensland Press hopes that its Scholars' Library will be recognized by the scholarly and specialist community as a genuine effort to preserve the important role of the specialist book.

Acknowledgments

Many people in various ways have assisted in the formulation of this book. In particular the Methodist and Congregational churches of New South Wales must be thanked for permission to use their archives in the Mitchell Library. A great debt is owed to the staff of the Mitchell Library, the Archives Office of New South Wales, and the Library of New South Wales where much of the research for this project was undertaken. My appreciation must also be shown to Professor Jack Gregory for his encouragement, and Professor Ken Cable and especially Dr Heather Radi for their suggestions and careful criticism of various drafts of this book. Needless to say, its shortcomings are my responsibility alone. Mrs Shirley Gordon has my special thanks for the professional manner in which she executed the final typing. Lastly, without the interest, typing aid and editorial help of both my parents and my wife, Margaret Donnan, this study would never have seen the light of day. Any merits this work may have are for them.

Introduction

On a hot Saturday in Centennial Park, Sydney. on 1 January 1901, well over eighty thousand people, many of them children wearing red, white and blue rosettes, filled the morning air with the sounds of "O God Our Help in Ages Past". Appropriate prayers were followed by speeches, cheers, guns and the running-up of the new Australian flag. It was a marvellous way to herald the birth of a nation! Certainly churchmen thought so. Religion formed a significant part of the ceremony and the new Australian constitution itself contained an acknowledgment of Almighty God.

However, such optimism did not always fill the religious mind. This is a history of the Protestant churches in New South Wales in the fifteen years from 1900, a period when Protestant churchmen felt particularly ill at ease with the world. It examines the responses these men made to the difficulties they saw around them. It is a story of faith and hope, but not always charity.

In the early nineteenth century Australia was never noted as a religious society; there was too much pioneering to be done. The colonies first of all had to suffer the trials of convict and predominantly masculine influences, and were then infested by adventurers and exploiters in the form of traders, whalers, sheep entrepreneurs and later gold miners, most of whom seemed to hold religion and high culture at a discount. By the 1850s the British working class, which supplied the bulk of the first colonists to Australia, was already lost to the Church at Home, and there is no reason to believe that the sea voyage to Australia made them any more pious.(1) Australia was for much of its early history crazed with get rich quick values – after all making money was the immigrant dream! Few at all had come with a view to establishing a light on the hill, and those who did develop a vision on Australian soil usually shaped it around the idols of land, security and economic independence.

Even the colonial churches, which by the 1830s were firmly transplanted from the old world, caught the colonial lust for development and the need to display one's progress in material things. Few churchmen were content with humble and makeshift chapels, and as soon as there were a few houses a church would be erected. Church building became a major preoccupation, born of the desire to recreate the familiar in a strange land, to impress, and most disconcertingly, to compete with other Christian denominations. Rev R. W. Dale, a visiting English Congregationalist, remarked in 1887 that the colonists had built relatively more churches in two generations than the English had in twenty.(2)

As the century progressed, barbarism receded before the onslaught of development, women, middle class culture and other harbingers of respectability and religion. Australians developed a penchant for orthodoxy and conformity, no matter how radical they may have appeared in political and industrial matters. Many became convinced of the social needs of the religious rites of passage. Thus by 1900 almost all marriages in Australia were conducted by the clergy;(3) all but a few daring or indifferent parents had their children baptized; and most people mourned their dear departed from the pews of their local church. In the New South Wales census of 1901, ninety-eight per cent of the people declared themselves to be Christian — forty-six per cent were confessed Anglicans; twenty-six per cent Catholics; ten per cent each of Presbyterians and Methodists; and almost two per cent each of Congregationalists and Baptists. Non-orthodox religious adherents were infinitesimal in number.(4) Public morality was firmly based on Christian principles and only the courageous minority denied the platitude that religion was a necessary social cement. All this indicated considerable religious influence, but it was ceremonial, "once a year" religion. How many Protestants actually practised their religion once a week, let alone in daily life? Computations from church statistics reveal that by 1900 a little over thirty per cent of nominal Protestants regularly attended church services.(5) This was a considerable number and higher than contemporary attendance in England or the United States of America(6) — but stating this was cold comfort to clergy who wanted to create a Christian Australia.

The religious optimism encouraged by the Commonwealth inauguration ceremony was atypical, because the overall mood of the churches around 1900 was one of anxiety — of concern that the Church and the Age were at odds. This was not a new fear for Christians, but it was particularly acute at this time. These fears were partly illusory, conjured up by the false rosy pictures of the religious past which many church leaders held and expressed when they viewed the prospects of the new century. However, although they did exaggerate the problem, the churches were certainly running against the secular tide of history. Each scientific development seemed to chip away at God as the natural world became demystified by the works of man. The growing power of the modern state was more than a match for the Church, and as the new knowledge expanded, the Church was even forced out of education. Therefore, despite the fact that the Protestant churches still had considerable residual social power and strength, the secular forces were pressing them hard. Churchmen counted the number of heads in the pews and when they found over two-thirds of their nominal adherents missing, they were in anguish.

The thrust of this book is to examine the responses that the Protestant churches made to the inroads of secularism and the perceived loss of religious influence in the community. Their natural instinct was to extend their borders, so part of this work deals with problems of pastoral care and evangelism. Novel as well as traditional means were used in their efforts to evangelize the slums of Sydney, its suburbs, and the far back blocks of the state. The usually competitive churches even tried cooperative evangelism, while some visionaries within the churches made tangible proposals for church union. Besides extension and reorganization, the most significant moves made by the churches in response to their anxiety were first, to tackle the Catholics who they feared were making inroads into Protestantism, and second, to attempt to reform the moral evils which the Protestants believed were eating into society and turning the people from God. Unfortunately for the peace and quiet of New South Wales, the defence of Protestant truth degenerated into sectarian sniping which now became more than just the preserve of madmen and hard core bigots. Similarly, the moral reform crusade, seemingly so admirable and necessary, deteriorated into the excesses of cant and coercion which became known as wowserism. Even pastoral and evangelistic efforts contained inherent pitfalls.

Why was this so? Why had Christian exploits failed, run to excess, or turned sour? In a word, because the Protestant churches had become too embroiled in the world! This is of course the eternal problem of any religious system which has an other-world philosophy — yet has to exist in this temporal world. The Protestant embroilment in the world was specifically that they identified with a class view, instead of a Christian universalist viewpoint. Because of this, religious activity such as the espousal of Protestant truth or moral reform could be used as means to a class, not a religious end.

The social fact was that by 1900 (and well before), Protestantism was largely middle class in composition and nature. Of course the Protestant churches contained a nominal and active working class element, but the great bulk of active Protestants came from the middle class. As in England, the working class had largely abandoned Protestantism or been abandoned by it.(7) The best attended and most solidly built Protestant churches in Sydney were to be found in the outer suburbs. These were the affluent areas with the highest home-ownership rate,(8) to which the middle class had escaped from the older inner city. Here amid fresh air and open suburban space they built late Victorian and Edwardian bungalows, and enjoyed the respectability that came from neat houses and rising fortunes. Not only did these salubrious outer suburbs produce the most thriving Protestant churches, but the suburbs themselves could be classified as Protestant. Protestant numbers were ten to fifteen per cent above their state wide average concentration, while the numbers of Catholics in these areas were correspondingly up to fifteen per cent below their state average. Conversely, in the inner city areas where the bulk of the

The Religious Distribution Within Sydney and Suburbs 1901*

Above average Protestant

Above average Catholic

*See appendix 2 for percentage distribution.

working class resided, many of them in old style or dilapidated rented buildings jammed up against factories, wharves and warehouses, the Catholics were ten per cent above their state average in the population.(9) This relationship between religion and class which was reflected by residential patterns was also revealed by occupational stratification. In the 1901 state census, Protestants were over-represented in professional and skilled employment, while Catholics were under-represented in these jobs, and over-represented among labourers, domestics, farmers and the unemployed.(10) As the Catholic bishops lamented earlier in 1885: Catholics were to be found "wherever the hours are long, the climate merciless, the labour unskilled, the comforts few and the remuneration small".(11) Even by 1921, unemployment rates were highest among Catholics, and they were also under-represented among those who were employers.(12) Similarly the working class nature of Catholicism can be seen in criminal statistics. While Catholics represented only twenty-six per cent of the population, they formed forty-four per cent of all those arrested in 1901(13) — a rate not atypical in the years around 1900. The fact was that the rural, relatively uneducated background of the nineteenth century Irish immigrant meant that he experienced the lowest social mobility of all immigrants.

Protestants were over-represented in the middle class, and the most virile centres of Protestantism were in middle class areas. Again, working class Protestants were the most likely of all Protestants to stay away from church. The leading laymen tended to be prominent citizens. On top of this, the educational requirements for the clergy meant that the large majority of Protestant ministers were from middle class and higher educated backgrounds. Thus, despite the presence of working class elements, the Protestant churches were staffed, attended and controlled largely by the middle class. Protestantism was overwhelmingly bourgeois!

Therefore, the universalist Christian religion, at least in its Protestant manifestations in New South Wales around 1900, had become weighted down by the albatross of the values and mentality of one class only. Thus it was that the treasure of Christian ideals was compromised by the earthen vessel of the Protestant middle class in which it had to exist.

This history both complements and challenges the existing work of Australian historians of religion. It broadens the field laid down by J. D. Bollen's *Protestantism and Social Reform in New South Wales* by its emphasis on pastoral care, evangelism, union movements, ritualist controversies, sectarian conflict and moral reformism, all central issues to the churchmen of the time. This work also complements the fine studies of Catholicism in Australia, headed by P. J. O'Farrell. However it diverges from O'Farrell's view of Cardinal Moran and sectarianism, and challenges Bollen's argument that Protestantism's major interest around 1900 was social, not moral reconstruction.

1. The Problem of Religious Indifference

At the beginning of the twentieth century while radical and liberal Australians believed that a brave new world was emerging in the antipodes, their more conservative minded compatriots were inclined to believe that the world was becoming worse. The liberal looked to the new social legislation of factory acts, old age pensions, industrial arbitration, votes for women and the establishment of a minimum wage. Federation was now a reality, so what could possibly stop Australia from becoming a glorious and prosperous nation? Schools, churches, town halls, trams, trains and all the joys of civilization spread out from the cities to the dusty streets of new suburbs. Gas and electricity revolutionized home and industrial work. Life was becoming easier! Yet, on the other hand, the 1890s had been racked by unprecedented strikes; the worst economic depression since the 1840s; and from 1895 to 1903, the greatest drought New South Wales had ever known. Unemployment was still at six per cent in the early years of the century, and as prices of commodities rose with the drought, real wages fell far below the levels of the pre-1890 period. Besides all this, the political scene was in a state of flux, with the newly emerged Labour Party of the 1890s becoming the effective opposition by 1904. The conservatives viewed this as creeping socialism which threatened to end individual enterprise. All these upheavals, changes and troubles, appeared to many to mark the end of an era of prosperity and stability — an impression no doubt symbolized by the death in 1901 of Queen Victoria after a reign of over sixty years. Thus two views existed regarding the state and future of the country.

As many Protestants were evangelicals and the bulk of them middle class political conservatives, they generally adopted a pessimistic stance. Modern life seemed to them to be moving against the way they viewed the world. Not only was the nature of politics changing but the moral order was endangered. The latest craze in the early 1900s was mixed sea bathing, which to many was an outrage. In 1904 moral laxity appeared to be proven by the report of the Royal Commission on the birth-rate which alleged that the blasphemous and malicious practice of contraception was widespread. Others claimed that drunkenness, gambling and vice were rampant. Rev W. M. Dill Macky caught this mood when he lamented to the Presbyterian Assembly in 1900 that "Sabbath desecration — impurity and vice seem to me to be on the increase in spite of all our efforts."(1) It was the old but potent lament of the moral improvers and conservatives who were affronted by the barbarism they perceived in Australian society. Many Protestants believed that the crux of all these difficulties was that the modern age was one of religious indifference – that too many people were apart from God! This too was an old fear, but its age made it no less virile.

Around 1900, the prevailing mood within Protestantism, especially among clerics, was one of anxiety. Naturally, this view was not totally or consistently held. The Baptists who were the most inward looking and sect minded, and thus insulated from secular trends and influences, were often optimistic and shunned "those who tell us the world is getting worse".(2) The liberal-minded Congregationalists disdained those who wallowed in "pallid-hearted panic". Of the other churches, the Methodists were heartened by their rapid growth in recent generations, while the Presbyterians and Anglicans often took comfort in the strength of their long church histories.(3) However, the pervading tone of clerical addresses at annual church meetings, of countless sermons and church press editorials, was that religion was at a low ebb. Bishop Thornton of Ballarat, who presided over the 1898 Anglican Church Congress, declared that "below the surface, Australian town life is stained deep with intemperance, profanity and lust; even – it is terrible to record – among our children".(4) Bishop Cooper told the Grafton–Armidale synod in 1904, that while there was a cycle of ebb and flow of religion, "at the present time it is generally agreed that the tide is low".(5) Rev R. Bavin, the retiring Methodist President, told the 1904 conference that national vice was increasing while church going was decreasing, and he wondered whether Australia was a religious nation after all.(6) The Congregationalist leader, Rev J. Fordyce, called for no less than a complete restatement of Christian doctrine and the nature of the Church, if Christianity was to regain its authority over society and the unchurched.(7) The great catch-cry of the clergy was that a revival of religion was needed.

It appeared that the church press competed for the distinction of giving the gloomiest forecast of the religious condition of the people. The *Methodist* in typical evangelical fashion, proclaimed that "the tendency in all human things is deterioration, and this had been seen in the Church as well as elsewhere", because the Church is further apart from the world than previously.(8) The Anglican *Church Standard* also typically stated that "there is a comparatively small percentage of the community who do regularly attend Divine Service on Sunday, yet they are after all only a select few; a remnant, as it were, when compared with the vast masses who spend the day in idleness or pleasure seeking".(9) Though the evangelicals were most inclined to see things in a pessimistic light, even the high church Anglican journal, the *Church Commonwealth*, commented that "it cannot be denied that of those professing to belong to the Church only a small percentage systematically attend Divine Service, and that this percentage is decreasing".(10) The realization that Australian society was becoming secularized and the churches were no longer of concern to the majority, was dawning on most churchmen by 1900.

Those who actually tried to count heads believed that about twenty to thirty per cent of the population attended church regularly, and that this proportion was diminishing. Religious indifference was of course not a new problem, but many clergy, especially the older ones who looked nostalgically back on their own religious upbringing, believed indifference was growing. Archbishop Smith, the Anglican Primate, said bluntly that the people had "forgotton God" and that ninety per cent were indifferent to religion.(11) No doubt the increasing pace of modern society encouraged others to accept this "decline mentality". They saw the world around them in a state of flux, an age "of immense mental activity, or bewildering advance in all directions . . . an age where the energies of men are strained to the utmost in commerce, in political and in social life".(12) Materialism and hedonism seemed to be the dominant values, because the bulk of the people preferred to picnic or laze in bed of a Sunday, instead of attending church. One Methodist layman lamented that even Christians "are too often as eager for a full cup of fleshy gratification as the mere worldling".(13) However, business and civic obligations as well as pleasure, kept people away from church services and meetings.

Most clergy were quick to recognize that it was worldliness and indifference rather than intellectual opposition which kept the people from church. "A careless, idle negligence" and "a listless apathy" were some of the phrases that clergymen reached for in describing their apathetic brethren.(14) Fordyce made one of the clearest statements of this view, when he told a meeting of the Evangelical Alliance in 1900, that "the vast mass of what is sometimes called intellectual opposition to Christianity is simply moral and spiritual indifference. This is, I admit, one of the deadliest forms of opposition, but it is not intellectual, and it cannot be reached by mere argument. It is simply dull, leaden, unspiritual inertia, and it becomes vocal only when it seeks to ward off attack or to justify its own attitude. And then its speech is largely make-believe. It may use the catch-words of intellectual unbelief, but it uses them not intelligently, or with conviction, but simply to justify its own attitude".(15) Compared to the more genuine opposition of sincere intellectual unbelief, indifference would prove to be a difficult problem for the clergy — perhaps as deadly as a wrestle with old Satan himself.

This Protestant anxiety was not confined to Australia, but was also prevalent in England, where the religious mind similarly lamented that Christianity was in decline.(16) Rudyard Kipling voiced this general concern in his poem "The Recessional", which he wrote in 1897. Kipling begged Britons not to turn their backs on their Maker, lest the Empire decline:

> God of our fathers, known of old,
> Lord of our far-flung battle line,
> Beneath whose awful Hand we hold
> Dominion over palm and pine —
> Lord God of Hosts, be with us yet,
> Lest we forget — lest we forget!

The insecurities of the English Protestant clergy were prominently featured (like all other English religious news), in the Australian religious press, and they added to the local anxieties. Indeed, the Australian press was often gloomier, because a typical rider to an English lament was that "in Australia the state of things is probably 10 per cent worse".(17)

However, internal factors were more important than the overseas influence in formulating this anxiety. The general economic and political tensions in New South Wales society in the 1890s and early 1900s, were quite important in creating pessimism among the middle class and Protestants. The turn of the century also encouraged long forecasts and reassessments, and the churches were forced to look at the realities of religion in a growing secular society. Empty pews in their churches and the secular tone of much of the world around them could not be ignored.

The publication of the census in 1901 was one of the most notable instances which forced the clergy to confront the bare facts of their hold over the community. While there was some initial supercilious satisfaction at the slight decline of the proportion of Catholics in the population, Protestant clergy expressed alarm at the vast difference between their nominal strength and those actually attending church. Congregationalists regretted the loss of some members to Anglicanism, and Methodist spokesmen believed that Methodism had not kept pace with suburban growth.(18) However, it was the Presbyterians who expressed the most sustained alarm. Two years before the census, the then current Moderator of the Presbyterian church, Rev J. Burgess, had expressed great dismay that his church was only in contact with 70,000 of the 130,000 nominal Presbyterians in the state.(19) Correspondents to the Presbyterian newspaper only marginally disagreed with his figures and all were upset that the "lost Presbyterians" formed sixty per cent of all nominal Presbyterians.(20) The census revived these fears and caused the *Messenger* to remark that "it would be optimism of the silliest kind to imagine that even one third of these [nominal adherents] are strongly gripped by Christian principles or are true in any high sense to the Christian faith".(21) Rev J. Walker who was the Moderator in 1902, stated that 50,000 Presbyterians never attended church! To counteract this, he called for a large amount of money to finance a massive building programme to provide 28,000 more seats in churches and the necessary number of ministers to man them. Above all, Walker pleaded for a new religious spirit among Presbyterians, who must "see the careless, the supercilious, the religiously indifferent, face to face, and for their soul's sake, for Christ's sake, with tact, sympathy and courage, have it out with them, and at least excite their interest".(22) Not only the Presbyterians, but all the Protestants, expressed a sense of urgency at this time about capturing the indifferent. Their assessment of the census figures encapsulated the general unease felt by concerned Protestants about the social changes around them and forced them to look about and to confront the great gap between things as they were and as they might be.

Apart from the problem of the numbers of the flock outside the fold, churchmen were worried by deficiencies and changes within the churches themselves. These shortcomings ranged from large questions to trivialities. The problems of inadequate manpower and insufficient finance were central to the churches' difficulties and these will be discussed in the next chapter. The clergy were perpetually engrossed in administration and fund raising, so much so, that some pleaded that they were "in danger of being hustled out of their spirituality by the business routine and the social matters they are expected to attend to".(23) A growing minority urged denominational cooperation and unity instead of fierce competition between churches, to overcome these problems of resources. Perhaps on a lesser level, there were complaints about the nature of church services, although this was an important issue to those who had to sit through them. On hot summer days, many found sermons longer than half an hour a trial, while the older generation complained that sermons were now too short and not as good as they used to be. The clergy were also chastised for not visiting their adherents often enough, or not visiting the right ones. Other complaints focused on numerous liturgical matters, the absence or presence of church music, particular hymn books, clerical clothing, choirs, extempore prayer and "amens".

Some believed that private devotional life was on the decline. The former practice of family prayers and Bible reading was said to now be fading away. Clergy complained that people only read collections of biblical tit-bits and commentaries and not the Bible itself. The more rigid criticized those who lounged and were inattentive in church, or the young who giggled and flirted in the back pews. The older generation also lamented the increasing tendency to attend only one service, not two, on Sundays. Similarly, the Wednesday night meetings were struggling to maintain adequate numbers. One Methodist layman was so concerned that he personally paid for several thousand copies of a pamphlet entitled, "The Revival of the Week-Night Service" and had them distributed. Clergymen tried to introduce changes to win people back to the Wednesday service, but even here secularization drove relentlessly on. Rev W. Allen began discussion sessions, but found that it was difficult "to keep discussion on spiritual and off polemical lines".(24) Only by the introduction of a myriad of social clubs with a religious tinge, did the churches hold the interest of many churchgoers through the week. The criticisms of the churches were thus numerous; yet many were only harmless wistful thoughts. Congregationalists resented the increasing centralization within their church, Methodists debated the merits of fixed orders of service, low church Anglicans were worried about popish ornaments being introduced into their parishes, while high Anglicans wanted more frills and weekly communion services.

One change which was of more consequence to the clergy was that admittance to church membership was gradually becoming quicker and easier. Some feared that this would mean that churchgoers were less pious and devotional than their parents had been. Allen remarked in 1906 that "unless I greatly err, admission into a Congregational church was never so easy as it is today".(25) Even the Baptists now allowed the prospective church member to be questioned in private about Christ, salvation, and his own conversion experience, rather than in front of the whole congregation. Anglicans entered their church by infant baptism and confirmation, and yet complaints were frequent that confirmation was too much of a mere formality. Similarly, while the Book of Common Prayer had ordered that communion be only given to those who had presented "their names to the curate at least some time the day before", recent liturgical trends meant this directive had fallen into disuse and fifty per cent of Anglican churchgoers took communion weekly as a matter of course. There was now more ritual but some feared that it counted far less; that a more frequent taking of communion perhaps meant it was a less moving and sacred experience.

Increasingly it took less time and effort to become an inner church member and this trend was most marked in the Methodist church. Traditionally, Methodists only held church membership if they had experienced a spiritual conversion and attended class meetings regularly, where fervent extempore prayer and personal religious testimonies were expected. However, as the Methodists moved up and away from their working class origins and the enthusiasm of those early years, these emotional and very personal exchanges of the class meeting fell out of favour with many. Their middle class distaste for enthusiastic piety and public professions of their personal religious feelings, led to a marked decline in the class meeting by the late nineteenth century. Circuit stewards complained about the neglect of the class meeting. By 1902, only one-third of all Methodist churches and preaching places had class leaders and therefore presumably classes.(26) Many of those that still existed, barely functioned. Rev C. J. Newman rather typically reported that only four of the ninety-one enrolled members at the Parramatta church actually attended the class meeting.(27) A belatedly concerned Methodist Conference in 1902 appointed an investigating committee which reported that the pace of modern life, competition from other church societies, and the poor standard of the class meeting itself, had led to its imminent demise. Yet, it could recommend no other criterion for church membership and alluded to the potential financial value of the weekly class contributions. It urged that the class be revitalized by new methods and young blood, and that the duty of attendance be impressed on the laity, because "there must be no word of retreat, no word of giving up".(28) The Conference must have agreed, because it adopted the report. However, within a year it had reversed its decision by recommending to the General Conference of Australia that while the class be retained, church membership should depend upon repentance, faith in God and attendance at the Lord's Supper as testimony of this new life.(29) After some emotional debating, the General Conference accepted (by seventy-eight votes to twenty-nine), a wider criterion for church membership than attendance at class, by accepting as members those having "faith in the Lord Jesus Christ, their lives also being in harmony therewith".(30) At first the *Methodist* attacked this "cheapened" standard, but then performed an about face in true denominational fashion, claiming that the new membership requirements merely showed Methodism's flexibility and accord with modern trends.(31) However, this attempt to appear liberal hid a deeper unease among many Methodists.

While the most caustic attacks on the Church came from the radical press like the *Bulletin* and the *Worker*, one of the most virile critiques at this time came from within the Church. It was launched by "Anglicanus", who published a series of articles on Anglicanism in the *Daily Telegraph* in July 1900. These articles stimulated a large correspondence, mainly from enraged and defensive clerics, which "Anglicanus" successfully parried. The thrust of his attack was that Anglicanism was in decline and doing very little about it. He claimed that most Anglican bishops and clergy lacked intellectual and moral energy and were unable, or unwilling, to provide sufficient leadership to their church. Many of them were ill-trained, or rendered ineffective by old age or other difficulties. "Anglicanus" added that "many of them have no conception of the Church and her mission, and are but sorry expositors of her teaching". The clergy transmitted little enthusiasm to the laity, who in turn responded with little interest and meagre financial support. Many country parishes were too huge for the clergy to be able to reach many of their parishioners and he recommended the use of itinerant bush clergy, gospel waggons and a well prepared group of lay evangelists. The city churches fared little better, because "Anglicanus" pointed out that less than twenty per cent of Anglicans attended church; most churches were only half full;

and over 200,000 Anglicans in Sydney alone never attended church. Furthermore, Anglicanism undertook no aggressive evangelism; little organized rescue work among the poor; and showed no marked interest in social reform questions. The young were neglected, because they were poorly tutored in their catechism and ill-prepared for confirmation.

It was little wonder this spirited attack brought forth equally hostile denunciations of "Anglicanus". The *Telegraph* published census and church attendance figures in support of "Anglicanus" and believed that while his articles were somewhat exaggerated, they were in essence true and that Anglicanism was "too self-satisfied, too self-contained".(32) It is important to recognize that these criticisms were not new at the time, nor confined to Anglicanism. Indeed, these were complaints that the clergy often made themselves, although in a milder, less public, and more scattered form. The only difference was that "Anglicanus" had brought all these criticisms together, and tinged them with venom.

The clergy were usually vague about specifying whether any groups in particular predominated among the seventy per cent who they now acknowledged were beyond the bounds of organized religion. However, many did agree that it was hardest to reach men and this question was debated at length several times in the period. The argument usually revolved around whether men were careless and sinful (which was the corollary to the view of women as morally superior), or whether the fault lay with an uninteresting and unmanly clergy and Christianity.(33) Only a minority of clergy at this time suggested openly that one class in particular was more absent than others from the Protestant churches. Rev R. G. Macintyre was one who ventured an opinion and he suggested that "the difficulties of the work lie at the two extreme ends of the social scale − the rich and the poor, the selfishness of one class and the stolid indifference of the other".(34) Probably there was a shyness about using the word "class" in a society which until recently had enjoyed a good standard of living and was committed to social mobility and the egalitarian ideal; an ethos which had only been shaken in the 1890s by industrial conflict and depression. Also, the clergy were loath to admit that they had lost the working class and that their faith which had been meant for all men, had become largely a religion of the middle class and "the decent people". Certainly, an aura of respectability epitomized by the "Sunday best" surrounded churchgoing. A few fearlessly admitted this fact. Mr W. White, a leading Baptist and self-made bread manufacturer, complained that the poor "would not be welcomed by the majority of churchgoers".(35) The Presbyterian *Messenger* stated in 1906 that church "membership is mainly confined to the middle classes of the community − the Church has practically lost whatever hold it ever had on the masses of our industrial population. To the overwhelming majority it does not exist".(36) How slow the churches as a whole were to pick up this fact!

Ever since the mid-nineteenth century, the more socially aware clergy and laity had realized the Christian Church was out of touch with the working class, and perhaps had never really held them. On a practical level, English evangelicals like Lord Shaftesbury and liberals like the Christian Socialists, F. D. Maurice and Charles Kingsley, began to sympathize with, and work to alleviate, the condition of the poor and the working class. They began from different theological positions to formulate a social gospel which urged social reform to create a heaven in this world as well as the next. The evangelicals stressed the "golden rule", because all men were brothers and equals under the Fatherhood of God. On the other hand, liberals like Charles Gore stressed that men could approach God's perfection through evolutionary process, and therefore must strive for social as well as spiritual reform.

However, these ideas only penetrated Australia in the late nineteenth century, and despite J. D. Bollen's emphasis on the growth of the social gospel in the 1890s, it seems to have only influenced a mere handful of clergy.(37) Rev W. I. Carr-Smith told the Sydney branch of the Anglican Christian Social Union in 1899 that the churches "had more or less applied Christ's teachings to spiritual conditions, but they had grievously fallen short of the height of their mission when they came to consider the bodies of men, their temporal needs, their social circumstances".(38) Advocates of the social gospel argued that the churches should attempt to influence social, economic and industrial affairs. In 1901, the Methodist President, Rev W. H. Beale, urged Methodists to follow Christian Socialism and be concerned with all aspects of human affairs.(39) However, the word "socialism" and the thought of being embroiled in political questions struck terror into the hearts of most Protestants. Only a few clergy ever called themselves Christian Socialists and some of these, like Archbishop Smith, were clearly not socialists, but merely desired a socialized Christianity which would concern itself with all human affairs. Only a minority of clergymen ever accepted the social gospel in the years prior to the first world war. Most clergy came from comfortable backgrounds and worked in solidly middle class churches, so that they had limited understanding and thus sympathy for the conditions which demanded a social gospel. The Protestant view was that social reform depended on individual regeneration rather than changed social conditions. A popular Protestant dictum of the time was that "the soul of reform was the reform of the soul". This was basically a self-improving, morally self-righteous and middle class view of the world. Thus, within Protestantism as a whole around 1900, there was a lack of a strong social concern for the working class and often an unwillingness to face the problem square on. Even some of those who advocated the social gospel and special evangelism among the working class, did so, not out of a strong sense of social justice, but merely as a means of capturing the working class.(40)

The Protestant churches by 1900 were rapidly becoming suburban churches, because it was to the suburbs that the middle class and affluent had been moving since the 1870s. But so engrossed were most of the clergy in this great suburban enterprise, that most were blind to the decline of religion in the inner city. Yet if they had cared to look there, as few did, they would have realized that the bulk of the seventy per cent outside the churches were from the working class. Canon Boyce, Anglican incumbent of St Paul's, Redfern, was distressed at the exodus of the wealthy from his parish, which left it in a struggling financial state. The Methodist, Rev J. E. Carruthers, lamented that this movement of people had closed seven Methodist city churches.(41) A Methodist committee of 1898, on the condition of the inner city churches, had urged their amalgamation, to save resources, and also called for the expansion of the Central Methodist Mission to attract the working class. Unfortunately, vested interests in each local church prevented amalgamation. This attempt revealed some awareness of the working class problem, but it was largely an awareness based on fear and contempt of the working class, rather than understanding. The 1899 Wesleyan Methodist Conference issued a pastoral on the matter in the following terms: "It is surely time, too, that the wealthy and propertied class of Sydney took a more active concern (in the interests of public safety and order; to say nothing of public morals) in the attempts which are being made by Christian organizations to reach and reclaim those whose practical heathenism is a growing menace to all the best interests of our life".(42) The Presbyterians had only six churches to cater for the 7,500 nominal Presbyterians in the inner city area. Three of these were usually well attended, but mainly by suburban commuters because many travelled to the fashionable church of St Stephen's; to the Welsh community church at Chalmers Street; or to hear the Protestant champion of the day, Dill Macky breath fire at Scot's church. Therefore, this left the three other churches to cater for the bulk of the 7,500 nominal Presbyterians. But there was no great crush in church! Only ten per cent of inner city Presbyterians ever attended church services.(43)

The alienation of the working class from the Protestant churches at this time is most clearly demonstrated in the findings of an Anglican committee appointed in 1900 to investigate the condition of Anglicanism in the Sydney area. The committee consisted of Canon Boyce, temperance and social reformer; Rev Carr-Smith, liberal and professed Christian Socialist; strong evangelical Rev C. C. Dunstan, who was frank to the point of rudeness; and Rev W. Hough. The committee reflected a nice balance of interest; two evangelicals and two high churchmen, half of whom were from the inner city and half from the suburbs. Before the committee even reported, its chairman, Boyce, attacked his church for a lack of aggressive inner city work,(44) and the committee as a whole compiled its report with "a feeling of responsibility which has been deepened by the inquiries made".(45) The evidence revealed that the Church of England in the inner city was grossly undermanned and in a very poor condition. There was church seating for only a quarter of adult nominal Anglicans. However, this distressing situation was tolerable because in fact only five per cent, and in a few cases, ten per cent of the nominal Anglicans in each inner city parish ever attended church. Only a few churches thrived; St James' and Christ Church St Laurence attracted many from the suburbs with good sermons and colourful Anglo-Catholic liturgy. While the committee thought no clergyman could adequately handle more than 3,000 parishioners, the ratio of clergy to Anglicans was usually one to 10,000 and as high as one to 20,000 in the inner suburbs. It was little wonder that the clergy were able to contact personally only a few of their flock. The committee urged a massive building programme with sufficient clergy, curates and lay evangelists to match. It recommended that prime consideration be given to the poor and crowded inner city parishes "consisting almost wholly of the working class of people". Here it claimed lived the "white heathen" of Sydney, most of whom never went to church and among whom "immorality abounds and drunkenness is frequent".(46)

On the other hand, the evidence collected by this Anglican committee revealed that the Anglican churches in the outer suburbs were flourishing. Church finances were healthy and often large enough to support a curate to help the incumbent and thus reduce the clergy-parishioner ratio to reasonable proportions. Church attendances were also much stronger. In the affluent parishes of Darling Point and Neutral Bay, and also the more modest middle class parishes of Bondi, Croydon and Kogorah, between twenty and thirty per cent of adult Anglicans regularly attended church services. Vastly different to the five to ten per cent attendance in the inner city! So it can be seen that the strength of Anglicanism increased with the distance from the inner city and the working class. This was true of all the other Protestant churches whose activities were generally few in the inner city, with perhaps the exception of the Methodists. But even here, as a report on suburban Methodism by Carruthers revealed, the outer suburbs were bursting at the seams while inner city Methodism was depressed. Indeed, Sunday school enrolments and church attendance in the new and outer suburbs threatened to outpace church building and the available supply of clergy.(47) Possibly half of the middle class never darkened a church door except on ceremonial occasions, but this was a far greater proportion than the working class. Therefore, the religious problem for the Protestants in the outer suburbs was one of resources rather than stolid indifference.

The religious condition of the bush areas was less clearly defined than in the city. The problems were shaped by the vast distances and climate

as much as any perfidious tendency in man to scorn the Christian truths.
Clergy had to cover circuits and parishes, hundreds and sometimes thousands of square miles in area, on horseback or by buggy or bicycle. This
was an arduous task especially to the newly arrived English clergy. The
churches were perpetually understaffed and lacked sufficient finance
to employ more men even if they were available. The Methodist Sustentation and Home Mission Society reported in 1904 in a familiar vein
that "we lack both men and money and are compelled to turn a deaf
ear to the calls of distant places".(48) The perpetual problem was just
to reach the people, let alone any influence that might be conveyed.
However, Bishop Stanton of Newcastle believed that churchgoing in the
bush was strong.(49) Similarly, Rev W. L. Patison wrote that Congregationalists at Eccleston would leave "their work in the fields at the busiest
season to attend some church meeting".(50) Many clergy believed there
was a great spiritual thirst in the outback which would be expressed if
only the people could be reached. As Rev A. Deans (a city cleric) wrote
of a service with a bush family who had not seen a clergyman for some
years: "As we read the sacred page the Holy Ghost Himself the Comforter
spoke to us direct. We sang a simple hymn, and then the little circle was
upon its knees".(51) Others acknowledged that church attendance was
poor. Some like Bishop Cooper of Grafton and Armidale diocese claimed
that the hard, monotonous and pragmatic life style of the bush discouraged spirituality, and added that the demands of dairy farming left little
time for church.(52) A few were more sceptical. Rev W. Robertson who
had been a bush parson for thirty years remarked: "This is not a religiously inclined people. In fact they seem rather afraid they should even appear
so. One hour of public worship goes a long way."(53) Complaints concerning the gambling, intemperance and Sunday desecration of bush
dwellers were numerous from clergy and laity alike.

While the indifferent outside the churches, be they town or bush
dweller, working class or middle class, were the Church's greatest problem; especially since the publication of Darwin's *Origin of Species* in 1859,
the clergy could not take it for granted that a Christian and a churchgoer
would always remain a believer. Also, the historical investigation of the
origins of the Bible and especially the radical, so called, Higher Criticism,
similarly threw doubts on the literal truth of the Bible. Much of this
debate on the truth of the Bible was scholastic and tedious, but with the
help of the popular polemicist, all could comprehend the question of
whether the earth was created in six days, or whether Jonah could exist
within a whale's belly or whether Balaam's ass could have spoken to him
or not. If Jonah was not swallowed by a whale, or the world not created

in six days, did God Himself exist? Some groups like the Baptists and the Catholics refused to countenance the problem, while others like the Anglicans, Congregationalists and Presbyterians, prepared to face the music. Some of the clergy and the laity adjusted, but who could tell how the majority felt? The brunt of the controversy was felt in Australian in the 1880s,(54) and yet the new scientific thought and biblical criticism could still unsettle many minds well into the twentieth century.

The years around 1900 formed a transitional stage in attitudes towards the Bible and the acceptance of the new scientific knowledge and biblical criticism. The retreat of the clergy from dominance in higher education and their loss of control over knowledge in the face of the scientific revolution was now far advanced. Many clergy marvelled at scientific discoveries as much as the uninitiated, and speculated about life on other planets or the eccentricities of the earth's orbit. It was all a part of the wonder that proved to them how astounding their God was. Such was their fascination with the new knowledge, that evolutionary terminology was frequently used in the pulpit. However, despite this acceptance of the new scientific laws, many of the clergy at the same time still held a firm belief in Divine Providence. The great drought and the bubonic plague outbreak at the turn of the century were both seen by many as Divine retribution for careless and sinful behaviour. A lot of evangelicals had changed their view of the Bible, but many Methodists and Baptists still held a literal interpretation and thus found it impossible to accept evolutionary theory. In 1900, the President of the Baptist Union, Rev F. Hibberd, carefully put the conservative case. He accused the Higher Criticism of the Bible of being utterly destructive of the Christian truths, and believed the struggle had come down to "whether the Bible is God's word, or whether the Bible contains God's word". Hibberd cried out — "Who is on the Lord's side" and made no mistake in outlining that he believed it was the literal and complete word of God.(55)

In the same year, the Congregational Chairman, Rev G. Campbell, expounded a more liberal view, which supported honest scholarship. He argued that historical criticism only appeared destructive in the short term, because it would not harm, and could only enhance, "the truth of the inspiration and reality of the Divine authority of the Bible". Campbell added that "the old and long-accepted mechanical theory of verbal inspiration received its death blow at the hands of the historical critics, though it had been dying a slow but certain death, and would doubtless linger still for a long time in the heart of Christendom.(56) Certainly his last remark was prophetic. The reason that the question of the Bible's truth was not discussed a great deal by the clergy around 1900 was not because they all accepted the new ideas, but because the bulk were unskilled in discussing such problems and were unsure of the answers. They preferred to keep silent and adopt the approach of Principal Shairp who wrote:

>   . . . while the sea of doubt
> Is raging wildly round about
> Questioning of life and death and sin,
> Let me but creep within
> They fold, O Christ, . . . (57)

Archbishop Smith was one who tried to circumvent these difficult questions by stressing positive issues and pointing out that it "should be borne in mind that after all the Bible is not our Saviour", but Christ alone.(58) However, despite these tactics, the question of the truth of the Bible did cause some unsettlement of faith in the 1900s, and compounded the problem posed by religious indifference.

A major factor in the concern over the Book of books was the presence of liberal Protestants like Rev A. Harper, who arrived in Sydney from Melbourne in 1902, to take up the principalship of St Andrew's College. He was an Old Testament scholar of some standing, having edited the volume on the Book of Deuteronomy in the Expositor's Bible series. This immediately marked him off from most clergy who had limited high-powered scholastic education and interests. Harper had definite liberal views on the Old Testament. In his inaugural lecture delivered to the theological faculty entitled "Modern Methods of Teaching the Old Testament" he rejected verbal inspiration, believing the Old Testament to be compiled over a long period, truth by truth, by inspired men subject to human frailties and contemporary knowledge.(59) In an address to the inter-state Presbyterian Fellowship convention a year later, Harper spoke along the same lines. He threw doubt on the authorship of some of the books of the Bible, and the acquiring of the Law by Moses at Sinai, but declared that while Revelation may now prove slower and lower than supposed, the Bible actually now could be said to contain more of God. Harper rejected the "left wing" analytical critics and declared modern critical studies "will not rob Christ of His Crown".(60) Outspoken to some, his views were blasphemy to conservative evangelicals.

Mr W. Adams, B.A., drew a large crowd to the Protestant Hall where he replied to Harper in the best "either-or" traditions of Victorian conservative apologetics. Adams stated that as Christ himself believed the Bible to be literally true, the Higher Critics who viewed the Bible differently, were anti-Christ. So interrelated was the Bible, he argued, that rejection of any part must "logically entail the rejection of the lot as spurious".(61) Canon M. Archdall, a Cambridge M.A. and incumbent of St Mary's, Balmain, was also moved to reply to Harper's heresies. Archdall who read the Bible in both Greek and Latin appeared an intellectual match for Harper. Certainly the *Methodist* thought so, because it urged university men to attend Archdall's lecture to see how baseless the Higher Criticism was.(62) Archdall argued that while the Bible was not inerrant, it could only be interpreted by men infused with the spirit of God. He added that Harper and the Higher Critics were not men of God, because he claimed they denied the supernatural basis of the Scriptures.(63) This was a gross distortion of Harper's beliefs, but under such an attack, Harper was forced to give a public denial. To the delight (and perhaps relief) of his listeners, Harper affirmed that his views were those learnt at his mother's knee, "that God so loved the world, that He gave His only begotten Son, that whosoever believeth in Him should not perish, but have eternal life."(64) The conservative evangelicals seemed please with Archdall's reply to Harper. The *Australian Churchman* commented "that there must have been cases in which unsettled souls were re-established in the faith by this instrumentality".(65) The daily press did not comment but indicated their liberal leanings by only summarizing Archdall's address, whereas they had printed Harper's in full. In general the controversy had revealed a solid core of religious conservatism and unease about the literal truth of the Bible.

A manifesto concerning the Higher Criticism of the New Testament arrived in New South Wales early in 1905, and signatures in support were solicited from Anglican clergy. It was partly a product of the Modernist movement within the Church of England which aimed to free religion from ecclesiastical dogma and assert the freedom of enquiry. Modernism sought to investigate the nature of God and man, and thus it questioned miracles (especially the Virgin Birth), which were taken as self evident in the Creeds and the thirty-nine articles of the Church of England.(66) Although the authors of the manifesto affirmed their faith in "the spiritual foundations to which Christian experience and the creed of the Church alike bear testimony", they expressed concern that Anglicanism was uncritically rejecting the Higher Criticism of the New Testament and barring ordination to such sincere seekers of the truth.(67) They stated in typical Modernist terms that trained scholars, and not the Church itself, should decide the historical validity of the New Testament. The Anglican hierarchy in Australia showed considerable restraint in the face of such radicalism. The bishops were generally tolerant, though Archbishop Smith's silence was as much caution as forbearance, because he stated that a "bishop should be cautious, an archbishop doubly so".(68) However, Bishop Frodsham was quite alarmed and issued a directive to his clergy forbidding them to sign the manifesto.(69) While many of the bishops and other Anglican clergy supported the valuable contributions of the Higher Criticism, both high and low parties within Anglicanism opposed the radical inference of the manifesto that the truth of the Virgin Birth was debatable. This doctrine was so central to orthodox Christianity that it was not to be doubted by good Christians for one moment. The controversy over the manifesto brought forth touching affirmations of faith. Canon Jones who was the respected principal of Moore Theological College, declared: "For my part, I am a little child in my beliefs, and I intend to be that. I believe that St Luke wrote by the inspiration of God, and that what he says is the truth".(70) The Anglicans clearly rejected the radical stance of Modernism, but were uneasy about what criticism of the Bible and creeds they would accept, and were determined that this disruptive question receive as little discussion as possible. Archbishop Smith expressed the general relief when he briefly told the synod in September 1905 that fortunately few Anglican clergy had signed the manifesto.(71)

Other churches were drawn into this controversy because it involved the veracity of central Christian beliefs. Rev W. Cunliffe-Jones did nothing to calm evangelical fears when he spoke in a liberal manner on the doctrine of the Virgin Birth in his presidential address to the Congregational Union in May 1905. He expressed personal reservations about the truth of the Virgin Birth and did not see that it was essential to the truth of the incarnation of God into man.(72) The Congregational journal supported the right of critical inquiry and private judgment, and urged the need to stress the positives of Christ's coming to earth, rather than the method of his birth.(73) The *Messenger*, which was now edited by none other than Harper, agreed that positives must be stressed and that the Higher Criticism could generally provide these. However, Harper revealed how moderate he really was by opposing the view of the Anglican manifesto that final judgment on the origins and truth of the Bible should pass from the Church to the biblical scholars. Harper also stopped short of the quagmire created by questioning the miraculous Christian beliefs, because he said that the Virgin Birth was beyond mortal judgment. Harper affirmed a personal belief in the Virgin Birth and claimed it was a crucial Christian doctrine, because it "is one of the supports which have upheld the popular faith, and if it be removed much more may be lost than might at first appear".(74)

On this issue, many liberals sided with the conservative evangelicals. The *Methodist*, speaking rather hysterically for the conservatives, charged the Higher Critics, the manifesto, and even Cunliffe-Jones with attempting to undermine the Christian faith.(75) A short but intense correspondence broke out in the daily press. Half of the correspondents supported the investigations of the Higher Critics but added, as did Harper, that these Critics were not qualified to pronounce on miraculous events.(76) Most Protestants would not tolerate any questioning at all of the events surrounding Christ's life. The general level of theological knowledge of the correspondents was low, the arguments being more emotional than intellectual. About one-fifth espoused "either-or" apologetics, T. O'Reilly writing that the Bible "is either the 'word of God' or it is a lie from beginning to end. There can be no middle ground".(77) Rev G. Martin, who termed himself one of the "simple minded Christian people" (which some antagonists no doubt took literally), came out in support of verbal inspiration and thus represented the feelings of a large number of conservative evangelical clergy in all churches.(78) Conservatives believed that any clergyman who doubted the Virgin Birth should leave the Church, because even sincerely held doubts were a rejection of the Creeds and a danger to the Church at large. The controversy subsided after three weeks leaving the correspondence columns to debate other "conspiracies" such as socialism.

Unlike the doubt and turmoil that wracked the Church in Britain, few clerics in Australia appeared to experience intellectual difficulties about their faith, or perhaps more correctly, refused to air them in public. Clearly, a number rejected the Virgin Birth but only a handful openly said as much. The doubt of others like Rev T. Roseby, the son of the prominent and scholarly Congregational cleric, Dr Roseby, was known only to a few confidants within the clerical ranks.(79) Rev J. Watsford claimed that a number of Methodist clergy disbelieved the doctrine of eternal damnation, which was "known and yet allowed, and so is doing great harm in many ways".(80) The fact was that the Australian clergy and churches as a whole were not strongly intellectual, and a few like Bishop Frodsham were blunt enough to say as much.(81) This was due to the inadequate training of many clergy and the pastoral demands of overworked and expanding churches. Besides, anti-intellectualism was a strong element in Australian society as a whole. Therefore, theological debate was usually carried out by only a few, and often at a superficial level and in overseas terms. If doubts did pass through clerical minds (and hopefully such stimulating questioning did occur), they chose to keep it to themselves out of fear of the consequences, and pity for their unsuspecting and ill-equipped congregations.

Certainly many churchgoers resented theological and highly intellectual sermons, preferring a religion of "plain and simple" discourse and biblical exposition. Some just plainly could not comprehend intellectual sermons. Canon Archdall of St Mary's, Balmain, often lost his congregation with his scholarly discourses. One member stated he understood the sermons as much (or as little) as his eight year old son. Another praised Archdall's enthusiasm which kept him awake "something like a song in Italian or French, or some other language we do not understand the words of". He added rather touchingly: "We know too that he was not talking nonsense, although his sermon was so much above the range of our intelligence".(82) Thus for twenty-six years the congregation of St Mary's sat dutifully each Sunday, impressed, yet unnourished, by words which they heard, but could not comprehend. Perhaps this was not typical, because Archdall's fine scholarship was atypical — but this is partly the point.

In the early 1900s, Protestants modified their views of the Bible only very gradually. Indeed, the change from a literal to an allegorical view of the Bible came less from a rethinking by individuals, than with the growing generation who believed this as a matter of course. Certainly liberal Protestants believed the young must be taught the allegorical nature of the Bible as early as possible.(83) Even the *Australian Church-man* which had taken a conservative line against Harper in 1903, advised this by 1909. Theological students also felt the change, or demanded it. In 1907, a palace revolution erupted among the third year Presbyterian theological students, because they claimed that the conservative theology of their lecturer in Systematic and Biblical Theology, the fiery Protestant Dill Macky, failed to equip them to deal with modern thought. Claiming that the insidious Higher Criticism was thriving in the very vitals of their church, Dill Macky uncharacteristically resigned in a huff. This Protestant Ulsterman usually urged "no surrender"!(84) Joint theological lectures among Presbyterian, Methodist and Congregational students began in 1907, and the following year the Methodist Ministerial Examining Committee voted six to four (to the disgust of the conservatives) to allow Methodist students to hear Harper lecture on the Old Testament.(85) The liberal views of Harper and Principal Thatcher of Camden (Congregational) College were thus disseminated widely, since Anglican students joined in the joint lectures after 1910.

However, though the conservative belief in the literal truth of the Bible was on the wane, liberal Protestants still urged caution lest the foundations of faith of the older generation be disturbed. As one of the perplexed layman of the old guard had written in 1905: "What has the higher critic to give us in place of simple faith in God."(86) On the whole, the Higher Criticism did not cause great harm to the churches at this time. *The Church of England Outlook* remarked that "it means just as much to the bulk of our clergy and laity as the eruption in Martinique. They heard that it did a lot of damage, but are too busy with a day's work to question further."(87) Rev J. Penman similarly assured the 1908 Methodist Conference that they were "not visibly disturbed".(88) Certainly the percentage of the population who declared themselves to be of no religion, free thinkers, agnostics, or who objected to state either way, fell from 2.19 in 1891 to 0.56 in 1911.(89) However, several times in the period, the challenges to the Bible had worried an already beseiged Christianity. These issues also revealed the entrenched conservativism of the Protestant churches which slowed and shaped any responses the churches might make to the major problem of religious indifference.

Yet, while the extent of indifference and doubt concerning Christianity suggested that the churches were beginning to flounder in a secular society, most clerics were by no means in despair. They took heart from St Paul's words to the Corinthians: "We are troubled on every side, yet not distressed; we are perplexed, but not in despair". Though they were anxious, active Protestants were basically optimistic, because they still firmly believed that the churches were a majority movement in society.

Almost every person in the street in 1900 declared a belief in God and one in three went regularly to church. The Christian Church might not have been actively a majority movement, but latently it held great power. Great events in public life, such as the birth of a nation, and the funeral service of a beloved Queen; or in private life, such as births or marriages, still had a religious aspect. It was claimed that the services held to pray for the end of the great drought in 1902, attracted some not "seen in church for many a long day".(90) In April 1906, 300,000 people, a number equal to half the population of Sydney, filed past Holman Hunt's "The Light of the World", then on loan to the Sydney Art Gallery for one month. Poems, hymns and sermons greeted this painting which was probably the most famous religious art work of the Victorian era. The *Messenger* enthusiastically hailed the painting as "a greater evangel of salvation" than any revival preacher.(91) It certainly hit the religious nerve of the people, and explained why the churches could wield such social deference and influence in a society well on the way to becoming secular. No matter how indifferent many were to organized Christianity, it was deeply embedded in them, and it still formed the basis of social values around 1900. The religious instinct, no matter how vague, was an indelible part of Australian culture.

Whether the clergy understood the complex relationship between the personal religious instinct and an outwardly secular society or not, they certainly believed the common man had an inherent religious instinct. As the *Messenger* typically argued — "the man in the street is not by any means opposed to Jesus. On the contrary, he fully recognises the sublimity and beauty of His character".(92) Perhaps they were right, because even the labour press which was antagonistic to organized religion saw the Nazarene carpenter as the first socialist, and definitely a worker. Thus, the clergy's starting point for the problem of religious indifference was that every living person was inherently religious. Therefore, Protestant churchmen were never in complete despair. Most Protestants believed, and they may have been right, that the churches did not require clever arguments to win the people back, but earnest men, and plenty of bricks and mortar, in order to reach and capture the indifferent with the plain and simple word of God.

2 The Quest for Men and Money

Orthodox Christianity has always had a strong Messianic quality coupled with an institutional emphasis which has created a perennial demand for an adequate supply of manpower and finance. The Carpenter of Nazareth Himself prefigured these needs when He chose disciples and called upon all men to meet and worship in His name.

Clergymen are vital life forces to the Church and yet around the turn of the century they were in perpetual short supply. Congregations without clergy withered because only clerics administered the sacraments and provided the necessary pastoral and administrative focus to church life. The Anglican church with proportionally the least clergy(1) had few actual vacant ministeries, largely due to the immense size of many inner city and rural parishes. The other denominations were less fortunate, because often a significant number of their churches, especially in the bush, were vacant for years on end.(2) Over ten per cent of all Presbyterian and Congregational churches were vacant from 1900 until 1908. The Baptists were in similar difficulties until 1906 when a reorganization of training kept them fully supplied thereafter. The Methodist church had few actual shortages, solely due to the wide use of lay local preachers and of a circuit system in which one clergyman was shared among several churches. Thus a considerable number of Methodists lacked a direct and continuous clerical oversight. Indeed, many other Protestants suffered the same fate. Most denominations utilized lay preachers and many theological students were conscripted into parishes during the middle of their course.

Despite the growing demand for Australian born clergy, the churches were often tempted to counteract clerical shortages by importing clergy from Britain. Most of the churches had unofficial agents at "Home" whose sharp eyes snared a few young idealists for colonial service. Occasionally official requests for help produced small batches of clergy – seven Presbyterians arriving in 1903 and six Methodists in 1910. The Anglicans also "transported" willing clergy for five years servitude in a colonial bush pastorate. However, despite repeated efforts the British supply was dwindling, not only because the home churches were themselves short of clergy,(3) but because a more settled Australia no longer attracted those wanting adventurous missionary service. Thus the Australian churches gained an Australian clergy partly by default and by 1900, sixty per cent of the Anglican and Methodist clergy, fifty-three per cent of the

Presbyterians and about forty per cent of the Congregational clergy were Australian born or trained. The churches were quite assimilated because only sixty-five per cent of all adult males were Australian born at this time.(4) This Australianization of the clergy continued to grow, though for a long time to come, clergymen still dressed and thought like their British counterparts.

Although it was ridiculous to imagine that this clerical shortage was a new phenomenon, many ministers believed it to be just that — and they argued that it was caused by the materialism of the present age. Parents and even church schools were admonished for guiding their young men into lucrative professions and commerce, instead of a life of Christian service and denial. The *Church Commonwealth* calculated that one Anglican school in fifty years had only produced twenty clergymen out of 4,000 boys, and thirteen of these were actually the sons of clergy.(5) Many were mortified at the dearth of candidates. Dill Macky, the Presbyterian Moderator, queried in 1899: "Has the love of God waned cold amongst us, and are the love of money and worldly position the most potent forces in deciding the choice of our youth."(6)

Certainly it was true that the stipends of the clergy were by no means generous. However, they shied from public discussion of the level of their salaries because it smacked too much of worldliness. Only a handful dared to refer to the "quiet poverty" and "wretchedly inadequate" wages of the clergy, all too often paid well in arrears.(7) Rev T. E. Clouston, a lecturer at St Andrew's Presbyterian College, reminded a group of students that the clergyman "will always be a poor and hard-worked man, with the constant worry of being obliged to maintain the position in society for which his means are inadequate" and that this tension often ground down his spirituality and zeal.(8) Surveying clerical stipends, the *Sydney Morning Herald* concluded that "in nine cases out of ten the pay of a clergyman is exceedingly poor".(9) While a few received over £500 per annum, and a larger number under £200, most clergy received between £200 and £300 per year — the Anglicans and Presbyterians being at the top end of the scale and the Baptists at the bottom. Often a house was provided and a small pension of less than £150 a year paid on retirement. It was a stipend equal to the wages of a medium grade clerk, a then poorly paid teacher, or a third grade engineer, and not the £700 of their often equivalently educated professionals.(10)

They were poorly paid in terms of the respectability they had to exude and the continual demands for handouts from the poor at the backdoor of the parsonage. Few luxuries such as a horse or even a bicycle were evident among the clergy, while many sported the shiny seats and elbows of well-worn suits. Their wives, who were not paid at all, organized numerous meetings, cooked countless cakes for fetes and generally ran the parsonage with the thrift of a working class wife. Was it any wonder that the religiously inclined who also valued material comforts avoided the clerical life? Also, few scholarships existed for theological study, and it was claimed that this prevented some from becoming clergymen. The colleges themselves were run on a shoe-string budget — Camden (Congregational) College actually turned candidates away in 1906 because of lack of funds. The Baptist Union allocated the ludicrous sum of £3 for theological education in 1903. Other men were discouraged because they were considered to be too old, too unsuitable, or not sufficiently well educated. However, it is unlikely that intellectual turmoil caused by the Higher Critics of the Bible prevented many from becoming ministers.

It seemed that the churches wanted the best possible men at the cheapest price. The expectations demanded of the clergy by society and the Church itself, were high. Besides the necessary prerequisite that the candidate and others believed that he had a call from God, the intending minister was expected to possess a whole range of personal traits and abilities to enable him to function efficiently as an emissary of his God. Rev John Walker warned St Andrew's students that the clergyman needed "true piety, high moral character, charity, sincerity, competent training and equipment, independent manhood, faithfulness" as well as skills of tact, patience and self discipline.(11) These were sorely needed because the clergy usually conducted a whole range of religious societies including Sunday school, bible classes for all ages, sporting and debating societies, as well as being enmeshed in the intricacies of church financial and management meetings, civic functions and the assemblies of the wider church. They were in fact asked to juggle numerous balls at once. Pastoral visits were their constant task and potentially the most demanding, as visits were made to people from a wide spectrum of social groups, often in moments of their greatest joy or despair. This was an aspect of their work which no matter how often it was done, never satisfied some people who would have liked to trap the parson or curate for tea every afternoon.

Ministers continually had to write sermons and deliver them in an interesting manner, because some of the congregation were quick to find fault or fall asleep. To speak well, the cleric had to continually read theology and good literature and spend considerable hours in his study. Walker remarked that "ignorance and narrowness of intellectual outlook are an inexcusable handicap in the pulpit. In general culture, in knowledge of literature and the arts and sciences, the preacher must at least be abreast of the more thoughtful of his people."(12) Besides all these demands, most clergy tried to be good familymen and devoted husbands. In what amounted to a cruel double standard, clergy were expected to set an example in their morals and manners. Sexual propriety and sobriety were so taken for granted that they were never mentioned. However, clergy were generally advised to avoid tobacco or at least its use in public. In an age where cleanliness was next to godliness, ministers were warned to carry out the daily ablutions of bathing, shaving, nail scouring and teeth brushing. Walker advised students that: "Dirty linen, down-at-heel, untidy boots, and a coat retaining the grease-stains of many a carelessly eaten dinner, are a hopeless and altogether an unnecessary handicap in the work of any Christian minister." He added that a change of clothes should be carried in country areas, in case one is invited to dinner, especially to the table of a squatter. At the table, over-fastidious manners should be avoided as well as the taking of greedy portions of food and masticating with open lips "which indicates unmistakeable appreciation of the victuals — but also more than smacks of vulgarity".(13) These men were expected to be angels, yet not all lived up to these standards, and others refused to try. Unfortunately, church life was poisoned or weakened by those who spoke behind their hands about their cleric's weaknesses.

This image of perfection was one of the factors behind the considerable social standing that clergymen held, despite their meagre salary. Admittedly there were differences — Anglican clergy, because they held more tertiary degrees and their leaders had access to Government House, had more status than Baptists — but in general, clerics were given considerable deference. Partly this was due to the close connection believed to exist between religion and morality by a society obsessed with social control and respectability. When clergy spoke on morals and manners they were listened to because religion was akin to respectability, though if they spoke on politics and social justice they were often disregarded. Certainly, the middle class and churchgoers showed them the greatest respect, but as ninety-eight per cent professed a belief in God, most people truly called them "reverend."

However, there were exceptions to this general rule. The popular image of the clergy in Australian literature and journalism was either of a somewhat effeminate or ill-equipped innocent who was duped by the mischievous bushman, or of a person who was a fanatic or hypocrite.(14) Increasingly after 1900 this was supplemented by the image of a narrow minded killjoy who was termed a wowser. He was sketched as bespectacled and dressed in clerical black, with thin ascetic features, a sour expression, and, ladylike, sporting an umbrella with which to ward off moral evil. With the excesses of moral reformism and sabbatarianism in the 1900s, this image became more powerful with the help of the widely read *Bulletin*, which never ceased to make fun of the clergy. This image was at the bottom of the frequent calls by clergy for a more manly type of minister. Secularization, which separated religion from daily life, aided the view that the clergy were a race apart and this was most prominent in working class and rural areas. Anglican bush brother, Rev C. H. S. Matthews, referred to the silence that always fell on a group when he entered a hotel or bush camp wearing his clerical collar — "a silence born partly of suspicion, partly of shyness in the presence of an unknown quantity".(15) It was this barrier that the clergy had to continually confront and try to dismantle. Yet, all in all, clergymen were respected if not always liked, and even the bushmen in popular literature who were cynical about organized religion, always gave a "bob" to the parson.

Churchmen also pointed to the need for a more qualified clergy. Archbishop Smith wanted ministers full of evangelical zeal, but also ones with "theological attainments, powers of teaching, ability to handle philosophical, philanthropic, and social problems".(16) Men with all round abilities were needed, as an Anglican, Rev A. E. Colvin wrote after a tour of the state in 1906: "The laity everywhere are most emphatic upon the necessity of having clergymen who are gentlemen scholars, and leaders of the people. They complain very much of too many inferior men nowadays getting into the Church."(17) Perhaps this was nostalgia on the part of middle-aged churchgoers, though more likely it reflected the improved educational standards of the community since the 1880 Education Act.

The churches responded to these demands, and theological education experienced rising standards throughout the 1900s. This was not uniformly the case, as Moore College in the Sydney Anglican diocese had to abandon the matriculation as its entrance standard in 1903 due to the lack of suitable candidates, though this prerequisite was restored again in 1911. However, St John's College established in the Armidale diocese in 1898, and the correspondence courses through the (Anglican) Australian College of Theology thrived in the period. There were no major changes in the three year course at St Andrew's (Presbyterian) College, though several new chairs were added and a theological library opened. The addition to its staff of Professor Andrew Harper from Ormond College, Melbourne, gave more intellectual lustre to this institution. Camden (Congregational) College experienced a similar fillip when Dr A. W. Thatcher, a senior tutor of Mansfield College, Oxford, and world renowned semitic scholar, arrived in 1911 along with his personal library of 10,000 books, to take up the principalship. Thatcher, who was to become an intellectual force among Sydney Protestants, quickly raised the academic standards of the college. All these colleges offered training in the classics, philosophy, mathematics and literature as well as the normal theological subjects.

Unfortunately, the Methodists and Baptists still suffered from the old evangelical view that books were the work of the Devil and that ministers need only study the Bible to be effective. The Methodists received a totally inadequate training at a provisional college set up in a house in Stanmore. Even the Principal, Rev E. J. Rodd, acknowledged that the two year course in elementary and practical theology meant that "anything like a finished training is beyond us".(18) However, the situation was to be remedied finally in 1915 with the opening of Leigh College to celebrate the first century of Methodism in Australia. The Baptist Union similarly strengthened its theological training from almost nil to a choice of either their own four year course with university subjects as options, or a course at the Victorian Baptist College. Overall, theological training suffered continually from financial shortages and too many overworked part-time lecturers, who had to guide a congregation as well. However, greater financial support was gradually forthcoming, and the combined theological lectures established in 1907 eased some of the strain on the human resources.(19)

Therefore, the trend was unmistakably towards a more intellectually equipped clergy. In 1900 one-third of the Anglican, Presbyterian and Congregational clergy had university training, one-third had theological training and one-third no formal academic training at all. The latter group were certainly not incompetent, because all the churches only ordained men who had the necessary theological knowledge and pastoral skills. However, it is true to say that men with no formal training made life hard for the churches in a tolerably well educated community which also had great religious needs. Only about five per cent of Methodists and Baptists had university degrees and only half had any training at all. The upgrading of theological training, plus the introduction of correspondence courses by the Anglican, Presbyterian and Congregational colleges, meant that by 1914 a higher proportion of clergy had received some academic training and the quality of that experience was higher.(20) Hand in hand with a better qualified clergy came the increasing rejection of the use of lay preachers. Many congregations showed a distaste for local preachers. The latter complained that it was difficult to obtain appointments in the city area.(21) As this was partly due to their poor education, the churches responded by introducing theology classes for their lay preachers. However, the main reason was simply that they were not clergy, and the fact that well educated, middle class city congregations were affronted if their services were not conducted by a minister. The numbers of local preachers stagnated by 1910 and this worsened the clerical shortage in the churches, especially in the city, although the "locals" still bore much of the burden of country work.

With the end of state aid in 1880, the churches in New South Wales depended on the voluntary giving of their flock. Frequently the needs were so pressing that, ironically, a Christianity which preached "lay not up for yourselves treasures upon earth", often became obsessed with the quest for money. While few clergy asked that the biblical "tenth" be given, most urged that giving be regular and proportionate to one's means.

They believed too few gave enough, especially in relation to the amounts spent on pleasure and luxuries. Rev J. Colwell lamented that the £3000, paid in one night by fight fans to watch world champion Tommy Burns batter Bill Squires senseless in 1908, could have erased the whole debt of the Methodist Home Mission Society.(22) Clergy claimed that adequate giving brought the giver into closer communication with his Master and the Church, while poor giving created a "leanness of religious life and a narrowness and sordidness of soul".(23) Their own stipends depended on how much went into the plate on Sundays, but they rarely couched their pleas in such terms. Indeed, Archbishop Smith confessed to being embarrassed when talking about money.(24) Giving was also to be direct and not from tainted sources. Bazaars, raffles, grab-bags, dances and concerts smacked too much of worldliness for clerical sensibilities, and reflected the desire to get something in return for one's giving. As Jesus had expelled the money changers from the temple, so Archdeacon Moxon disbanded a church bazaar because his zealous parishioners had committed the sin of running a raffle to raise funds. The Methodists and Presbyterians actually forbade such sacrilege by church law. Yet high ideals were sometimes corrupted by the need for money! Although smoking was regarded as one of the minor sins of the flesh, the usually morally strict Baptists did not refuse the generous donations from church member and tobacco manufacturer, Hugh Dixon.

Sometimes building debts moulded much of the financial and religious energies of local congregations. The main commitments were for a church building, a church hall and a residence for the minister. The role of women in aiding church finances was crucial, because large amounts were raised by incessant sales of handicrafts and products of the kitchen, as well as by church concerts, garden parties and gypsy teas. No less important were the coppers or small silver tied in the corners of handkerchiefs and produced as young voices sang:

> Here the pennies dropping,
> Listen while they fall;
> Every one for Jesus
> He shall have them all.

Archdeacon Abbott of Tamworth and Rev J. Auld of Ashfield were just a few of the clergy who transferred to other parishes or retired early, worn out by the strain of unmanageable congregational debts.(25)

Church building, however, continued at a strong rate, aided by a buoyant economy after 1905. Most churches developed from a meeting of a few of the faithful or from a watchful cleric who saw a need in a new area. Services were initially held in private residences or a local community hall until a large enough congregation was gathered to consider building a church. Usually a generous donor provided the core of the building fund to erect a modest wooden or brick structure to seat one hundred or so. Affluent congregations hired a contractor to erect the church, especially if it was to be large and imposing like the Waverley Methodist church, to which Mrs Schofield gave £7,000 and Hon E. Vickery M.L.C. £15,000. In poorer circumstances the church members did much of the work themselves, the wooden Baptist church at Auburn being erected in a single day by the congregation. All too often the building fund fell short of the needs or pretentions of the collectors and a large debt remained. Nor did financial commitments end there! There were always repairs; the need for additions to provide for the Sunday school; and the necessity to rebuild in brick as the wooden structures became beneath the congregation's dignity or simply dilapidated. The Baptists of Woollahra were finally forced to rebuild as showers of dust rather than heavenly grace descended upon them from their ageing roof.

What forces were there within these churches to cause them to expend so much energy and money in throwing up bricks and mortar? Indeed the Englishman, Anthony Trollope, remarked in 1873: "wherever there is a community there arises a church, or more commonly churches . . . the people are fond of building churches".(26) Primarily, the impetus in the 1900s was due to the current anxiety which many churchmen felt regarding the number of Christians who were purely nominal or indifferent. However, this was based upon a longer tradition of virile competitiveness among the Protestants for the souls of the colonial population. This competition was often ludicrous and destructive because it endowed the tiniest communities with a church of every brand, all to be paid for, and all sparsely attended. The lust for souls led to a desire for fine churches to attract customers and this manifested itself for instance in the creation of a Presbyterian architecture advisory committee whose efforts resulted in the building of "a considerable number of handsome, artistic buldings, both in town and country".(27) The Parramatta Methodist church was one of the many instances where congregational vanity to create a local landmark with brick arches and buttresses of a great height, produced such a debt that the vigorous efforts of a decade kept up with little more than the interest payments.(28)

The insecurity created by the act of migration also contributed to the large number of fine churches. The Englishman, Rev Dale, attributed the large number of churches he saw to homesickness, because "to see a Genevan gown again and to hear the Scotch Psalms would be almost as good as to tread once more the purple heather of the old country and to breathe the fresh air of the hills; and as soon as a half a dozen Scotchmen settle within reach of each other they build a Presbyterian church. It is the same with the members of the other religious denominations."(29)

Church building was part of the community sense of identity. Donations to church building were often across denominational lines — even at times the Protestant-Catholic gulf. The church stone-laying ceremony was a civic and festive occasion, often accompanied by brass bands and gymnastic displays by the young. Church buildings were essential to communal and personal identity, as well as religious faith, but too often they were pretentious structures rather than functional and cheap affairs. It was the old story of the mixing of heavenly and earthly aims, because while they sincerely glorified God, they also expressed the vanity of man and the worship of Mammon. It was a tragic comment on Christian ideals that so much energy was expended on church building debts instead of spreading the Word and giving material comfort to those outside who were in spiritual and physical distress.

With such a foundation of congregational pauperism, it was little wonder that central church funds were always inadequate. The clergy continually appealed for money for home and foreign missions, theological colleges, rescue and orphan homes, church restorations, ministers' retirement funds and all sorts of other schemes. Their demands were a tribute to their incessant need to be initiating projects in this period. One columnist in the *Church Commonwealth* commented: "It is a pity that bishops, priests and deacons have to busy themselves about money so much as they do, and that the laity should so reasonably come to the conclusion that it forms the chief object of their quest, as it is in other people's."(30) Most church agencies existed on small budgets, and the home mission societies whose purpose it was to promote church extension, spent everything they had and more. Frequently they were in debt and were forced to temporarily curtail their activities until more money was forthcoming. Rev Luke Parr, the organizing secretary of the Anglican extension society, spent much of his time just raising funds, and he remarked with some bitterness that he had "not enjoyed the work of begging money from men about the city. Many of them, though not all, have been hard and unreasonable." Only a quarter of the 350 businessmen he visited in his first year responded. Then again, only a quarter of the clergy gave anything, and apathy was so great in some parishes that Parr had difficulty in getting someone to act as collector for the society.(31) In the years between 1903 and 1909 all the other churches appointed full time secretaries for their extension societies, to increase the financial as well as administrative efficiency. These men were piqued at the large sums raised for foreign missions, often as large as those for home missions. Rev A. J. Waldock, the Baptist organizer, believed that the "heroism of home missions has not seized our imagination", while Archdeacon Greer of Bathurst was annoyed that "the home mission is swamped on this wave of sentiment in favour of the far away, the unknown, and the mysterious".(32) Certainly the black skinned "heathen" had a romance about them. Foreign mission tales were always a favourite with Sunday school children who aided missionaries in China, India and the Pacific. The grownups also shared this fascination, and in one single night of enthusiasm Methodists promised the enormous sum of £2,353 to the newly formed Indian mission. The money was there if only it could be coaxed from the laity's pockets in the right manner. The successful cleric was also an entrepreneur.

Fund raising that was organized and tenacious was generally the most successful. Once the zealous assistance of the ladies was enlisted, the Anglican and Congregational home mission funds were doubled. Similarly, the Grafton—Armidale diocesan fund was pitiful until the newly arrived bishop introduced an envelope system which greatly increased the contributions.(33) The church funds initiated to celebrate the advent of the new century also revealed the need for efficiency. Congregations only gave token amounts until the organizing secretary visited and whipped them into action. The Methodist and Presbyterian century funds fared the best. The Anglican church fund, carried on without an organizer, only received donations from half of the parishes. Whereas the Presbyterian fund raised about £54,000 over six years, and the Methodist fund £42,000 over three years, the Anglican effort only raised £42,000, despite this church being four times the size of these other two. The Baptists raised only about £1,000 while the equally small Congregationalists raised the enormous sum of £14,000. The Congregational effort was so successful, not so much because of better organization and an affluent congregation, but because it was orientated to the more attractive goal of eliminating local church debts rather than bolstering central funds. The current economic recession may well explain some tardiness in giving, yet only a quarter of all Methodist and Presbyterian churchgoers gave anything at all to these special century funds, which suggests a certain lack of enthusiasm in their Christian giving.(34)

The reality was that the churches depended for their survival on a few large donors. For instance, only 10,000 Presbyterians donated at all to the century fund, and of the £54,000 received, £11,000 was given by twelve people, Sir Samuel McCaughey M.L.C. alone donating £3,000.(35)

The foremost Christian philanthropist of the period was the Methodist and self-made man, the Hon Ebenezer Vickery, M.L.C. He was a landed gentleman, wealthy merchant, company director and Wollongong colliery owner whose belief in the Protestant work ethic had enabled him to amass over £800,000 by 1902. Vickery arrived in the colony from England at the age of six in 1833. His mother was the first woman in the southern world to lead a Methodist class meeting. He was associated with every significant Methodist and secular charitable enterprise for fifty years until his death in 1906. Vickery was a founder and life treasurer of the Y.M.C.A., and helped manage the Sydney Rescue Society, the City Mission, the British and Foreign Bible Society and other such societies. Among his larger gifts were £15,000 to his local Waverley church, a single donation of £10,000 (one of many) to the Methodist Home Mission Society, which he helped found in 1859, and over £20,000 to maintain the tent mission of 1902–03. In 1905, Vickery purchased and renovated the seven story old Lyceum Hall at a cost of £90,000, which, after the prostitutes and "two-up" schools had been removed, symbolically became the head-quarters of the Central Methodist Mission.(36) Between 1859 and 1908, Vickery, Wollongong businessman John Bright and Rev W. Schofield together gave half of the Methodist Home Mission Society's total income of £300,000!(37)

Fortunately for the other churches they had their own generous bene-factors. By 1904 the Sydney Anglican diocese held six hundred endow-ments yielding £1,200 yearly. Presbyterianism was well served by pastor-alist David Berry of Shoalhaven, who gave £30,000 for church extension, Sir Samuel McCaughey, Mrs Hunter-Baillie, Robert Logan and Colonel J. H. Goodlet and others who constantly gave large sums. Sir James Reading Fairfax owner of the *Herald*, and medical men Sir Phillip Sydney Jones and Sir Arthur Renwick, all generously aided Congregationalism. Prominent Baptist, Hugh Dixon, founder of the Conqueror Tobacco Company which marketed the popular "Yankee Doodle" brand, gave continuously to his church's funds, including £10,000 for extension in 1900. Both William Buckingham of Buckingham's Emporium, Oxford Street, and William White, a bread manufacturer (till he "went to glory" in 1903) gave generously, especially to purchase land for new churches. Some of these may have given with the pride and the motivation of the pharisee, yet most of these men also faithfully served on their church's committees and were prominent in secular charity work. Despite the utter dependence of the churches on these large donors, the children's pennies were proportionally as great a gift and were equally a delight to the clergy. So from the mighty and the meek money flowed, yet the clergy were always wishing there was more and still more, as financial worries deadened and distracted their minds.

Despite the difficulties of a shortage of resources, the churches were in closer communication with the people in 1914 than 1900. With each passing year, the various church agencies became more professional and more efficient. The Presbyterian church typified this by its transference from small rented church offices to its own three storey building in Wynyard Square. Similarly, the number and range of church societies and benevolent agencies rose as the churches responded to new problems, or old ones more adequately. Each church had its own weekly newspaper which provided overseas and Australian religious news, comments on politics and articles on spiritual matters. The Methodist and Presbyterian weeklies had a circulation of about 2,000, equal to five to ten per cent of the number of churchgoers. The Baptist monthly journal sold 1,500 copies, equal to about twenty per cent of churchgoers.(38) However, because one copy was usually shared among families and sometimes friends, the readership was wider than these figures imply. Besides, the daily press also gave considerable coverage to church news, and so the church scene stretched further than the religious press.

Parallelling this growing sophistication of management, church extension was progressing aggressively and at times competitively. Churchmen were always on the lookout for new possibilities, the *Methodist* typically commented on the new church in Cardigan Street, West Kingston: "The undertaking is a serious one, as there are but few Methodist families in the locality. It is a case of getting a building in the hope of getting the people. But the place is growing rapidly, and there is no other church just at hand".(39) Most of the churches had special committees which purchased prime building-sites in new suburbs for future extension. Red-bricked Queen Anne styled or neatly painted weatherboard churches dotted the new suburbs or stood on small rises in rural areas, challenging the open spaces around them. Crosses and spires could be seen from vantage points in most Australian streets.

The expansion which marked this period reflected the churches' anxiety about religious indifference. The growth rate of church building and new clergy was over thirty per cent in the decade after 1900, which exceeded the state's population growth rate of twenty-two per cent.(40) The Baptists were the Christian success story of the decade because their building and manpower growth approached seventy per cent. Therefore, in spite of a lack of resources, the churches had achieved a robust expansion. Yet they were to need imagination and a congenial message as well as buildings, if they were to recapture their lost sheep!

3   Pastoral Care in the Slums and the Bush

The strength of Protestantism in New South Wales was uneven, and it was this fact that had made churchmen around 1900 anxious about the state of Protestant Christianity. In the middle class outer suburbs of Sydney and in most large country towns it was strong — even assertive. However, most concerned Protestants acknowledged that the churches had little contact with the working class, or their thinly dispersed flocks beyond the fringes of the country towns. Of course there were problems of pastoral care in the fast growing suburbs, but these were ones largely of resources. The problems of the slums and the bush were qualitative more than quantitative, and they demanded new directions rather than just more of the same.

The condition of the working class in Sydney around 1900 revealed that the earlier dreams of an Australia where all enjoyed social and economic equality had not been fulfilled. Of course if one wanted to make comparisons with European societies as did Sir T. A. Coghlan, the government statistician, it could be argued that in Australia "wealth is more widely distributed and the violent contrast between rich and poor, which seems so peculiar a phase of the old world civilisation, finds no parallel in these southern lands".(1) Certainly overseas visitors took this view; the Frenchman Metin, in his *Le Socialisme sans Doctrine* (1901) remarked that "more and more one can observe the external difference between the worker and the bourgeois diminishing except during working hours".(2) However, to emphasize this comparative view is to promote the idea that Australia was a workingman's paradise, which obscures the real social and economic deprivation that the working class suffered. Although labourers earned high wages, work was not always available, and in the 1890s the economic position of the working class deteriorated with the coming of economic recession and industrial unrest. Unemployment stood at over thirty per cent at a time when "there was no dole, no pension, no child endowment, and no health scheme to assist them".(3) When a man's savings were exhausted, he was at the mercy of private charity. Country people at least subsist in most depressions, but this one coincided with the 1895–1903 drought — till then the worst in New South Wales's history. Over thirty million head of stock died and many graziers were forced off the land, and on to the road and the charity of the Lord Mayor's fund which distributed the large sum of over £23,000. This drought delayed economic recovery, forced food prices up, and wages down, and maintained unemployment at six per cent well into the 1900s.(4)

Despite the successes of unionism in the late nineteenth century, life in the factory around 1900 involved long hours and hard work. Most factories were small, over seventy-five per cent of those in the Sydney area employed less than twenty people. Many were simply old sheds or converted houses which were consequently cramped and ill-equipped. In these conditions, workers laboured for at least fifty-five hours a week, for around £2 per week. Women workers who constituted a third of the factory workforce were only paid about £1 a week. The worst factory conditions at this time in New South Wales approached the excesses of the English industrial revolution, because not only were long hours worked in dangerous and unsanitary surroundings, but children and sweated female outworkers were employed. Significant reform came in 1896 when the Factory Act reduced the hours of work for children and women to forty-eight, laid down basic sanitation standards, required machinery to be fenced, thus reducing the number of limbs mangled by machines, and instituted the registration and inspection of factories. However, the Act neglected outwork in people's homes altogether and though the inspectors tried, many of the standards could only apply when factories were rebuilt. Inspectors reported the existence of ill-ventilated, damp and dilapidated workrooms, where the natural order was one of filth and junk. Some buildings had rivers running under their floor-boards, non-existent or inadequate fire-escapes, and unsanitary rest rooms, often without separate facilities for women. The Act provided no powers to regulate unique industries like bone-crushing, rag and chemical works, so lung diseases and poisonings continued. Women soldering tins in a jam factory had perpetual ulcers or "birdseyes" on their fingers, while inadequately fenced machinery still occasionally nipped off a finger. It was difficult for injured workers to gain compensation under the Employers' Liability Act and payments were a long time in coming. Those who were injured were forced to dip into their usually small savings and thus slowly went into debt.(5)

Not all the city working class laboured in factories and thus a number were found in the transport and construction industries where they not only worked long hours, but often laboured in all weathers. Carting goods and building materials, and constructing roads and houses was arduous work before the existence of lifting devices. Work was not easy wherever it was! The bulk of the hired domestic workforce were women who rose before six o'clock and prepared meals, washed, scoured, and swept out those cluttered Victorian households, and then often prepared the master's children for bed. This fourteen hour day passed without the aid of modern household devices.(6) The other nine-tenths of households were cared for by wives and mothers who did the same work for no payment at all, except the glories of motherhood. The shop-assistants were as poorly unionized as the domestics. They worked up to seventy-two hours a week, on their feet all this time, until six o'clock closing for shops was introduced in 1900. Illicit after-hours trading continued for some time in working class districts. Some working class wives were bad organizers, while others either worked during the day or lacked the domestic help to allow them the freedom to shop before six.

The living standards of the working class complemented their depressing working conditions. The English observer, Francis Adams, remarked that. no European manufacturing city could boast of more hideous inner suburbs than Sydney, which contained a "congerie of bare brick habitations, which is just as much an arid, desolate waste as the mid-desert. Utterly unrelieved by tree or grass, they oppress the soul and shrivel up every poor little instinct and aspiration towards natural purity and beauty in man, woman and child."(7) Dr Herbert Moran, who grew up in Chippendale in the depressed 1890s, commented that "in the nineties games were rarer among the very poor. These children had been spawned in misery and then spilled out like slops into a dirty street from insanitary houses."(8) His own early life was made even the poorer by his mother's death from septicaemia during childbirth. Death rates were thirty-six per cent higher in the inner suburbs than in the outer suburbs and the country.(9)

The Chinese who formed the lowest rung of the working class existed in the worst conditions in rented premises in the Haymarket and dock areas, and in Alexandria where they owned market gardens. Some premises had no water laid on and the drainage was usually defective, making the area smell offensive. The ten by twelve feet backyards of some of these premises had been covered in and cooking facilities and cess-pits were found within feet of each other. One boarding house inhabited by aged Chinese was divided into cubicles of which all had defective ventilation and some were only six by five feet in diameter. The cubicles in the cellar were almost completely devoid of light and air. The significance of these living conditions uncovered by a royal commission is firstly that the commissioners blamed these conditions not on the Chinese, but on the inadequate and unpoliced building codes, and on the owners of the premises, many of whom were "well known Europeans". Secondly, the Chief Medical Officer of the Board of Health and also the Inspector of Nuisances both claimed that a considerable number of Europeans lived in similar or worse conditions.(10)

It is little wonder that in these miserable conditions bubonic plague broke out several times around 1900, claiming 112 lives. There was one consolation — the unemployed earned six shillings a day fumigating and whitewashing the whole Darling Harbour area and razing some of the wharves to the ground. They killed rats for a penny a scalp until the

Health Department halved the bounty and the unemployed declared the "game" black.(11)

Certainly many of the working class aspired to a quiet respectability in neat three-roomed cottages with tiny gardens. However, over seventy-five per cent of this class rented their dwellings (which meant they were generally below standard), as opposed to a rental rate of less than fifty per cent among the middle class.(12) Also, rents were ten shillings weekly, or a sizeable one-quarter of the labourer's wages. Besides this burden, around 1900, food and commodity prices were increasing, while real wages were declining. While the average family had five children, working class families were above this average size and so had more mouths to feed from lower wages.(13) Many old, single, or destitute people of this class lived in boarding houses, while whole families of the very poor lived in ill-furnished single rooms. Mince meat, rabbit, a few vegetables and plenty of bread and dripping formed their diet.(14) It was these conditions which created the misfits and larrikins who upset the more respectable. Henry Lawson saw the links in his *The Captain of the Push*:

> For they spoke the gutter language with the easy flow that comes
> Only to the men whose childhood knew the gutters and the slums.

Several parliamentary committees revealed that the crowded, insanitary slum conditions of the nineties persisted through the 1900s. A spokesman for the Sydney University Christian Union's committee of investigation into slums, told the commission into Sydney's urban growth in 1913 that in the "blind lanes, narrow streets and acres of old and dirty houses" of the inner city, there were many instances of families living in one room. The infant mortality rate per 1,000 here was 135, while only 82 in the outer suburbs and 70 in the country.(15) Ironically, in the ensuing four years, 417,000 Australians enlisted and rushed eagerly overseas to right wrongs.

With unemployment at over thirty per cent in 1892 and still six per cent ten years later, there seemed little justice for the unemployed. Henry Lawson in the 1890s observed the homeless unemployed sleeping out under "Domain Blankets" (known to most as newspapers), and crowding the soup kitchens and sixpenny restaurants. He believed this to be a "Great Wrong" and poured out his heart to:

> The pallid stream of faces in the street —
> Ebbing out, ebbing out,
> To the drag of tired feet (16)

Some did care — over sixty charities gave sustenance and support to the destitute. However, the prevailing philosophy held by charity workers, was that only sufficient should be given to keep the poor from starvation, otherwise they would become too dependent on this aid and lose the will to work. Thus, the rations were carefully planned — a woman with three children was able to collect once weekly from the Benevolent Society, five loaves of bread, two pound of flour, three pound of meat and some tea, sugar, arrowroot and rice, and blankets and boots if needed. The president of the society, Sir Arthur Renwick, admitted a wave of poverty had swept the country — the number of people his own society supported increasing by 150 per cent in the 1890s.(17) Overall, the number classed by the government as destitute increased by fifty per cent and as late as 1904, 37,000 people or seven per cent of Sydney's population, were receiving outdoor relief.(18)

The 1896 select committee on pensions was informed by the Inspector General of Police and charity workers that many of Sydney's destitute were formerly sober and respectable workingmen who had been unable to provide for their old age. Canon Boyce's evidence referred to a number of typical cases of aged people. Many of them were ill or had no one to support them, some had even sold all their possessions for food and fuel, and then resorted to begging. "J. B. and his wife live together, one is 74 years old and the other is 72; they are both very weak and practically destitute; they have been begging for the last three or four years; they are very respectable people, and lost their money through the failure of one of the building societies three or four years ago."(19) A small aged pension of ten shillings a week was instituted in 1900, but owing to a twenty-five year residence clause and a means test, only 20,000 received it. Therefore, privation existed among many of the aged and the destitute who had not reached the qualifying age of sixty-five.

Many of the working class had the feeling that they were born tired, and was it little wonder that some turned to alcohol and gambling in their despair. Some drank "brutishly and in bursts of dipsomania. It brought fantasy and romance, appeasement to their griefs, forgetfulness of their failure".(20) Their children had narrow lanes and factory sites for playgrounds or were compelled to play about in the gutters. It is a wonder that more did not reveal their resentment by drifting into larrikinism. It has been seen that the working class stayed away from church. It was not only that they were indifferent to religion, but many did not have the energy to go to week night meetings, or the resolve to forsake their Sunday chance to linger in bed and later to go on a picnic, simply in order to attend church. The likelihood was that if they did go they would not hear things to their comfort, but condemnations of their lust for drink and the sins of the flesh, because most churchmen placed the need for moral reformation above social justice. The challenge to the churches was that the working class needed material sustenance and a gospel that preached social reform as much as comfort for the next life. Would the "organ grinders" (as the larrikins called them), respond?

Canon Boyce was very influential in developing the interest of the Anglican church in the working class and the destitute. Perhaps he owed his sympathy with the poor, who always struggled so tenaciously for life, to his narrow escape from drowning in the wreck of the *Earl of Charlemont* off Barwon Heads in 1854. Boyce was then ten, the son of an accountant who like many others flocked to the golden lands of Australia. His social concern developed when he moved from the country to Pyrmont in 1882 and then to St Paul's Redfern in 1884, both inner city, factory and slum areas. In 1900 he wrote that a section of his parish was "a very poor one, and there is no sign or probability of its becoming richer. Many of the children are poorly clad, and dozens run about without stockings or shoes. The thrifty people are continually moving away to the outer suburbs."(21) Boyce's feelings for the people and the aged, which he admitted "at times I had been inclined to regard as a nuisance", were further sharpened by the chance purchase from a railway bookseller of Charles Booth's *Old Age and the Poor*. By the mid 1890s, Boyce was preaching and writing in support of old age pensions, and furthered this cause as much as the other champion of the aged, Senator Neild. Twelve years later, Boyce was publicizing the state of Sydney's slums before an urban planning inquiry. He took the Lord Mayor, Sir Allen Taylor, on a tour of the slums. Taylor was so shocked that he declared that he had "seen houses which are not fit for dogs to live in".(22) The resulting demolitions by the city council, plus those stimulated earlier by the plague scare, and the building of Central Railway, eradicated some of Sydney's worst slums by 1914. Even Boyce's suggestion of cheap housing for the poor was partially taken up by the council. Canon Boyce was also president of the New South Wales Temperance Alliance for twenty-four years until 1915 and founder and president of the British Empire League in 1901. However, his action over slums was historically the most important of his work, because in 1900 he stimulated and led an Anglican church inquiry into the inner suburbs of Sydney.

The ensuing report disclosed an alarming degree of religious indifference, because less than five per cent of Anglicans attended church in these overcrowded and understaffed working class parishes. It recommended the use of mission halls, lay evangelists, deaconesses, the Church Army and more curates.(23) Some, including the Archbishop, felt that greater needs existed in the bush, and others feared that the organization needed to promote this inner city work might threaten the vested interests of the older Church Society.(24) However, Boyce's persuasive powers and the support of the well respected Archdeacon Langley of St Phillip's, who expressed astonishment at the miserable religious condition of the working class, won the day. A Mission Zone encompassing the five square miles of the inner city from Woolloomooloo to Alexandria, and from Redfern across to Camperdown and Newtown, was established as a sub-branch of the Church Society. The prospectus issued by the Zone committee apologized to the "host of worthy and respectable people" who had been included in this area, but affirmed that it was here "that the battle for Christ had to be fought primarily in New South Wales". Conjuring up a vision as black as Dante's hell, it declared that it was here that the bulk of the criminal class and prostitutes resided; here that a third of the state's convictions for drunkenness had their origin; and here also were to be found the majority of the city's poor. Continuing, the prospectus claimed that in this area the "little waifs, the street arabs and the children that beg about every day, and late into the night, are mostly found". The people were poor, living in sin and were apart from religion. The Church "should effectively carry the banner of the Cross into every narrow street and slum, and by teaching Christ's words . . . endeavour to raise the metropolis that religiously, and so morally, it may be an example to Australia".(25)

It is patently clear that the Zone committee held a middle class and evangelical view of the slum problem! Those who were morally upright and religious were classed as "worthy and respectable" whereas the sinful and the poor were apart from religion and therefore they were immoral. This view held that poverty was caused by laziness and dissolute habits, and not the social and economic environment. The Zone committee seemed as much concerned with cleaning up the drunks and the prostitutes for the national good, as with preaching the gospel for the sake of their God. Thus the work of the Mission Zone, which was the creation of a few idealists concerned with the poverty and religious indifference of the working class, soon began, in the hands of the wider Church, to take on a moralizing tone. It was in danger of being ineffective from the start, because it exhorted the poor and the criminal classes, who were a "menace to the state", instead of understanding and comforting them.

The task of the Mission Zone was immense. The area contained 170,000 people, 70,000 of them being Anglicans. Church seating existed for less than 9,000, though as so few went to church, there was no scrambling for seats. The clergy and the lay missioners sallied forth from fifteen churches, six mission halls, one tent, a shop and a disused factory. Services, meetings and Sunday school classes were held and tracts distributed. Lunch hour factory services consisting of a short address, with musical interludes, were a regular feature. Spontaneous open-air services were apt to spring up in any of the narrow inner city streets which the missioners frequented. Then groups of bare-footed, grubby children would collect to listen to biblical stories and sing "Jesus Loves Me", and some adults would drift from the hotel steps or their front doors, to hear a few earnest words and receive a tract or two. On one occasion, Mr W. H. Croft, a missioner, was knocked down and kicked. However, he believed his greatest problems stemmed from the Mormons who he lamented were winning "ignorant" people in Erskineville.(26) In a pre-mass media era, people generally attended street meetings and this was especially so of the working class, who spent more time in the street to escape their cramped and ill-ventilated dwellings. Therefore, simply the activity of a mission meeting provided entertainment value, apart from the music and sermons. However, the missioners preferred to believe that the children and adults listened earnestly at the outdoor meetings.

The Zone's work branched out in many new directions. At the same time as the middle class parishes were rejecting lay preachers, the Zone stressed their role and used them to good effect. Face-to-face confrontation with the population was achieved through home visiting by the Mission's evangelists and bible women, who believed that this was the best way to confront the religiously indifferent. In 1906, seventeen workers made 35,000 personal home visits, in 1909 the number was 42,000, and in 1912, twenty-five agents made a total of 100,000 home visits.(27) Besides this one-to-one communication, the missioners held services which forced small groups to confront the Christian message. In 1906 the long established work of Rev George Soo Hoo Ten among the Chinese in the Haymarket area was extended by the appointment of Rev A. W. Schapira to evangelize the Asians and Syrians in the dock areas. Though the report's recommendation of a deaconess's institute was not taken up, the Church Army, which had been established by the cornet playing Rev Wilson Carlisle in London in 1882, was introduced into inner Sydney. Archdeacon Langley invited Captain Robinson, a Church Army worker from Melbourne, to come to work in the Mission Zone. Robinson, with predictable evangelical zeal called for recruits:

> Wanted! Men of faith and fire!
> Men whose zeal will never tire;
> Men who dare leave father and mother,
> Business, pleasure, sister, brother.
> Louder let the summons ring
> Wanted, wanted for the King.(28)

Nineteen men offered themselves for the three months' training programme. Robinson worked in St Luke's, Sussex Street city, and the Dauntless Hall of St Silas, Alexandria, and attracted Saturday night crowds of up to 400 at the corner of Botany and Raghlan Streets, Waterloo. However, the attempt failed and there were even suggestions of his incompetence.(29) Robinson lingered on with a handful of followers, until he and his flock were accepted into the Congregational Union in 1909. The Church Army might have failed, but the work of the lay evangelists and bible women thrived.

Not all house visitation was directly spiritual, because at least one-eighth of these visits were to the sick and dying. The tenth annual report of the Zone had specifically stated that the "Mission Zone agent is expected to pay special attention to the sick and the dying and those in poverty".(30) The missioners daily visited those in need of food, shelter and medical treatment, as well as emotional comfort. The agents often discovered unknown distress during their visits. One missioner found a family of four where both parents were incapacitated, the two teenage boys supported the family with fourteen shillings per week, of which ten shillings was needed for rent. He wrote: "When I found them they were in a pitiable state. No furniture of any kind, boxes used for seats and table: almost bare of clothing; the woman's feet covered with old felt hats to keep them warm; no blinds, but paper used for the purpose, and no floor covering. The district nurse attributes the wife's illness to want of proper food."(31) To the Anglican church's honour, it not only challenged the people in the Zone to heed the Word, but also afforded them comfort. Food and clothing were distributed – 17,000 garments being given out in 1913, as well as mattresses, air pillows and hot water bottles. Also, to relieve the distress of poverty, worsened by increasing unemployment in 1913, a labour bureau was established and jobs found for 1,200 men in that year.(32) Such work reflected credit on the Church of England.

However, if the aid was given in a paternal or self-righteous manner, the poor could be resentful and thus not amenable to the gospel message. L. C. Rodd who grew up in a tenement in Bourke Street, Surry Hills, recalled a visit from a charity worker at Christmas time: "The female said, not to my father or mother, but to the room in general, 'We are from the Benevolent Society. We have investigated your case and decided that you are entitled to the Society's charity'. From the bag she took a few miserable packets and placed them on the table . . . and waited expectantly for some effusion of gratitude." It came in the form of the articles being pitched over the balcony onto the pavement, such was the fierce pride and independence of his invalided father.(33) Many of the destitute were not loafers, but hard working people who could not cope, or had been overtaken by tragedy.

If Canon Boyce, strong evangelical, social reformer and temperance advocate, set the tone of the Mission, Rev R. B. S. Hammond solidified it. Hammond was a curate under Canon Archdall and Archdeacon Langley, two of the foremost evangelicals in the diocese, before he became the missioner in the Zone from 1904 to 1910. In those six years he personally conducted 31 parochial missions of two weeks' duration, held 375 lantern slide lectures, addressed 3,000 meetings in halls, factories and streets, and raised £7,000 for the Zone. Hammond also revived St Simon and St Jude's, Surry Hills, and packed out the services with a tenfold increase in attendance. In 1908 he established the Pilgrim's Home, a night refuge, in Newtown. The Governor-General, Lord Dudley, paid tribute to his work by spending a night at the Home in 1910, where incidentally, he met one of his old Oxford colleagues who had fallen by the wayside due to alcoholism. Hammond's greatest gift was his physical vibrance and the sheer force of his presentation during addresses, which compelled men to listen to him. He held the interest of a meeting of strikers by speaking to them on sin, after gaining permission to speak "about a man who went on strike because the wages were too high". Hammond had great rapport with the working class and the unchurched and as he remarked himself: "I spent a lot of time cultivating the non-churchgoer. I liked him. I soon found that interesting sinners were much better company than some stale 'saints'. I found among the non-churchgoers a willingness to serve — often a fine generosity, a kindly consideration and a delightful frankness."(34) One wayfarer stated in his testimony at the Pilgrim's Home that Hammond's work had "taken religion out of a book where I always knew it was, but where it neither touched nor interested me and showed it in the life of my fellow men, and I have been compelled to acknowledge both its power and attractiveness".(35)

In 1910 Hammond resigned from the Zone. He was a man who did not suffer fools or trivia gladly, so that friction soon arose over the administration of the Zone. Tension also mounted because the Mission Zone was so successful that it threatened to outgrow its parent body the Church Society. Hammond moved to St Barnabas's where he continued his work among the destitute. Later in the 1930s he was to found a unique retirement village near Liverpool which bore his name.

The Mission Zone survived without Hammond and achieved a great deal by 1914. However, its energies were always divided between providing material relief, spiritual comfort and moralistic exhortations. Temperance meetings and "Men Only" meetings where the sex question was delicately alluded to, were a feature of the Zone's work. Boyce was the leading temperance light of his day, and Hammond also took up this crusade and edited his own weekly temperance journal, *Grit*, for thirty-six years. Personally, both these men successfully combined temperance with their social reformist views, yet as a whole the Mission Zone did not achieve such balance. The Zone's committee specifically urged its agents to promote temperance work, and the 1905 annual report baldly stated, in terms alien to the social gospel, that "the problem of these overcrowded parishes will largely be solved when the Liquor Traffic is thoroughly reformed".(36) Though Boyce and Hammond would have denied such a simplistic statement, the committee promoted the idea that drink caused poverty, and that the destitution of the working class was due to immorality. In support of this, the Anglican newspaper declared the Mission Zone to be "a special attack upon the enemies of society in the shape of immorality, drunkenness and all those evils which are the source of misery and crime and which are a reproach to our nation".(37) The Zone which was conceived as a coherent attempt to reach the unchurched in the inner city, came to reflect the split between the liberals who saw poverty as the cause of vice, and the conservatives who believed vice caused poverty. The Zone at times was more a moral policeman than a comforter to the poor, and the wider Church certainly saw it as saving the community's morals. But those on the receiving end were less impressed by temperance sermons than ones which preached the golden rule. However, while the moralistic element weakened the Mission's effectiveness, the tens of thousands of personal visits, the hundreds of services, the material relief broadcast, and the words of comfort given each year within five square miles, showed the working class that Anglicanism was finally caring. To some it was too little too late, but a few returned to the Church, and the others at least heard the Word and felt its compassion!

Methodism had working class origins in early nineteenth century England, and although it had become significantly middle class by 1900, it still had some rapport with the working class. Rev W. G. Taylor, a thin and dreamy evangelical Yorkshireman, began the Central Methodist Mission (C.M.M.) in the Centenary Hall in York Street, Sydney, in 1884, and the enterprise met with such success that it expanded to the larger Lyceum Hall in 1905. The C.M.M. approached the new overseas concept of the institutional church, which ministered to the body as well as the soul, by material aid and entertainment. It operated homes for inebriates, foundlings, fallen and friendless women, seamen, homeless men, and the aged, and a training centre for its evangelists. It also provided devotional groups, sporting and youth clubs, and fostered a musical society and a brass band. Five other mission churches were opened up by the Methodists in the inner city and one in Newcastle by 1912.

These mission churches provided a base for outdoor relief and evangelism in street, home and factory. Food, clothing, rent assistance and medical help were given to the needy. Even the inner city churches which were not designated mission churches gave this kind of sustenance. Always it came with a kind word, a bit of humour and of course a religious message, because Taylor believed "philanthropy severed from evangelism should never form a part of the Church's propaganda".(38) Therefore, if sick or poor sailors were visited as part of the seamen's mission, a religious tract was always given out and an attempt made to get a conversion and a temperance pledge. Taylor's reminiscences are scattered with accounts of marvellous conversions of alcoholics, ex-boxers and criminals. His evangelists followed suit because their open-air meetings usually had a moral purpose firm in the view that vice created destitution. One evangelist wrote: "Our lantern service in the slums on Wednesday last was a contribution to the solution of the problem of temperance reform — it was seed sown by the wayside, it was bread cast upon the waters, seen in after days." He was certain a "surrender of hearts" had followed the singing of "When We All Get to Heaven" and "All to Jesus I Surrender".(39)

The mission churches were generally well attended. The Lyceum Hall attracted 1,000 people, and it was claimed the Montague Street Balmain mission which held its services in an old ice-skating rink captured a similar number.(40) To an extent this was due to the attractions of the sporting facilities, reading rooms, brass bands and the use of newfangled devices, such as phonographs and lantern slides. The pleasant Sunday afternoon of musical entertainments and Christian addresses proved popular because as one C.M.M. evangelist remarked: "It is a bare statement of fact that scores of families find the only break in the dull, monotonous round of the week's work in the entertainment provided at the Halls. Many a time we have met those who had to watch so closely every penny of their income that the smallest amount could not be spared for anything outside of the food and clothing bill."(41) These mission churches were attended mainly by the working class, the poor and "horny-handed" people and were avoided by the "respectable" and middle class. One church trustee of Balmain West End church remarked that the recent alteration of his church to become the Rozelle mission "caused us to lose a number of families who prefer to worship in regular churches elsewhere".(42) However, on the other hand, despite Taylor's denial, there are suggestions that the services of the C.M.M. itself were attended by many suburban middle class commuters, who came to hear the foremost Methodist preachers, Taylor himself and Revs P.J. Stephen and W. Woolls Rutledge, and to hear the hundred strong choir.(43) Indeed, a New Zealander who preached at the C.M.M. expressed disappointment that the congregation "was so respectable".(44) Were the meetings for the outcasts held at midnight for their convenience, or in consideration of the sensibilities of the respectable eight o'clock congregation? However, the C.M.M. was still the focus of Methodism's considerable philanthropic efforts and the record of its work is sprinkled with conversions from among the inner city dwellers; 175 surrendering after one fourteen day's mission in 1905. Like the Mission Zone of the Anglicans, this rescue work and open-air evangelism, put Methodism in touch with many hitherto unreached inner city dwellers.

The other churches made far less organized and concerted attacks on the working class problem. Leading Presbyterian, Congregational and Baptist clergy, some of them liberals, advocated new methods for inner city work and discussed the merits of the institutional church and evangelistic techniques. The Presbyterian church even set up an unwieldly committee of fifty-two members on this question, and although it did not recommend the establishment of an institutional church like the C.M.M., it urged that existing churches use such methods.(45) This small group of aware clergy made little impact, because the Presbyterian and Congregational churches as a whole were too caught up in a middle class view of the poor, and lacked a strong background of slum work which the

Methodists and Anglicans possessed. The Presbyterian Home Mission Committee in 1902 remarked of the inner city: "Here it is not physical difference that separates the people from the ordinances of religion, but moral antipathy, indifference, contempt, distrust, debased personal habits, unhappy domestic conditions, chronic poverty, drunkenness, open traffic in sin, pursuit of luck. Of churches there is plenty, but of full congregations a sad scarcity."(46) The Moderator in 1902, Rev Walker, believed the "problem of great cities was everywhere the problem of Christianity". Yet he appeared to lack a real empathy with the destitute, because in 1905 he warned theological students "to be careful in giving money to beggars. My painful experience during a long stretch of years is that nineteen out of twenty, if not forty-nine out of fifty, who ask for money at the manse door, do not deserve it, and a very large proportion drink it."(47) Also, many Presbyterians and Congregationalists were too well educated and too theologically sophisticated to support the emotional "heart religion" and simplistic evangelism which was needed for house and street evangelism in the slums. The evangelistic committee affiliated with the Presbyterian century fund commented on the prejudice in many congregations to missions and added: "crude methods and cruder theology do not commend themselves to our ministers or people".(48) On the other hand, the Baptists distrusted the entertainments given at institutional churches and street meetings, because their rigid evangelical views held that amusements or even attempts at moral elevation obscured the real message of the gospel.

Despite this reticence, these churches did some slum work. The Presbyterian Women's Missionary Association in 1905 switched from its preoccupation with foreign missions and supported the efforts of two deaconesses at Palmer Street church, Woolloomooloo.(49) The affluent St Phillip's church, Macquarie Street, supported a missioner to the sailors and city hospitals. The Pitt Street Congregational church ran a mission and soup kitchen in Sussex Street, though it had dated as far back as 1852. The Baptist churches in Burton and Bathurst Streets began institutional methods and the latter employed a mission sister for home visitation, who claimed to have brought many new faces to chapel "to hear the Gospel in all its purity and truth".(50)

However, it was a miserable effort in terms of the increased needs of the 1890s and early 1900s! It might be said that G. E. Ardill, the prominent Baptist who organized and managed twelve rescue and aid societies, did more in this direction than the remainder of his denomination as a whole. Many Christians did local and quiet work for the poor outside the churches. Some lent their administrative skills. Congregationalist Sir Arthur Renwick was honorary president of the Benevolent Society, and James Stedman, an active Anglican and manufacturer of sweets and "Kiss Me" chewing gum, directed several aid societies. It is true that the Anglicans and Methodists did a considerable amount for the working class, but much more could have been done if these suburban middle class churches had stretched their imaginations and mobilized their supposed Christian charity. But then they were busy building churches and was not that also a work of God? Yet was it an appropriate one in terms of the current needs?

The great Australian bush has proved an unyielding environment for the efforts of countless men and women, and likewise the endeavours of Christianity. The influence of the churches was countered by two things: the barbarism that pervaded rural society, and the huge distances that typified the Australian backblocks.

At the base of the barbarism was the sheer hard task of carving out the land and working it. The rural workforce of miners, and pastoral and agricultural labourers, who formed a third of all breadwinners, generally worked the daylight hours for six days a week. Therefore, men toiled for up to fourteen hours a day, at times in searing heat or miserable rainy conditions. The shearers, many of them still preferring the blade to the newfangled mechanical shears, bent up and down and wrestled with over a hundred sheep a day, for sixty hours a week from July to December. In the remainder of the year they joined the rest of the rural workers digging "spuds", harvesting, fencing or splitting timber. Much of the rural workforce was itinerant, so those with families often left them behind on a selection somewhere. These men would return with some cash if they managed to avoid the pubs, to eke out an arduous existence on their farms, becoming leathery before finally falling victims of arthritis or heart disease.(51) Their women all the time beside them, as Lawson wrote in "Past Carin' ":

> Through flood and fever, fire and drought,
> And slavery and starvation;
> Through childbirth, sickness, hurt and blight,
> And nervousness an' scarin',
> Through bein' left alone at night,
> I've come to be past carin'.

The railway navvies, bullockies and carriers, tasted the tang of sweat and the weariness of long hours. The miners gouged at the earth in dusty open-cuts, or worked for fifty hours in the steamy bowels of the earth, risking death like the ninety-four men entombed under Port Kembla after an explosion in 1902.

Where the work was hard, and muscle the valuable commodity, there was no time for higher things like religion, nor little value placed upon them. Many of the rural working class spent their spare hours drinking and gambling, because they needed excitement and numbness to forget the agony and monotony of their daily lives. Some claimed mateship as their only religion. Others like Joseph Jenkins, a well educated Welshman who spent twenty-five years as a swagman, professed an undogmatic belief in God through the reading of the New Testament.(52) The evidence suggests that only a small number of the rural working class went to church, or read their bibles and attended home prayer meetings. In many parts of the outback, religion was left to the owners of stations who aspired to maintain some elements of civilization.

In the country towns the situation was much better and the shop-keepers and middle class generally, maintained a church life similar to that existing in the suburbs. There were numerous churches in most country towns, but Sunday was generally a busy day, not entirely given over to churchgoing and respite. It was the only time for the bachelor workers to do their washing, and the only chance for many to visit town and do some purchasing. Also, as Steele Rudd sardonically commented: "we always looked forward to Sunday. It was our day of sport."(53) Young men headed for the bush with guns and their dogs, or escorted ladies around the town, while others drank as they played cards or dice. Joseph Jenkins said "some go to church or chapel" but the "stay-at-homers" outnumbered all the other denominations.(54) The clergy sadly admitted the prevalence of sport, intemperance, or work as usual on Sundays, all carried out right under their very noses. Rev Waldock lamented that "it is by no means an infrequent experience for our men to be conducting Divine Service on the Lord's Day, while a tennis or football match is in full swing outside the building".(55)

The vastness of the Australian bush made a mockery of the parish and circuit systems which were more suited to the smaller scale of the English countryside. In the bush the large distances between settlements, which were themselves often too small to support a clergyman, meant that minister's visits were few and far between. The clergy often had to choose between ministering to the town or the bush, and for convenience chose the town. Small settlements close to country towns had services at least once a month, but those further out might only see a clergyman twice a year, or not for years on end. Many had to attend services of another denomination and combined or union churches were common in the bush. In these circumstances people drifted into religious apathy or despair. Rev Patison remarked that the people on the Gloucester River "are tired of burying their dead without even the semblance of a service, and they often long for a minister to visit their sick".(56)

The life of a clergyman was hardest in the bush! Like all bush people, the cleric had to confront an unpitying environment and ultimately himself. Rev Matthews, a newly arrived Englishman who worked between Dubbo and the Paroo River, reflected thus on the life of a bush missionary: "Loneliness sometimes becomes a burden greater than he can bear, the loneliness which consists often on his journeys in an almost entire absence of all human fellowship of any sort or kind, and a corresponding sense of the vastness of Nature which is always depressing to sensitive souls."(57) The bulk of the bush clergy travelled up to 6,000 miles a year on horseback, pushbike or buggy. By 1914 the more courageous took to the country roads on motorcycles. Heat, hardship, loneliness and the prospect of becoming "bushed" were just some of the common problems. Rev J. Adams of Blayney, survived several flooded rivers only to be thrown into a fence by his horse where he hung unconscious till rescued. The shock and the injuries caused him to resign his pastorate.(58) Rev G. Laverty of Wilcannia used to bicycle twenty miles to give services, only stopping "to remove the green scum from a stagnant pool to quench his thirst".(59) Bush parsons often wrestled with the elements as much as with old Satan. Rev T. Morgan slogged across the black soil plains in a buggy, and Rev P. A. Smith coaxed a gospel van across stony ground amid dust storms, to discover settlements without bibles and Presbyterians unministered to for over ten years.(60)

If life was hard for the clergy, it was toughest for the older ones, some of whom ended their sojourn on earth alone on a country road. The Anglican and the Presbyterian clergy were worst off in contrast to the three or five year pastorates of the Methodists. Some spent their whole life in the bush, not always from choice, but because they were not called to a city church. By no means rare was the case of Rev T. Johnstone who spent forty-three years at Armidale and had one holiday to England for six months in that time. The *Messenger* remarked of several of the eight clergy who passed away in 1904: "if they could have been given changes of spheres a few years ago, it seems to us that they would not have died".(61) Presbyterian country clergy at a ministers' conference in 1905 spoke of hardships, one lamenting that he had not had the pleasure of worshipping as a member of a congregation for ten years.(62) Anglican and Presbyterian committees which considered the question of long term pastorates could never agree on alternatives. The matter always lapsed and a number of clergy continued to be trapped in the outback.

Once again it was the Anglican church which made an imaginative response to the problem of religious indifference among many bush dwellers, and the difficulty posed by the vastness of the territory to cover. In 1903 the Brotherhood of the Good Shepherd was founded in the Bathurst diocese. It was modelled on the similar unique experiment begun in 1898 in the Rockhampton diocese. The brothers who were originally Englishmen serving a five year term in Australia, were to cover an area of 50,000 square miles bounded by Walgett, Dubbo, Cobar, the Paroo River and the Queensland border, and minister to all those untouched by the parish clergy. They received a token £25 per annum and for obvious practical reasons rather than theological choice, were pledged to remain unmarried during their stay in the brotherhood. It was not a religious community because the bush brother was "one who is sent out to fraternize with all and sundry",(63) and besides their work meant that they rarely saw each other at their base in Dubbo. Rev E. S. Hughes stressed this fact to the Church Congress in Adelaide in 1902, to scotch evangelical criticism of the creation of the brotherhood, but to no avail. Canon Archdall maintained it would debase church life and the Orange element in the Sydney diocese lamented that Bathurst was on the way to popery.(64)

In 1900 the Mudgee Methodist circuit introduced a similar concept of an unmarried circuit missionary to cover the outer fringes of its boundaries. His itineracy allowed him to traverse untouched ground and his bachelor status meant a smaller stipend which could be more easily accommodated by his impecunious church. The Methodist conference which was increasingly concerned about the expense of extension, enthusiastically approved of this innovation.(65) In 1905 there were fourteen circuit missioners and in 1914 about twenty, one of whom was Rev H. Doust who zipped around the Riverina by motorcycle. Inspired by Canadian precedents, the Presbyterians in 1906 created a mission district in the Bourke area, manned by lay agents under the guidance of a clerical superintendent.(66) The Presbyterians seriously discussed whether these unordained men should be allowed to administer the sacraments. This was resolved in the negative, but they did at least tacitly allow them to baptize and endeavoured to train them by correspondence for the ministry.

The churches made other innovations in an attempt to reach those in outlying areas. The non-denominational New South Wales Bush Missionary Society had used gospel waggons since 1856 and the churches adopted this itinerant method after 1900. The Methodists were first with a van in the Riverina area, which reached some untouched for many years. However, the work soon ceased due to the exorbitant cost of horse feed during the great drought. The Anglicans had a van in the Grafton district in 1903 and the Presbyterians in the Bourke area in 1905. These vans were usually well equipped with lantern slides and Christian literature. However, they were expensive to run. The Baptists had to delay such work until the Sunday school children were able to raise enough money to buy a horse for Rev Kay's van, which they named "Junior". As the Baptists were so small a denomination, Baptist churches in the bush were rare, and thus Baptists often worshipped with other Protestants. It was little wonder that Kay wrote: "I have often seen the name on the car looked at askance".(67) It was only by 1914 that the Baptists, and to a lesser extent the Congregationalists, were penetrating country towns, especially those of the north coast.

Within the context of hardship and frustration, the bush parsons, especially the new itinerant variety, carried out energetic Christian work. If some faltered like the Anglican, Rev C. Lumsden, who resigned after two years gospel van work, it was either because the body was weak, or the soul destroyed by the disappointment. The parsons visited homesteads, small towns, shearing sheds and isolated, transitory timbercutters' camps. They gave lessons at any bush or Sunday school they sighted, though dedicated laity often preceded them on their own initiative. The clergy baptized, confirmed, married, buried, exhorted and comforted in their journeys of thousands of miles a year. Confirmation classes were begun on a promise to return "soon". Bibles were shown in shearing sheds for the first time.(68) The Presbyterians in the north-west received quarterly rather than yearly visits after the establishment of the mission in that area. The three encampments of railway navvies near Helensburgh received the services of a full time lay Anglican missioner in 1913. By 1914, the Brotherhood of the Good Shepherd had seven priests, five laymen, a community of sisters at Gilgandra, twenty-two horses and two motor-cycles.(69) With a slowly declining rural population on the one hand, and increased church activity on the other, the churches were in closer contact with the people in the bush by 1914. However, did these people care more about religion?

Perhaps not even the clergy themselves could have answered this question. It seems that in the country town, religious life was at least healthy, if not universal, and Christians could enjoy a corporate church life approaching that offered in the city. In the remotest areas, the clergy always claimed they were well received. "All the missionaries report universally good receptions and kindly treatment by old friends and new" was a typical report.(70) Certainly this was true of most of the homesteads where they were welcomed as educated, respectable and civilizing forces. Mr A. Lawrie of Rawdon Vale Station, near Barrington, told Rev Patison that he was willing "to support any Protestant minister".(71) Parsons even described their audiences in the sheds as attentive! However, perhaps this was due to bush hospitality, or the hearing given to a stranger with a good yarn, rather than a "hungering for the Bread of Life". Among the workers there was an air of reticence and the bushmen have been traditionally seen as anti-religious.(72) One bush song has as its chorus:

> Why, strike me pink, I'd sooner drink
> With a cove sent up for arson
> Than a rain-beseeching, preaching, teaching
> Bloody, cranky parson.(73)

However, not all bush parsons were moralizers. Some of them had the intelligence to stress the positives of the golden rule. A number of clergy had an immense respect for and rapport with the bushmen, even though they openly disapproved of their irreligious ways.(74) Other bushmen believed they had little need for the parson, because they had developed the golden rule of mateship from their own experience:

> No church bell rings them from the Track
> No pulpit lights their blindness —
> 'Tis hardship, drought and homelessness
> That teach those Bushmen kindness.(75)

In his own account of his four years in the Brotherhood, Rev Matthews referred to steady development and "ups and downs", rather than large gains. The Principal of the Brotherhood in 1911 sanguinely hoped that their work would tide the Church over until closer and more frequent contacts could be made, and concluded that "if we can say that our occasional visits to remote places prevent deterioration, it is something even if there are no positive results to record".(76) If the remote areas only received the bare essentials, at least it was an improvement, because before the itinerant innovations and the greater efforts by the church extension committee, not even the bare essentials were offered. If there were no great gains for Christianity, there were certainly no significant losses!

In both the city and the bush the children were of crucial concern to the Church because here lay the future of Christianity. The clergy generally agreed with Bishop Camidge of Bathurst that "once win the children, once sow in the virgin soil of their young hearts the good seed of the Word of God . . . and we shall have laid a foundation upon which the true Christian life may be built, a foundation which can never be altogether destroyed".(77) The home was seen as the cradle of Christian influence, but many anxious clergy believed that modern life meant that parents were too preoccupied to teach their children effectively. Rev Walker suspected that nowadays home religion amounted to little more than the Lord's Prayer and "Gentle Jesus Meek and Mild".(78) Therefore the burden rested on the churches to reach the children in day or Sunday schools.

The biggest challenge to the churches lay in contacting the children in the state schools. This was due to the fact that the Protestant churches had largely retreated from the education field since the passing of the Education Act of 1880 had placed education in New South Wales on a firm footing. Indeed by 1900 only two per cent of all school children attended Protestant private schools. However the Protestant educational influence should not be dismissed. Protestant church schools all but monopolized secondary and thus tertiary education until 1914.(79) Here, hundreds of civic leaders and their cultured wives were manufactured by physical, moral, religious and secular education of a high, if regimented, standard.(80)

Even though the 1880 Act had made state education secular, and the Catholics derided this system as "godless", there was still room for an important Protestant presence in state education. This was made possible by the particular definition of "secular" in the Act which allowed for undogmatic bible readings by teachers and also one hour per day of denominational instruction from visiting ministers. The embarrassing fact was that the 800 Protestant clergy in the state could not hope to visit the 2,800 state schools regularly, let alone every day. This was the challenge for the Protestant churches!

In 1903, the Minister for Public Instruction, Mr J. Perry, criticized the churches for their laxity, pointing out that the Anglicans averaged only six visits per school per annum, the Methodists and Presbyterians one, and the others less. The clergy indignantly refuted his figures, but their own statistics only revealed that about half the schools were visited once a fortnight, while the others were never touched.(81) It was hard enough for the overworked clergy to visit the suburban schools, and it was almost an impossibility to reach the many scattered bush schools. Increased efforts by the Anglicans, who had ten paid workers and some voluntary teachers to help the clergy, only resulted in half of the city schools and a third of the country schools being visited in any regular fashion. With smaller budgets, the other churches reached even less and had to fall back on combined Protestant classes, especially in the country areas. The worth of these lessons, even when given, can be questioned, as the clergy were often quite incapable of handling school children. The *Messenger* commented that some clergy are "so unskilled that they grow discouraged, and give it up".(82) Militant Protestant, Rev Dill Macky, certainly had no intention of ceasing, and he remarked that he had "no fear that the children in my class will ever become Roman Catholics".(83) No doubt Dill Macky spiced his lessons with anti-papist propaganda! The churches certainly made renewed efforts to cover the schools after Perry's criticism in 1903, because while 19,000 visits were made by clergy to schools in 1900, by 1904 the number was 40,000, and in 1912, 52,000.(84) However it was clear the churches were unable to mobilize enough resources to reach the children, as only half received regular lessons, and these were of dubious value. Greater hope lay in the Sunday school where the help of the laity was more readily available.

The Sunday school was probably one of the most effective agencies for christianizing the population that the churches possessed. About half of all Protestant children were enrolled in Sunday schools and over forty per cent actually attended.(85) Younger children and girls were the best attenders. Yet Sunday schools were not without their problems. The attendance at the Methodist morning schools declined, although the afternoon classes remained healthy. In 1910 the *Methodist* lamented that the children could no longer be introduced to church membership simply by marching the whole morning school over to the church service.(86) Undaunted, the Methodists established a Young Worshippers' League in 1914 which encouraged attendance at the morning service and within a year it had 14,000 members.(87) They also introduced a catechumen ticket which gave junior, and finally, full church membership to the Sunday school member. This stemmed the leakage from the Sunday school back to the church.

While crayons, cut-outs, songs and bible stories may have implanted simple Christian truths, there was little doubt that the schools could have been educationally much better. There was a continual shortage of teachers and consequently the young, the inexperienced and the do-gooders were prominent. The Presbyterian committee commented that "the problem is to find teachers of any sort and it is little wonder, therefore that the teaching is not what it ought to be".(88) Rote learning of the Scriptures was a feature and Mr T. K. Abbott, an Anglican Sunday school examiner, complained of a lack of lesson preparation by teachers and insufficient use of the question and answer technique.(89) Yet these teachers were a dedicated group despite their shortcomings, and the *Messenger* with much justice commented that "there is no body of workers from whom the church expects more and for whom she does less".(90) Generally they worked under difficult conditions, in schools which were poorly equipped and usually did not have separate class-rooms.

The 1900s witnessed a growing interest in Sunday school teacher training and better educational methods in the schools. Since 1890, teachers could subscribe to the *Australian Sunday School Teacher* which gave hints and lesson aids, to supplement the weekly meetings presided over by the minister or Sunday school superintendent. Modern educational ideas filtered in from America and England, the most notable being better equipment, graded lessons, separate class-rooms and the use of child psychology. After 1905 the church press and conferences began to disseminate the new thinking. The Rockdale Methodist Sunday school pioneered graded lessons and other innovations in 1908. However, change came slowly. The 1909 Methodist Sunday school conference focused on the use of cradle rolls for recruitment and how best to manage decision days, and only briefly mentioned graded lessons.(91) The visit in 1912 of Mr G. H. Archibald of the London Sunday School Union Teachers' Training College accelerated the change, with more schools adopting graded lessons and acknowledging Archibald's influence.(92) Sunday school teachers by 1912 were offered night courses in educational principles. Reflecting these influences, the Methodists appointed a clergyman to supervise Sunday school work full time in 1912. He encouraged the new ideas, and for the first time in a decade the number of Methodist pupils measurably increased.(93)

The churches spawned numerous clubs and societies to further bind the young to the corporate life of the Church. There were young men's and women's fellowship societies, bible study groups, missionary support groups and a whole range of less religiously orientated bodies. These groups were supposed to blend the religious and the recreational, but often the former suffered. An investigating committee reported that in the Anglican young men's societies "the spiritual element is wholly in the background while in a few it is omitted".(94) Many of the churches' clubs promoted good citizenship rather than Christianity. The various sporting clubs were clearly to build vigorous bodies for national defence, and even the mutual improvement and debating societies, and the host of temperance groups, including Bands of Hope, Sons and Daughters of Temperance, were to meet civic as much as religious needs. Still, if the religious element survived it was a good way to keep the young in contact with the Church. Though most individual societies had a precarious existence, added together they formed a considerable body of Christian influence.

Perhaps the most remarkable youth group of the period was Christian Endeavour, which was founded in Portland, North America in 1881 and begun in New South Wales in the early 1890s. Its motto was "For Christ and the Church", and its members were pledged to read the Bible daily, and attend church twice a week. Besides spiritual and social activities, the groups supported foreign missions, and senior endeavourers took flowers to the sick, distributed tracts during open-air evangelism, and visited the La Perouse Aboriginal settlement. Membership increased from 12,500 in 1900, to 16,000 in 1911 and then flattened out. Not all members were zealous, because about forty per cent of the endeavourers were associate members, more interested in the social aspect.(95) The bulk of its members were female and over half were Methodists, although proportionally the Congregationalists and Baptists were a little stronger. Not only were these churches staunchly evangelical (with the exception of Congregationalism), but they did not have strong youth groups of their own. This partially explains the small Anglican and Presbyterian involvement, as these churches already had fellowship groups.

Liberal Protestants were reticent about Christian Endeavour for several reasons. Firstly, this society exhibited a certain slickness of organization and methods due to its American heritage. The existence of aggressive "look out" committees for new recruits, showed that American business management was part of its ethos. Secondly, the society typified the conservative evangelism of the time. It was fervent and stressed the relationship between good citizenship, morality and religion. Mr M. W. A. Roberts said to the society's Australasian conference in 1903 that "if we don't organize the children for work against sin, Satan will organize them in schemes against righteousness".(96) The society was extremely pious —

encouraging tithing and home prayer meetings. The secretary of the Balmain group wrote in 1913: "I am sure we have spent some very good and helpful meetings, and have found comfort, strength, and encouragement many times when we needed it".(97) However, thirdly, Christian Endeavour also tended to encourage self-righteousness and "religious excitement and precocity".(98) One redeeming feature for the liberals who sought church unity was that it reflected the strong common Protestant spirit of the times.

Driven on by a sense of anxiety in the face of religious indifference, the churches had tackled extension work with energy and considerable imaginative innovation. However, they still found it hardest to touch and help the working class, as was to be expected in a middle class Protestantism obsessed with moral reform. The ability of man to sympathize with other men different from himself is the hardest of all tasks. The church building and quiet pastoral work brought the churches in greater contact with the people in all areas of the state, but there was a sense that they were doing little more than keeping pace with the tide of indifference against which they rowed. Were short term dramatic efforts a better way to attract the indifferent?

4 Missions and Evangelists

Jesus of Nazareth did not spread the gospel in a regular and localized manner like an ordinary cleric, but moved about creating brief and dramatic impressions, much in the style of an evangelist. The clergy believed that such special and intense efforts should play a part in the daily life of the churches, especially in their work among the indifferent and the unchurched. The "natural religion", that ministers believed all men possessed, was best appealed to by dramatic means. After all, had not St Paul been instantly converted on the road to Damascus when confronted with the voice of God? The evangelicals laid special emphasis on evangelism — "Every preacher an evangelist, and every service a special service", declared the Methodist Conference Pastoral in 1905.(1) They placed great emphasis and value on the conversion experience, which was the basis of their evangelical faith and faith in their evangelism. Most local churches of all denominations held special missions at least once a year and some more often than this. Missions were thus a part of normal church life. What is distinctive about the evangelism of this pre-war period, is the new emphasis on large-scale missions and, more uniquely, interdenominational missions.

It must be stated from the outset that compared to religion in other new societies such as North America, the churches in Australia were basically conservative and unemotional. Sir Charles Dilke when visiting Australia in 1867 noted the absence of new sects and added rather neatly that the colonist likes "to pray as his father prayed before him, and is strongly conservative in his ecclesiastic affairs".(2) Therefore evangelism in Australia was always a shadow of the more enthusiastic efforts overseas.

Only the Methodists had proved capable of real religious fervour, but even amongst them it was in decline by the late nineteenth century. Rev Watsford wrote of a revival at Goulburn in the 1840s: "The whole assembly was mightily moved, the power was overwhelming; many fell to the floor in agony, and there was a loud cry for mercy. The police came rushing in to see what was the matter."(3) At another revival in Wagga in 1877 "strong men wept; and class leaders and local preachers in tremendous tones told of how they had been living at ease, and making an idol of means only, devoid of the real power of God in their souls".(4) However, as Methodism became more respectable and middle class in nature, such outbursts became less frequent and the decline of the class meeting was truly evidence of the demise of religious enthusiasm. Rev Carruthers, who arrived in the Ryde circuit in 1888, noted a "backlash" against the protracted special services of the previous minister, a fervent revivalist, and added that "not a few of the young people especially were perceptibly shy of any attempt to repeat the efforts they had passed through".(5) Unemotional religion was the dominant strain within Australian Protestantism, paralleling the basic stoicism of the Anglo-Australian temperament. A few sought religious fervour, but they were a tiny minority. The Salvation Army which comprised the largest pocket of sect-like fervour in the state only numbered 9,585 in 1901.(6) However, while the general temper of Protestantism was unemotional, there was still a place for special efforts within Protestant worship — for evangelism, if not emotional revivalism.

The Evangelical Council of New South Wales sponsored much of the large scale, interdenominational evangelism carried out in the 1900s. This Council was an interdenominational clerical and lay body, formed in 1899 on the model of the British Free Church Council, to express the common Protestant concern regarding moral problems and the inroads of popery, and to counter these by positive evangelistic enterprises. It had emerged directly from the desire of leading evangelicals to show more aggression towards the enemies of Protestant Christianity! The Council had the support of most evangelicals, but was dominated by the Methodists. The Anglicans generally remained aloof, though they sometimes cooperated with the Council's activities. Indeed, two prominent Anglican evangelicals, namely Canon Boyce and Rev Hammond, were at one time presidents of the Council.(7)

The Evangelical Council in mid-1901 decided to make an assault on the problem of religious indifference by holding a unique interdenominational mission in Sydney and its suburbs in the coming November. Dubbed the simultaneous mission, this effort was to extend nightly for two weeks in over fifty centres. The services, where possible, were to be held in tents and mission halls rather than churches, because the aim was to capture those who never attended church and were perhaps shy of stained glass and steeples. The organizer, Congregationalist Rev W. Allen, had great hopes that the mission would encourage further united efforts. Preparatory prayer meetings were held, 160,000 invitation cards were distributed by house to house visitations, and 60,000 special hymn books were printed.(8) Considerable interest was aroused in religious circles by all this activity. The *Australian Christian World* predicted that it would be the biggest mission held in the southern lands.(9) Even the daily press took notice. Attendances were large, totalling 30,000 nightly, 4,000 alone flocking to the central tent in Hyde Park. The *Daily Telegraph* estimated that 200,000 had been reached by the simultaneous mission, which was an extravagant claim as the metropolitan population of Sydney was only about 500,000.(10) The *Sydney Morning Herald* believed the mission to be one of the biggest religious movements hitherto attempted in Sydney and commented at its close: "There is something inspiring in the spectacle of a metropolis given over for a time to the consideration of things spiritual."(11) Even some in the government were inspired by the efforts of the clergy. The Premier, Sir John See, defended the mission's right to erect tents in public parks on the grounds that the movement would "benefit the conditions and improve the morals of the people".(12) See was so pleased with the churches' efforts for community righteousness that he arranged a free and relaxing harbour cruise for the missioners on the government's yacht, the *Victoria*. It was only two years after this that militant Protestants with short and bigoted memories attacked See for allowing the Catholic Primate, Cardinal Moran, to use the *Victoria* merely to reach the shore when disembarking from overseas.

The clergy to a man were enthusiastic about the results of the simultaneous mission. Rev H. Gainford in typical vein wrote: "A wave of spiritual influence has reached Sydney. Thousands of people of all shades of social, commercial and religious and non-religious character have flocked to the various and many mission meetings held in and around the city."(13) Dr Roseby considered that the tents, which had been used to attract the unchurched and the working class, had succeeded in appealing to the pioneering spirit existent in Australian breasts, and had helped to break down class and denominational barriers.(14) Other clergy thought the unchurched had been reached in the inner city to a greater extent than by any other means. The simultaneous mission gathered in the not inconsiderable number of 4,500 enquirers. Besides, as Rev J. Copeland remarked: "Hundreds have been helped who did not go near an enquiry room".(15) Also the mission had some success in terms of its aims to reach the unchurched, because half of the enquirers came from the fifteen tents, and seventy per cent of all enquirers were men.(16) Therefore a number were conceivably reached among working class males, the group considered to be the most indifferent. However the great majority who attended the mission, and even the tent missions, were regular churchgoers. Rev Hammond was so disgruntled by this fact that at one service he asked the congregation to leave the front seats vacant for the unchurched.(17) Also, as quite a number of people were at the services on more than one occasion, the *Telegraph*'s estimate of a total attendance of 200,000 people seems rather inflated. Still, the mission attracted some of the unchurched, and certainly leavened and strengthened the churches themselves, as many church members renewed their dedication to Christ.

The simultaneous mission was certainly a milestone in Protestant cooperation! Fifty centres had been manned by clergy from all the Protestant churches, including the Church of England. Indeed a united communion service was held at the conclusion of the proceedings. Most commentators in both the secular and religious press believed the mission had expressed the essential unity of evangelical Protestants. The *Methodist* even claimed that during the services it was impossible to distinguish the denominational affiliation of the missioners.(18) Common Protestantism appeared to be strong and increasing in esteem.

The Anglican church however remained officially apart, because Archbishop Smith felt unable "to send official representatives to an outside council for conducting missions" and also believed that the large-scale nature of the mission could lead to artificiality.(19) Nevertheless he added that he hoped Anglican clergy would participate on a local and unofficial level. A few actually did so, and several even defied their church laws by participating in the united communion service. It is clear that Smith was not objecting to evangelism as such. Indeed, at the suggestion of Canon Boyce, the Anglicans held their own simultaneous mission which brought about conversions, "crowded churches and deep spiritual movement".(20) What Smith objected to was official cooperation with those outside Anglicanism in an enterprise over which his church would have little control. Despite the evangelical nature of Sydney Anglicanism, it always retained a certain exclusivism and aloofness from the other Protestant churches. Therefore the Protestant unity manifested by the simultaneous mission was largely confined to non-Anglicans.

In 1902 and 1903, the rural areas of the state were not only gripped by drought, but touched quite deeply by a tent mission which scoured the countryside for "seekers after Christ". It sprang from the desire of staunch Methodist, the Hon E. Vickery, to match the 50,000 guinea target of the Methodist century celebration fund with as many souls. Vickery, who was then a member of the Evangelical Council, perceived that portable tents would enable him to cover the whole state in a short time. The number of tents in use was increased from one to seven after the first mission at Illawarra had captured 2,500 converts.(21) The tents, several of which could seat up to a thousand people, were equipped with organs, appropriate literature, acetylene lighting and a staff of three. One commentator estimated the tent mission cost £70 a week to maintain, while others claimed the overall outlay was between £10,000 and £20,000.(22) The mission was organized for the efficient gathering in of converts for Christ. It was one expression of Vickery's long term desire to win Australia for Christ, and create a Methodism that would parallel the success of his own business empire.(23) It was sadly ironic that Vickery was the principal shareholder in the colliery company whose inefficiency and poor safety precautions contributed to the death of ninety-five miners in an underground explosion at Port Kembla in July

1902. One factor in the disaster was the failure to use inexpensive safety lamps.(24) Indeed, Vickery's expansion of the tent mission in late 1902 and his contribution of £90,000 to build the Central Methodist Mission in 1905 may have been influenced by remorse over the mining disaster; although it is undeniable that he had always been a generous Christian philanthropist. If these gifts were an expiation for the tragedy, it was a private appeasement, for at the time of the tent mission, few were aware that Vickery was its anonymous sponsor.

Though it was initially a Methodist enterprise, the tent mission soon became an interdenominational effort, which reflected the growing common Protestant evangelistic concern, and also the realities of country Protestants, who tended to worship under the one roof. Even Anglican bush clergy supported this mission. The mission continued for a period of two years and visited 200 centres, mostly in country areas. It was highly organized and was generally preceded in each town by considerable preparations. Dodgers, bill-boards, the press and personal invitations all proclaimed the coming event. Cottage meetings and church services of the faithful began to work up the necessary spirit.

At most places the missioners initially reported that the religious and moral condition of the people was depressed, and that there was considerable apathy to the mission. No doubt this was partly an image to create the right dramatic effect among the Christian readers back in Sydney. However such reporting also reflected the true state of religious indifference. Indeed, in some towns, namely Moree, Inverell and Grafton, the hostility encountered was lively, while at Devil's Corner in the working class suburb of Balmain in Sydney, the tent was fired and almost destroyed. In much of the Riverina, the mission was prejudiced by having to follow in the footsteps of that Protestant champion Dill Macky, who was currently touring there for the Protestant Defence Association, disrupting the community and setting some against the Protestant churches and religion generally. However, the missioner Mr W. H. Scurr persisted in his battle against Satan and often won through. In what became quite a typical report he wrote in true evangelical style of the Port Macquarie mission: "Indifference reigned supreme, but the men of God, strong in conviction, resolved in the name of their Lord to break it down . . . Still the fight was a severe one. At first the audiences were small, but interest grew . . . but even then there was a hardness and resistance painful to the lover of souls. The closing night of the mission brought a full tide of blessing and a longing for the mission to continue; but the tent had to be moved on."(25) Rev A. Graham, the local Methodist minister, was left with his soul on fire and the unenviable task of continuing the work.

The pattern was generally the same; or so the missioners claimed in their reports to the Christian press. A town, once indifferent and stained with sin, would slowly be awakened to showers of Christian blessing and conversion. At Wauchope 137 people decided for Christ, while at Taree 90 people came forward in the first three nights. At Lismore one sixth of the town attended the first service and 417 professed. It was even claimed that Sunday football was halted at Narrabri due to the mission. In the Hunter area the results were similarly astounding. A seventh of the town of Coraki entered the enquiry room and at Singleton it was a sixth. At the other mining centre of Kiera in the south the decisions numbered 300. Some of the reports emphasized the number of adults among the seekers — both respectable and care-worn alike. Others stressed the large number of young people among the enquirers. When Rev W. E. Blackwell gathered 300 youths together in the suburb of Granville, many under twelve responded to his appeal for a life in Christ. Children's services were invariably successful. At Lismore it was claimed that the young "converts" showed their "first love" for Christ by entreating their friends to make similar decisions. Rev R. Bavin, president of the Methodist Conference summed up the work as "gloriously monotonous for in each place there is the same record of faithful preaching of the truth and powerful preaching in prayer, followed by deep conviction of sin, knowledge of salvation, and the conscious witness of the Holy Ghost".(26)

Within the twenty-two months of its existence, the tent mission had gathered in 25,000 enquirers, an average of 125 in each of the 200 centres visited. Each of these had spoken personally to the missioner about their salvation, filled in a decision card and had their name forwarded to the church of their choice. These were more than encouraging results which moved Rev W. G. Taylor to comment that "although associated with evangelistic work all my life I have never known a revival of religion like unto this".(27)

It was little wonder that most Methodist circuit meetings acknowledged the mission's importance and influence. The Wagga circuit gave thanks for "the quickening of the spiritual life of believers and the conversion of others", and the Port Macquarie circuit resolved that "a large number of this district have been turned from darkness to light, from the power of Satan unto God, and the work of God has been generally revived".(28) The Grafton district synod, which in October 1902 acknowledged that the mission had "deeply stirred the spiritual life of the Methodist people", recorded a membership increase more than double that of the previous year.(29)   This was not unique, because many other circuits experienced larger than normal yearly increases in church membership. Membership increased in the Manning River circuit from 266 to 357, in the Singleton circuit from 97 to 120, in the Bega circuit from 80 to 145, and in the Camden circuit from 221 to 245.(30) The Glen Innes circuit was one of the few Methodist localities which believed that it had not been revitalized by the tent mission, but it "thanked God for what had been done for others".(31)

This revival of church life was not confined to the Methodist church. For instance, only 20 of the 100 converts at Parramatta were Methodists. Also the mission led to the establishment of prayer groups and Christian Endeavour societies beyond the bounds of Methodism. However, the gains for Anglicanism may have been small, because the Anglican clergy often remained aloof. Rev C. White wrote of the Anglican clergy: "They did not join the crew of the Mission Life Boat; but it may be taken for granted that they stood close to the shore, watched her every movement among the billows of a Satan-tossed sea with keen interest, and hailed with delight every soul rescued by her from the surging surf of sinfulness, in which they were being engulfed into eternal ruin."(32)

Although 25,000 souls were snatched from the "surging surf of sinfulness", how many of these were brought permanently into the churches? The Methodist church statistics revealed that about 1,000 new church members above the usual yearly increase were gained in the year following the mission. The only other statistics available are for the Presbyterian church and these show no significant change. One in every twenty-five appeared a poor survival rate, which might lead one to conclude that there was a leak in the "Mission Life Boat" itself. However the small number of new church members seems to be partially explained by the fact that churchgoers formed the bulk of the mission congregations. Methodist circuit records support the view of the Upper Manning *Presbyterian Record* that "unfortunately those for whom the mission was most intended did not attend the services, and . . . the congregations as a rule were made up of church-going people".(33) Many of the enquirers were in actuality believing Christians and churchgoers reconsecrating themselves to their Master. This fact should not be surprising, because the sudden conversion of Paul on the road to Damascus was atypical. Most scholars and theologians believe that most religious conversions come gradually, and so it was to be expected that many of the enquirers were people already interested in the Christian lifestyle and already formally within the churches. John Calvin pointed to this fact when he remarked that "men never so repent as not to have need of the continuing help of God. For we are renewed from day to day and little by little we renounce the desires of the flesh. We do not put off the old man in one day ... we are converted to God gradually and by sure degrees."(34) Though the actual number of new church members was small, a significant number of existing members were revived and became more committed, temporarily at least.

What of the unknown proportion of enquirers who were not churchgoers and chose to stay that way? It is highly likely that some outsiders who were at the mission made a decision for Christ, but later waned in fervour and never took up church membership. How are they to be counted in the Protestant battle for Christ? Professor Starbuck, who studied the psychology of religious conversion statistically in 1899, would have replied that their decisions for Christ in the mission tents were not worthless even if active church affiliation did not follow. Starbuck claimed that a decision experience brought "a changed attitude towards life, which is fairly constant and permanent, although the feelings fluctuate . . . In other words, the persons who have passed through conversion, having once taken a stand for the religious life, tend to feel themselves identified with it, no matter how much their religious enthusiasm declines."(35) There was no doubt that then, as now, there were many Christians who never darkened the church door. Whether the tent mission's enquirers were already in the churches or never joined them, does not alter the fact that the mission strengthened the cause of Protestant Christianity.

Part of the tent mission's impact was due to its atypical religious enthusiasm. The expectations and suspense created by advance publicity and prayerful preparations, often meant that the mission would gather momentum until the final meetings overflowed with emotion. Rev R. Robertson wrote of the mission at Milton: "The first few nights but little result followed the preaching of the Word; then there was a break through the dark clouds, and the sunshine of God's love and peace flooded the souls of poor distressed penitents, and many testified to the blessing they had received through the mission."(36) It was alleged that the serious minded were reached first and ushered to the enquiry room. Then came the more spectacular successes, as the rowdies, the cynics, the best (or worst) swearers in the district, the sportsmen and the Sunday desecrators — all moved forward to make a decision for a new life. There were denials by the clergy that the services were sensational, but the missioners were so persistent or poignant in their search for souls that tears often flowed. Mr Gilbert, who was the missioner at Dungog, described how, without any pressure, there was a rush for the enquiry room and here "were sights never to be forgotten. Members of families who had been at variance were hanging on each other's necks. Some of the leading business men of the town, who lately had been at law, were locked in each other's arms kissing one another . . . Old companions in sin were locked in each other's arms. Mothers and fathers embraced sons and daughters who had been wayward but had now come to Christ."(37) On this occasion, 212 declared that they were sinners, and 500 people during the ensuing week entered the enquiry room. Rev Colwell, who compiled the *Illustrated History of Methodism* in 1904, commented that "some of the scenes witnessed at the Tent Mission services are too sacred to be held up to the public gaze".(38)

While the level of emotionalism did not approach the extremes of nineteenth century American revivalism, the tent mission revealed considerable religious enthusiasm even for Australian Methodism. Certainly country centres were generally more religiously conservative than urban areas, and therefore less sophisticated, and less inclined to scorn religious enthusiasm than the urban churchgoer. However more than just religious conservatism lay behind the enthusiasm and the number of decisions gained by the tent mission.

There is little doubt that the missioners became skilled fishers of men after holding possibly 2,000 meetings in 200 centres throughout the state. They came to a strong understanding of the psychology of conversion and knew just how to gain decisions. After all this was their job! The report of the Kempsey mission related how Scurr "did not attempt to draw in the net in the first few nights", but when he finally made an appeal, there was a steady flow to the enquiry room.(39) Hymn singing and lantern slides softened up the congregation, and then an earnest plea to accept salvation persuaded many to come forward. However, there had been other missions and other missioners. Just how had the tent mission gathered in 25,000 enquirers and quickened church life? The answer lies partly in the compounding forces of a moral reformist upsurge and the great New South Wales drought and partly with the tent mission's own efficiency and the eternal power of the Word.

The tent mission, like other contemporary evangelistic enterprises, was influenced by the growing Protestant belief that the nation was in need of moral regeneration. For instance the parochial mission at St Andrew's, Seven Hills, held in December 1902, ended with a "men's only" meeting addressed by Rev J. Dixon who spoke of "Sowing and Reaping". Dixon's appeal resulted in thirty-three men of the forty-four who were present agreeing to discountenance drunkenness, gambling, profanity and impurity. However the tent mission probably stressed the moral reform aspect more than most other missions, no doubt due to its Methodist origins. Men's purity meetings were held as an integral part of the mission and White Cross purity pledges were sought especially from the single male. At Lismore 230 men (and perhaps women) signed pledge cards, at Ballina the promises numbered 108, and at Kempsey where the missioner finally ran out of cards, 138 people pledged to keep themselves undefiled. Given the relationship between conversion and the struggle between good and evil, and the fact that sexuality at this time was firmly suppressed as evil by much of respectable society, the missioner's appeal for both a moral and spiritual regeneration was a potent mixture. Some studies of Christian conversion have emphasized that many adolescent conversions accompany guilt feelings associated with growing sexual awareness,(40) and this may account for the large number of young enquirers captured by the tent mission. Certainly many churchmen saw a moral revival emanating from the work of this mission. It was alleged that some of the Mt Kiera miners stopped swearing, bad debts were paid, working men gave a fair day's work and the publicans' business at Coraki was adversely affected.(41) It is questionable how true these statements were, or for how long these conditions may have lasted, but these claims certainly revealed the faith in moral and spiritual regeneration of those who supported the mission.

Perhaps of more importance to the success of the mission was that it coincided with the state's worst drought which lasted from 1895 to 1903. Over two-thirds of all stock in the state died. Forty million sheep alone perished, some by design, like the 7,000 emaciated beasts slaughtered at Wagga in November 1902 for their pelts. The grain yield had dropped by over sixty per cent, and in 1902 not a sheaf was harvested in some areas. The leader of the state opposition, Mr J. H. Carruthers, commented that "in some of the country towns half the shops are closed. In parts of the interior the settlers, large and small, are leaving their homes and temporarily abandoning their holdings until a change comes. The water supply for domestic purposes has become exhausted in many places."(42) He claimed that quite a few people were forced to eat the bran sent to them for stock relief, tempered with treacle. In the western division of the state the conditions were the worst. The stock losses were heavy and here alone, seventy-three crown tenants had walked off the land and left six million acres to any rabbits that may have survived the drought. Business firms in Bourke and other western towns had only a third of their turnover of 1890, and as a result, land sales, construction, farm and station work and general employment were down by a similar degree.(43)

Even the mines were affected by the lack of water. The Sydney Lord Mayor's Drought Relief Fund disbursed £22,524 to stricken and hungry bush dwellers in 1903, and the state government provided £20,000 for water conserving relief works.(44) Mr A. Oliver of the Land Appeal Court, who travelled widely through the state, claimed that "at least three-fifths, if not seven-tenths, of New South Wales is at this moment desert lands".(45) Bush parson Matthews corroborated this official view when he remarked of the outback, "you might drive day after day for a month, and never see one blade of green grass or herbage. Here the whole surface of the black basalt plains was seamed with cracks."(46) One station owner who stayed on his land recalled that at this time, while "lying in my tent at night, I had a persistent nightmare of financial figures passing through my brain, and it seemed absolutely impossible that I could ever pay my debts".(47) The 1903 Methodist Conference alluded to the "high tension" in the outback due to the drought.

Many people around 1900 firmly believed that disease, drought and other natural disasters were a visitation from God. This was by no means confined to the clergy or churchgoers, because even the state government called for prayers for rain, as it did for peace in time of war. The government actually gazetted a public holiday for prayer and humiliation for the drought on 26 February 1902, and a day of thanksgiving to God when it finally broke in December 1902. While no actual tent mission addresses survive, it is inconceivable that the artful missioners did not allude in a providential way to the drought conditions all around them. One of the missioners, Rev Robertson, did remark in one of his reports to the press, that "the country is in a dreadful state. The temporal and spiritual are both in need of a downpour".(48) It is likely that the success and emotionalism of the tent mission depended upon and reflected the "high tension" in the outback at a time of unprecedented drought. A number of people doubtless saw the drought as Divine disapproval of their personal failings, and this, combined with their own economic distress and anxiety, can account for their often fervent decision for a new and more righteous life.

The simultaneous and tent missions had stirred the fires of revival in the breasts of Protestants. In 1902 Bishop Cooper urged an Anglican evangelistic mission to cover the whole of Australia, and all the churches were keen to do likewise. The Presbyterian Evangelistic Committee became active and had four full time missioners by 1910. The Congregational churches responded to the great blessings occurring in the Welsh revival of 1905 by holding their own missions. The Baptists carried out street-corner work with the aid of the donations of several prominent laymen. With touching zeal, the *Baptist* argued that if one man converted another, and each in turn did likewise, within just thirty-one years the whole world would be won for Christ.(49) The renewed evangelical zeal of this period was summed up by Rev B. J. Meeks, who said that "no true Methodist Church can content itself with the ordinary round of worship, while Godless, careless, churchless people whom it may influence and save are all around it".(50) Protestant anxiety did not cause panic, but on the contrary, greater effort! To aid this renewed dedication to save souls, the churches looked for help from foreign gospel practitioners.

In the years around 1900 a large number of overseas evangelists came to Australia and held missions in the Sydney area. The bulk of them were in the American mould of Moody and Sankey, who in the 1870s blended salesmanship and evangelism in highly efficient, large scale Protestant missions which moved England and America for a generation. Under the influence of Sankey's golden voice and Moody's earnest words, thousands decided for Christ. During their first mission in London in 1875, two and a half million people attended the services over four months. It was little wonder that by 1911 there were over 650 active professional evangelists in the United States, many of them graduates of the Moody Bible Institute of Chicago. By the late nineteenth century, Australia was on the "gospel trail" of these itinerant British and American evangelists. In the 1890s the most notable of these were Revs G Grubb, T. Cook and John McNeil, Drs Paton and Talmage, Messrs Gypsy Smith and Duncan Ross. This flow continued after the turn of the century. In 1905 alone, Sydney was graced by such gospel exponents as American Fred B. Smith, the New Zealander Rev J. C. Jamieson and the venerable General Booth. They seemed to drift in and out like the tide, often leaving few ripples on the sands of Christian conscience — yet they were generally well received by non-Anglican Protestant churchmen.

Large evangelistic enterprises were one of the hallmarks of the Christian world in the early 1900s. In 1904 and 1905 the great Welsh revival led by Evan Roberts thrilled Christians everywhere, while Wilbur Chapman and Charles Alexander, among others, spread the gospel in the great cities of Britian and North America. Protestants in New South Wales called for similar showers of blessings. One visitor of interest who responded to their call was Rev Torrey, Director of the Moody Bible Institute of Chicago, who arrived in 1902 for a fortnight "to revive the Church and drive the Devil out of Sydney". He was accompanied by Charles Alexander, the gospel singer whose book of gospel hymns adorned many a chapel in succeeding decades. Alexander so enthralled the congregations, that they astounded Sydney tram and train commuters by singing his "Glory Song" while homeward bound.(51) Alexander's impact in 1902 was important in determining the enthusiastic reception that he and Dr Wilbur Chapman received from Sydney Protestants seven years later.

Chapman and Alexander arrived quietly in Sydney in 1909, supported by a party of seventeen, to conduct a five week mission for the New South Wales Evangelical Council. Local clergy handled the spiritual preparations while the well oiled American machine began to organize the more temporal arrangements. The missioners were to occupy the Town Hall each night, while the local clergy were to hold simultaneous supporting missions in suburban centres. The religious press anticipated great gains based on Chapman's recent successes in Boston and Philadelphia, but carefully stressed that the missioners were not unduly professional or emotional. The *Methodist* cautiously pointed out that not all missions were revivals.(52) The *Messenger* defensively argued that even on the day of Pentecost, some organization and dramatization of the gospel was needed to captivate the people. Besides, it continued, if God gave us emotions was it wrong to express them in religion?(53) Rev Stephen, the convenor of the organizing committee self-consciously pointed out that religious indifference and the modern age demanded sizeable and professional missions, though he quickly added that these Americans were exponents of sane evangelism.(54) But others expressed real fears about the dangers of excessive emotionalism. Nationalists like Rev A. Burt were even concerned that a whole batch of converts might be produced, whose new found faith was expressed in Alexander's racy hymns and Americanism.(55)

From the outset, an unsuspecting Sydney witnessed packed services in the Town Hall each night and, as the mission gained momentum, the crowds seeking admittance grew to such proportions that overflow services had to be held in the Pitt Street Congregational Church. The concurrent Nellie Melba concerts were made to appear feeble by comparison. At one mission meeting, some zealous women listened to the service atop forty foot ladders at the back of the building. On another occasion, by no means unique, 7,000 people were waiting for the seven thirty service at four pm. As this number swelled, the police were called in, and they only narrowly prevented serious injury as hysterical young girls, determined old ladies who achieved wonderful speed, and others, all rushed the doors at once. It was perhaps predictable that in this climate over 1,500 people made a decision for Christ inside the Town Hall that night.(56) Of these "human Niagaras" one correspondent remarked: "Until one saw it with one's eyes, one could not have believed that these things were actually going on in Sydney."(57)

The Chapman—Alexander mission was efficient, neat and well organized for the gaining of decisions. These two men had already held many missions in England and America, where, as one scholar has remarked, Chapman's "genius for organization made his campaign in the great cities astonishingly successful and literally thousands professed conversion under his preaching."(58) Though Chapman seemed sincere enough, the mission had an air of slickness about it. The right mood was created, the religious nerve touched, and the decisions flowed. Alexander opened the 5,000 strong services in the Town Hall with rousing congregational singing, and swapped vaudevillian witticisms with the audience. Individuals were induced to sing solos from their seats, more patter and laughter followed, until the audience was receptive. Then, with the contrast of the second interrogator in a television police drama, the beaming Alexander gave way to the sombre, bespectacled, dark-suited Wilbur Chapman. He would give a quiet, sobering address, urging the congregation to confront the perfection of Christ, and on the other hand their own sinfulness. The congregation was urged to make a decision for a new Christian life. Those who did would move forward, shake Chapman's hand, and then move to another room where they would be addressed again, and counselled by one of the myriad of personal workers. A decision card would be signed and their name forwarded to the church of their choice. Neat and relatively painless!

Few could fail to be touched by the plaintive appeal of Chapman and Alexander. To a special men's meeting, Chapman appealed to the powerful image of home and family. "O men, come home! In the name of your father come home! In the name of your mother, come home! Come home!!" As those deciding for Christ came forward, Mr Naftzer sang "O Mother, when I think of thee, 'tis but a step to Calvary". The appeal to parenthood, to home and hearth, played upon the prevailing idealization of motherhood and the family in a message that appealed to the hearts, but not the minds of the congregations. The preaching often descended to the soppy and the sentimental. One of the most popular hymns of the mission was, "Tell Mother I'll be There".

When I was but a little child how well I recollect
How I would grieve my mother with my folly and neglect;
And now that she has gone to heaven I miss her tender care;
O Saviour, tell my mother I'll be there!

One day a message came to me, it bade me quickly come
If I would see my mothere ere the Saviour took her home;
I promised her, before she died, for heaven to prepare;
O Saviour, tell my mother, I'll be there!(59)

The clergy as well as the laity were mesmerized by the maudlin addresses of Chapman, full of moralizing about stereotyped reformed prize-fighters and wayward youths. At a special ministers' meeting, some overworked and spiritually flagged clergy, who suffered from strained idealism in the face of the religious indifference around them, broke down and "tears streamed down many faces unheeded". All those present were moved, and reconsecrated their lives to their Master.(60)

Ralph C. Norton, who was in charge of the personal workers, gave an insight into the missioners' professionalism when he described the "seige method" that he used in winning souls, which he had learnt while a book salesman. "The seige method", he explained to church workers, "means to approach the people, not with a rush, but warily, to have a plan; to get at them along the line of their own thought and habits."(61) The missioners certainly "got at" many people in a very successful way, through the profession of a heart religion, promoted with considerable professionalism and skill, and framed to the gaining of converts.

All the church press was caught up in the general fervour of the mission, and outdid each other with superlatives. The term "revival" was freely used. The *Messenger* believed that the Americans had outshone Nellie Melba; the *Methodist* declared it to be "Sydney's Pentecost"; while the *Baptist* shouted: "The Church had been quickened with a new energy, thrilled with a new joy, possessed of a new passion for souls, inspired with a new spirit of victory."(62) The *Australian Christian World* issued a daily mission edition; the *Methodist* splashed its pages with pictures, and likened the mission to the great Welsh revival of 1905. Rev Taylor, with breathless excitement, summed up the feelings of the evangelicals: "I find it extremely difficult at this moment to write with calmness. My heart is all aflame as I think of what would happen to our Church in this State were we all . . . to become dominated by the power of the Spirit of Pentecost."(63) At the time, many churchmen saw the mission as a turning point. Certainly those who attended the meetings found them thrilling. The surging crowds, the mad dash for a seat, the power of over 5,000 voices and the thrill and quiet emotion of Chapman's addresses, all made for a memorable night. Christians believed that they were a force in the land after all, and the less committed found it to be a train fare well spent. The large crowds continued until the end of the mission, and there was a steady stream of ashen-faced people to the enquiry room, where they confronted that decision between heaven or eternal damnation.

Most missions were geared to the gaining of decisions. What then were the numerical gains of this mission? It was stated that 3,500 enquiry cards were given out during the mission, which appears small in terms of the great crowds and the reports in the press.(64) A rough count from the press reports would place the number of decisions at perhaps 10,000, because it was claimed that 3,000 went forward at one service alone.(65) The statistics of the Methodist church revealed a membership increase of 2,000 in 1909, three times the normal, which implied a gain from the mission of possibly 1,000 people. Other churches reported increases and the Presbyterian church actually received 362 enquirers' cards and admitted 273 people to church membership.(66) Still the gains were not large in terms of the crowds, or the results of earlier, home-grown missions. As usual, the bulk of those attending were established church-goers, and many attended more than once, to be thrilled by the preachers. Even if they had wished to, the unchurched and footloose would have found it difficult to compete for seats with those who streamed off the suburban trams. The missions held simultaneously in the suburbs remained well in the background, though the attendances were swollen when Chapman and Alexander occasionally left the Town Hall to preach in the suburbs. Churchgoers also formed the bulk of the congregations of the suburban missions. As the convenor of the Woolloomooloo mission remarked: "Repeated house-to-house visitation, was not sufficient to draw them [the unchurched] through the doors of the churches. True there had been a goodly number of conversions, but these were almost without exception among church attendants."(67)

However all the churches still termed it a success, and reported increased attendances at church and the holding of special services. Despite the moderate number of enquirers, Chapman could still call the mission an unqualified success, because his stated aims at the outset had protected himself nicely: "This campaign is essentially a ministers' movement . . . We stand for the minister and the Church. Though we gain thousands for Christ, we do not count a mission a success, unless we can claim a revived Church."(68) There was little doubt that the mission would be able to get the churches on side, and enthuse them, and this in fact occurred. The churches were given a fillip, and perhaps this was success enough, provided that the excitement did not disrupt the churches thereafter, by making the hum-drum of ordinary church life appear boring. A throng of

2,000 people farewelled the mission party at Central Station. Chapman was presented with a testimonial from 140 Sydney clerics who declared that the mission had caused "the quickening of God's people and markedly so of many preachers of the Gospel, who had begun to lose hope through the lack of results".(69) The farewellers sang hymns till the train was out of sight.

The following months certainly witnessed a revival of evangelistic activity. The Methodist clergy formed a league of prayer to induce further religious revival and increase church membership. Services along evangelistic lines, complete with Alexander's hymns, were much in evidence. Taylor and Mr J. Gilmour held ninety-eight services throughout the New England area, to spread the "revival" to rural areas. They claimed that 4,000 "converts" were gained and that £600 was raised for the Central Methodist Mission.(70) In 1910 A E. Walker, a former member of the tent mission and one of a family of clerics and local preachers, was appointed as a full time Methodist evangelist by his church. The Presbyterian Evangelistic Committee received so many requests for its services that, even with five full time evangelists, it could not fulfil the needs. Dr Porter, a prominent Baptist clergyman, came out of retirement to undertake evangelism until the Baptist Union could appoint a full time missioner to continue the "revival". The Congregational ministers held several conferences to discuss methods of gaining and retaining members, and formed a men's fellowship to minister to the working class and backsliding members. Activity existed also on an interdenominational level, for both a Bible Success Band, dedicated to learning a verse of Scripture a day, and the Pocket Testament League, sprang out of the mission. A Tramway Men's Pocket Testament League with 350 members was spontaneously created during the mission. In all, the whole stock of 35,000 pocket-sized testaments brought by the missioners to Australia were sold. It seemed that Ralph C. Norton was still a book salesman, practising the "seige method", and one wonders how much the missioners made on each copy. But it was beyond doubt that the churches were revitalized by the Chapman-Alexander mission, if they were not greatly enlarged.

Yet, as the fervour of 1909 died, some of the clergy began to rethink the wisdom of going through another such intensive mission experience. In general there was, and always had been, some reticence towards emotional and sensational evangelism. Bishop Stretch summed up this view in 1907 when he commented that "a mission is a medicine, and a fairly drastic medicine too. If administered without careful consideration of the constitution of the patient it may go near to killing instead of curing."(71) Liberal Protestants were not only offended by religious enthusiasm, but also by the conservativeness of most of the evangelical missions which were "generally identified with the narrowest and most reactionary theology, and have been punctuated by attacks upon Higher

Critics, upon modern thought in all its branches, and upon some harmless customs in which many find innocent pleasure".(72) Others were concerned at the disruption of normal church life. Some believed that church finances had suffered during these missions. Still others were sceptical about the gains made during large-scale revivalist missions. This had proved to be the case with the Chapman-Alexander visit, and evidence from Wales suggested that in the long term the Welsh revival had weakened Nonconformity, not strengthened it.(73) Conservative evangelical, Rev Harry, and the liberal Congregationalist, Rev Cowling, were at one in believing that missions from within the churches were more effective than those of the travelling professional evangelist.(74) Certainly, the simultaneous and tent missions had been more quietly effective than the Americans' efforts. Some clergy were clearly jealous of the kudos given to evangelists and denied "the hard working minister, with his far more strenuous and exhausting toil".(75) Indeed, eloquent and powerful evangelists threatened the prestige and standing of the parochial clergy which had been built up by years of toil and dedication. In previous centuries, new Christian sects had often emanated from the charisma of one person, and no doubt for this reason alone many clergymen felt uneasy about the activities of these artful professionals.

The New South Wales Evangelical Council in late 1909 and early 1910, negotiated for the return of the Chapman-Alexander party in 1912. However, even the Council was uneasy about the book-selling activities of the recent mission, and urged that such commercialism be avoided in the future.(76) Others were more critical. Rev J. Mursell of Brisbane fired the first shot in a letter to the *Australian Christian World*, opposing the invitation for a return mission in 1912. Though Mursell conceded that good work had been accomplished in 1909, he maintained that 1912 was too soon for the repetition of such special efforts. He also guardedly raised questions about the character of several of the mission party.(77) The journal called for correspondence and published twenty replies "from a variety of sources". Though this journal had previously been an ardent supporter of the 1909 mission, the replies it printed were two to one in favour of postponing the proposed 1912 mission.(78) The majority rejected the sensationalism of "the advertising methods and extraneous excitement that characterised recent evangelical campaigns", and which disrupted church life.(79) Certainly, both within and without the Sydney Town Hall in 1909 there had been extraordinary scenes taking place. Most believed that the results were too ephemeral and brought "few, if any, additions to church membership".(80) Many clerics were obsessed with counting heads, and if the 1909 mission had gathered in more converts, they might have forgiven its sensational methods. As it was, it could only claim to have enthused church members. However, the whole purpose of the evangelistic enterprise in this period was to reach the unchurched, especially the working class and men, who formed the hard core of the religiously indifferent. One "minister of wide experience" (the journal did not identify the correspondents in this debate) claimed that the upper working class in his neighbourhood "generally regard such missions with marked unfriendliness, and some features of them almost with contempt".(81) Such antagonism would have been even greater among the less "respectable" sections of the working class.

As the invitation to Chapman had already been sent and accepted, all this talk was so much tilting at windmills. However it had given the churches a chance to confront the whole question of evangelism and its role in orthodox Christianity. On the eve of the return of the Americans, Rev Macintyre gave a spirited defence of emotionalism in religion, which was perhaps a little strange for a Presbyterian.(82) However, the bulk of Protestant opinion of all complexions lay with the *Australian Christian World* which had tempered its earlier enthusiasm for large-scale missions enough to warn of the "spiritual and moral dangers to the life of a community in working up emotional excitement".(83)

The Chapman-Alexander mission party spent three weeks in Sydney in July and August 1912, and undertook campaigns in Newcastle and Goulburn. The style was the same as 1909, with the same inspiring singing by Alexander and Naftzer, followed by Chapman's heart seeking preaching, laced with anecdotes of reformed pugilists and converted pickpockets. A choir of 800 voices was added to the packed Town Hall services which increased the spectacle, but reduced the seating available to the "seekers after Christ". The efficiency seemed greater than before. Always ready for a good story, the daily press showed more initial interest in the Americans that it had in 1909. However, although the crowds were still large, they were much more subdued, and so the press soon lost interest. The church press also took far less notice; its innocence had been lost in 1909. The *Australian Christian World* did not issue a daily penny issue this time, and only the *Methodist* conjured up any real enthusiasm. Many clergy were again tear-stained throughout the special ministers' meeting, but their former enthusiasm for the mission party had waned. Even Taylor did not speak with breathless excitement when he called on Methodists to extend "the fires of revival".(84) Significantly, he was the only one to use the term "revival" to describe the 1912 campaign.

The desire to "Go ye into the world, and preach the gospel to the whole creation" did not suffer from the reaction against large-scale, professional missions, but it did cause evangelism to assume certain forms. The clergy came to realize through the hard school of experience that the simultaneous and tent missions, which were locally inspired and controlled, and less sophisticated and organized, were more productive of results than the efforts of visiting professionals. But those who were perceptive saw that even the parochial missions only revived the churches and did not capture those outside them despite the fact that this had been the whole aim of evangelism in this period. In this sense the churches had made little or no progress. The working class was still largely outside the Church, and there seemed little that could be done by anyone to change this, especially by middle class churches. After 1912 the emphasis shifted to small denominational missions held by ordinary clergy, or the official evangelist of the denomination, who visited each local church one by one and carried out quiet work. Some staunch evangelicals fostered street campaigning, though these were local efforts. Even Mr G. E. Ardill, the president of the newly created Open-Air Gospel Mission, stressed that there was "no intention to conduct a huge campaign in the city of Sydney, and thus in any way disorganize church work in the various suburbs".(85) Religious fervour gave way to the Australian penchant for blandness.

However, while dramatic large-scale efforts had failed to gather in the lost sheep to the Christian fold, they had strengthened the existing flock. The Protestant churches appeared to have latent energy and a sense of purpose which some clerics around 1900 feared had vanished. One significant aspect was that all these campaigns were interdenominational in nature, which revealed the strength of the thinking at this time that the separate churches could no longer afford to go it alone. The problems of religious indifference and the secular world demanded one big Protestant church, and after all, had not the Christ prayed that "they all may be one"?

5 Unity and Schism within Protestantism

Christianity has been subjected to splits and unifications throughout its history, and these same trends were evident within Protestantism in New South Wales at the beginning of the twentieth century. On the one hand, there were centripetal forces working to increase cooperation between churches and form one large Protestant church, and on the other, centrifugal forces championing diversity. The most significant divisive influence at this time, besides the perennial impetus of denominational loyalty, was the high/low church factionalism within the Anglican church. This dispute over doctrine and its liturgical manifestations had implications far beyond the bounds of Anglicanism. Both these centripetal and centrifugal trends expressed the deeper anxiety within the Protestant churches at this time. The demands for unity were posed in terms of greater Protestant strength, while the arguments for diversity were couched in terms of the purity, truth and hence the greater virility of the various branches of Protestantism.

Early in the twentieth century, the Protestant churches in Australia experienced a strong movement for unity. This was due in part to overseas trends, but it also reflected local conditions which had reduced the uniqueness of each of the churches, and increased the need for common effort. The vastness of the Australian landscape, the levelling effects of the democratic ethos, and the backlash to the competitive spirit of the denominations, all played a part in creating common aims and methods among the churches. They all became structurally centralized, instituted comparable pastoral techniques, and were subjected to the same liturgical and architectural trends. The bulk of their membership came from the same social grouping, the middle class, and so, officially at least, they shared similar social and political viewpoints. Above all, they now found little to quarrel about on the matter of Christian doctrine. Few barriers of doctrine remained because evangelicalism was the dominant strand within the Protestant churches. The Presbyterians and Congregationalists had abandoned their strict Calvinist belief in the salvation of an elect number only. The majority stressed the evangelical truths that salvation came alone from faith in God and the recognition of mankind as an eternal backslider. Only repentence and the atonement of Christ, and not priests or indulgences, could save the sinner. Liberal Protestantism, which held a more exalted and optimistic view of man and a less severe view of God, was the minority strand within Protestantism. The evangelical-liberal split meant that evangelical clergy often felt closer to evangelicals of another denomination than liberal clergy of their own church.

However it should not be imagined that the Protestant churches were all the same, because denominational identity and loyalty were still strong. For instance, only about twenty per cent of Protestants' marriages were with those outside their own church. Yet there was a strong Protestant spirit abroad and it was encouraged by practical considerations as much as the Christian ideal "that they all may be one". A shortage of clergy and lay teachers necessitated the giving of common Protestant scripture lessons in the state schools. This intermixing also happened a great deal in Sunday schools. By no means rare was the Balmain Methodist Sunday school where forty per cent of the children were non-Methodists.(1) This blending occurred not only because of a lack of resources, but because the schools happened to be closer to home, or in a better part of the neighbourhood, or any number of reasons. Protestant parents were more concerned that their children receive a Protestant Christian education than that of any particular denomination. Lack of resources in the country forced people to worship in union churches or with a denomination other than their own. In urban areas some people attended different denominations because the sermons or the choir were better, the church more comfortable, or closer, or bigger, or nicer. Clergy who advertised compelling sermons and services encouraged this moving around. Some changed their church permanently because the new one suited their social status better. Rev G. W. Sharp, a Congregationalist, lamented that some "moneyed men and women of position with no convictions have left our churches and fawned on bishops, and made for heaven through Anglican doors".(2) The majority stayed put in their own church, but the minority who chose, or were forced to move around, added to the strength of common Protestantism, which was also energized by fear of the indifferent, the Catholics and the immoral forces in society. Besides, unity was in the air! One of the biggest questions of the 1890s was that of the federation of the Australian colonies.

In the late nineteenth century, Protestant clergy developed some knowledge of the benefits of cooperation in the ministerial associations that most suburbs and towns spawned. These were formed to provide fraternity, but also as a vehicle for a greater Christian presence in the community. From the late 1880s several of these groups existed to promote the Protestant view of a righteous Sunday. The council of the Churches was formed from all the Protestant churches in 1889 to lobby on public morality. Even the Anglican church was a member, showing the wide agreement among Protestants on moral questions. However, the Council was an official creation of the churches and could only act on matters when there was complete agreement. When strong minded evangelicals wished to tackle the Catholics in public controversy, this unanimity was not forthcoming, and the militants became disgruntled.(3) They looked for a more aggressive platform for their common views on evangelical and Protestant questions.

The Evangelical Council was formed in 1899 to provide evangelical cooperation to fight immorality and popery, and to evangelize those indifferent to religion. It was designed to be free from official church control to enable it to act quickly and positively in controversies. Its first president, Dr Roseby, stressed the advantages of Protestant cooperation "for the defence of our altars and our hearths, our religion and our homes".(4) The Council was born out of the great concern with the current needs of the churches. At its inaugural meeting, Rev F E. Harry gave an address on the religious condition of Sydney, in which he spoke of widespread religious indifference, prevalent materialism, pleasure-seeking, drunkenness, gambling, and the inroads of Catholicism.(5) Though few Anglicans and liberal Protestants joined the Council it became a potent force within Sydney Protestantism. Its list of clerical presidents read like an evangelical "Who's Who", for it contained the Methodists Taylor, Woolls Rutledge, Stephen and Carruthers, and Presbyterians Dill Macky and White. The Council's concern with moral reform attracted such Anglicans as Boyce and Hammond, and Congregationalist Roseby as presidents. Nor was it by chance that the Council's second president was the foremost Protestant champion of the day, Dill Macky. By 1904 one third of the 102 clerical members were Methodists. The fifty-four lay members included prominent Methodists, Hon Ebenezer Vickery, M.L.C. and Hon. W. Robson, M.L.C. militant Protestants R. Booth, M.L.A., and T. Jessep, M.L.A., and charity worker, G. E. Ardill.(6) As well as its united evangelism noted earlier and its militant Christian witness in public affairs, the Evangelical Council promoted and reflected "a feeling of fellowship and comradeship among ministers and leading men in the churches such as no other organization offered the means of doing".(7) It remained virile until the demise of strident evangelicalism around 1913, and lingered on in a moribund state until superseded in 1925 by an official church creation, the Council of Churches.(8)

While some clergy were clearly satisfied with interdenominational cooperative efforts like the Evangelical Council, others yearned for the organic union of the churches as the only real solution to the pastoral and evangelistic difficulties of Protestantism. In 1902, the Moderator of the Presbyterian Assembly, Rev J. Walker, encapsulated some of the current thinking in a poem entitled: "The Call to Church Unity", which went in part:

As when a streamlet, leaping from the hills,
Is broken by some rock to separate rills
Which henceforth parted flow, with each a name:
So is the Church divided; yet the same.

No Church may claim the patronage of Grace;
Each Chapel in God's Temple has its place;
Yet, when divisions 'pinge on Christian love;
Break down partitions! every barrier move!

Aye, and the soul-thirst of this land is deep,
And cannot be supplied by rills that creep
And trickle. These must join and make a stream,
Both broad and deep, in which Heaven's glories gleam.(9)

In the light of the essential unity of all Christians and the huge problem of religious indifference, many believed that the competitiveness of denominational expansion was madness, and argued that church union would bring greater power and strength by ending wasteful overlapping and thus enable the churches to speak with one voice. Given the evangelizing task of the churches, the *Methodist* believed "no earnest Christian will but regret the wasted energies that must result from the multiplying of unnecessary agents in one place, to their exclusion from other necessitous places".(10) Rev J. Fordyce, chairman of the Australasian Congregational Conference, declared that "unless we can secure a new determination of frontiers, and either a real federation, or a union of the churches, we shall be, indeed we are now, utterly baffled by the forces that are working against the kingdom of God".(11)

As the debate on the federation of the Australian colonies had only just been successfully concluded, arguments for church union in terms of both efficiency and sentiment were well understood. The Presbyterians had just reorganized themselves on a federal basis. Similarly, in 1901 the Methodist fragments completed their negotiations and formed the Methodist Church of Australasia. However, while the smaller Methodist groups were enthusiastic for organic union in order to overcome their weakness, the larger Wesleyan group had only approved of union by one vote. The negotiations had proved tortuous, and took ten long years of arguing over details of property and other vested interests. Still, in the end most Methodists and all the other churches welcomed Methodist union because they believed it would strengthen the Christian forces in society. Many saw it as a blueprint for wider Protestant union.(12) The *Sydney Morning Herald* caught the temper of the times when it stated that "the call for union has come, indeed, from a sense of weakness".(13) Yet anxious churchmen, who were attracted by the old maxim that "unity is strength", perhaps did not realize that fear was a much more fragile basis for unity than cooperation and understanding. For it was fear that underlay the push to union — and not only fear of religious indifference, but also fear of Catholicism, because the proposed unity was to be Protestant to the core!

The synthesis of these disparate forces for Protestant union came from Rev T. E. Clouston, a lecturer in historical theology at St Andrew's. In a bold move, he called for the Presbyterian General Assembly "to appoint an influential committee to devise a scheme for the federation of as many as possible of the Protestant Churches of Australia, with power to confer with the representatives of other Churches so as to promote closer fellowship and organized co-operation, with a view to the ultimate formation of one grand Church of Australia."(14) Clouston believed that cooperation and fellowship should precede organic union because they fulfilled urgent needs and also ensured the success of such union. However the Assembly, which supported the general idea and appointed a committee to consider "closer union", rejected this practical path to union for a theoretical approach. The Presbyterians were not prepared to drift into union, but wished to approach it head on through closely defined statements on doctrine and polity.(15)

The initial response from many quarters was warm and even enthusiastic. The Wesleyan Methodist Conference, then in session, indicated its willingness to discuss "Protestant federation" and the Congregational Union agreed to join negotiations for a "closer union".(16) The Presbyterian committee was appointed to consider "the closer union of the churches" and sent invitations to all the heads of the other churches. The Methodist and Congregational churches sent favourable replies, although the Baptists declined and the Anglicans failed to reply. Discussions began immediately.

The initial report of the Presbyterian and Methodist joint committee emphasized the great similarities between the two churches, especially under Australian conditions, and outlined the virtues of union. It stated that Christ's kingdom "will be more effectively promoted by the organic union", which would have a psychological and real impact on all aspects of Christian work by ending competition, and strengthening missions to "the lapsed masses of our great cities, the lonely dwellers of the bush, and the new populations which from time to time spring up in the states of Australia".(17) The report used the term "organic union", which suggested the complete disappearance of the old denominations, but others still continued to use "federation" when referring to the union movement, implying something less, and indicating an unwillingness to cast aside denominational loyalties. Still, the prospects were encouraging.

This early period was one of hopefulness and idealistic statements of Christian unity. The setting up of committees gave the union supporters the sense that they were achieving something. Church meetings passed encouraging motions of support for union, which were often accompanied by applause. However, at the same time, there was a note of caution and a vagueness about any firm commitment. Clouston was at times pessimistic, and Rev W. H. Beale, an enthusiast for union, told the Methodist Conference that it could take twenty years.(18) The Australasian Methodist Conference typically declared "such an organic union is eminently desirable, provided that a satisfactory basis of union can be formulated".(19) To provide satisfaction for all, was to be the challenge.

The general opinion was that the line of least resistance lay between the Presbyterians and Congregationalists, because creed subscription and the form of church government appeared to be the only major differences. Even these seemed less formidable since the joint committee declared that these traditional differences were fading. Whereas Congregationalism had formerly rejected adherence to any form of creed and fiercely stressed the autonomous nature of each local church, it now practised at least verbal adherence to a set of doctrines, and accepted considerable central control. Indeed most Congregational churches now handed over their church property deeds to a central committee.(20) Presbyterianism which had traditionally demanded written consent to the intricate Confession of Faith, now adhered to a shortened statement and appeared willing to accept verbal affirmations to this creed. However, a little probing beyond superficialities revealed that the so-called line of least resistance was meeting with firm denominational opposition. The Presbyterians appeared unprepared to abandon their cherished democratic and highly centralized tiered government, which they claimed gave adequate protection to local church rights.(21) Similarly, the Congregational loyalists mounted a strong attack on the concept of organic union itself at the interstate Congregational meeting in Brisbane in 1903.(22)

Besides the growing opposition from the loyalists, the union movement was rocked by the revelation that the Anglicans and Presbyterians had been conducting secret union negotiations in late 1906 and early 1907. This startling situation developed in the following way. The General Anglical Australian Synod, which only convened every five years, had not been able to consider the original Presbyterian invitation for talks until as late as 1905. However, when it did, it was decided to accept the offer and two conferences were held with the Presbyterians. Like the other union negotiations, agreement on the Scriptures, creeds and doctrines was reached quickly and relatively easily. The second conference predictably took up the ordination question, but amazingly, with only two of the eight Anglicans dissenting, it resolved that there should be a mutual recognition of existing orders, and that no reordinations would be necessary under the proposed united church. Bishops were to remain, but were to be elected — perhaps for limited terms. The Anglican delegation headed by Archbishop Clarke of Melbourne, and containing three bishops, three archdeacons, three canons and two laymen, by accepting the validity of Presbyterian orders, had moved far beyond the Anglican world guidelines for reunion with non-Anglicans laid down by the Lambeth Quadrilateral in 1888.(23) As the Anglican church was still connected to the mother church in England, it had to await a decision on these negotiations from the ensuing Lambeth Conference of 1908. The Presbyterians were prepared to wait, but declared that future talks must be conducted with the joint committee of the three churches.

It was at this stage that news of the negotiations leaked out. The Congregationalists and Methodists naturally felt excluded and were at first hostile to such treachery. Carruthers, who was a strong advocate of greater cooperation, remarked that the "self-respect of those churches has been wounded and the spirit within them that has made for union has been chilled".(24) The Methodist Conference felt piqued and sulkily changed a motion that "organic union was eminently desirable" to one which merely gave "continued sympathy with ... a closer union".(25) The *Methodist* only begrudgingly accepted Clouston's embarrassed explanation of the delayed acceptance of the offer to negotiate by the Anglicans.(26) The general view was that the Presbyterians had been imprudent, and some even suggested that the discussions with the Anglicans, which were bound to fail, were a deliberate attempt to sabotage the union movement.(27) At least they were correct in predicting that the talks would be fruitless. The Lambeth Conference rejected the radical suggestions of the Presbyterian-Anglican discussions. The upshot of the affair was that while the union negotiations were not wrecked, they were seriously disrupted.

Enthusiasm was difficult to maintain during the long years of thrashing out a constitution for the proposed united church. The tedious debates over the minutiae of church doctrine and polity were not of a type to instil fire. The *Messenger* did the most to maintain interest as the Presbyterians had initiated the movement. News items of parallel Canadian and Irish negotiations were highlighted, and editorials attempted to provide encouragement.(28) Pessimistically, the *Methodist* remarked that "sectarianism is becoming intenser and the lines of demarcation are being more deeply drawn while committee men are spending precious hours in drawing up academical constitutions".(29)

The long awaited Basis of Doctrine and Scheme of Polity was presented in 1910, after seven years of negotiations. Defining oneself out of existence had proved to be no easy task! The initial reactions from the church conferences were promising, although they were in terms of general approval only. The Methodists suggested further talks, because "the polity proposed is the result of large concessions by each of the churches represented".(30) From the outside the *Sydney Morning Herald* urged that "compromise and concession" could produce a strong united church which "would be manifestly a great gain to the moral life of Australia".(31) The Presbyterian negotiating committee stated that "some sacrifice of sentiment and practice is called for from each of the churches embraced in the present scheme, if union is to be accomplished" (32) But many were not prepared to make these sacrifices. Indeed, the union movement began to fragment at the very stage when something concrete had been formulated. In 1911 the Anglican-Presbyterian negotiations were renewed and then the Congregationalists and Baptists began discussions. The *Methodist* was livid and declared that negotiations must be "perfectly open and above board. There must be no coquetting with the other suitor behind the back of another."(33) It was a little like a teenagers' dance! In the midst of all this confusion a belated attempt to rouse popular support for the Basis at a public meeting in April 1911 chaired by the Governor General, Lord Chelmsford, failed dismally.(34)

Then came more direct opposition to the union movement. The *Methodist* printed a series of articles quite critical of aspects of the Basis, and the *Congregationalist* boldly attacked the very notion of organic union and suggested it was a greater evil than those it sought to end.(35) The concept of organic union which was idealized because it had the sanction of Christ, who prayed at the Last Supper "that they all may be one", was now savaged by the denominational loyalists. The church conferences had delayed discussion on the Basis in 1910 sensing the difficulty of the enterprise, but now the struggle was laid bare. The death blow came from the very Congregationalist committee that helped to draw up the Basis, though there were others with knives at the ready. It rejected the Basis of Doctrine and instead suggested a simple confession of faith in Jesus Christ. The committee also cast aside the Scheme of Polity because it did not give enough sovereignty to the local church.(36) Congregational committees were convened to consider these recommendations and finally in May 1912 it was agreed to end Congregational participation in the union negotiations.(37) The Presbyterians appeared willing to continue the discussions, but amendments to the Basis in the Assembly which mangled and Presbyterianized it, made this seem pointless.(38) The Methodists simply refused to give the dying Basis any close scrutiny until 1913 when the Australasian Conference finally killed it.(39) Carruthers, a long standing commentator on the union movement, wrote in November 1912: "With Congregationalism definitely antagonistic, Presbyterianism seriously divided, and Methodism non-committal, what is the use of going on?"(40) The negotiations were dead and although the ideal lived on, it was back to square one.

Church union from the outset had been hindered by a wrong approach. The churches had opted for a theoretical approach by agreement on a basis of doctrine and church government, instead of moving towards organic union via the back door of cooperation and amalgamation. This had several important consequences. The obsession with theoretical models reinforced the natural tendency for this to be a clerically led movement and completely isolated the laity from the negotiations. So the unity movement lacked strong grass-roots support. Those who adhered to the theoretical approach often believed that the advocates of cooperation were aiming at something less than organic union, possibly even deliberately, in order to sabotage the movement. Therefore suggestions for cooperation were received coolly by the advocates of union. The denominational loyalists certainly opposed common long-term efforts, because they did not wish to give away any denominational sovereignty. Despite the anxiety over the religiously indifferent and all the talk about the need to end overlapping, there was no attempt to rationalize church building or services. While there was common Protestant action against immorality, the Catholics, and the indifferent, by means of the Evangelical Council and other more ephemeral unofficial bodies, the only official cooperative efforts occurred in the united theological lectures given in Sydney. Truly, Rev Carruthers lamented: "we argue together and pray apart".(41)

Only after 1910 was there a reassessment by some unionists and an attempt to gain organic union through cooperative means.(42) Conferences initiated by Mr H. E. Wooton, a Melbourne Congregationalist, were held in Victoria in 1913, attended by the three negotiating churches and the Anglicans and the Baptists. They drew up plans for rationalization of manpower in rural areas as a prelude to union, but these were never implemented.(43) Cooperation certainly appeared to be the best strategy, because the parallel Canadian church union movement finally succeeded in 1925 after rejecting the theoretical for the cooperative approach.(44) But the reassessment of strategy in Australia came too late. By 1910 when some unionists were discussing cooperation, the mood of Protestant anxiety which formed the raison d'etre of the church union movement had waned,(45) and with it went the clergy's willingness to compromise their separate church traditions.

These denominational loyalties were based on several hundred years of tradition and commitment. They formed the very essence of Christian enterprise because, with few exceptions, Christian action was carried out in a denominational framework. Everyone in the community belonged at least nominally to a particular church. The label, "C. of E." or Presbyterian, formed a significant part of the self-concept of even the most indifferent. To the more religious, denominational allegiances represented commitments to a particular Christian vision. To others, these traditions were part of a cultural heritage — an expression of ancestor worship. The Presbyterian congregation at Port Macquarie stood to pray and sat to sing as they did at home in Scotland before they emigrated.(46) By their devoted Presbyterianism they revealed their fierce determination to remain Scottish.

Denominational loyalists had a certain inevitable self-fulfilment about them. Rev Penman declared that "he believed what every minister ought to believe, and what every minister must believe, who is loyal and true to his Church — that it was the best Church in the world for him".(47) Methodists sang the praises of their evangelism and spirituality; Presbyterians lauded their polity as apostolic, divine and democratic; while Congregationalists boasted of their apostolic liberty and intellectual freedom. Only three years after writing his poem, "The Call to Christian Unity", Walker confessed to Presbyterian theological students: "Well do I know the faults and weaknesses of Presbyterianism. But, with all its faults, I know no system of organised Church life so Catholic, so strong, so Scriptural, so regardful of the Christ-given rights and liberties of the Christian people; so ready to recognise the good in other Communions and other christians, and able to produce a better or more reliable type of character. Withal, for me, it is the Church of the stock from which I have sprung . . . I love the Presbyterian Church with a love apart — an intimate, intense, passionate devotion."(48) It was upon such unswerving and blind devotion that the church union movement foundered.

The union negotiations, which lasted a decade, appeared to indicate a strong idealism within the churches, but it was also a pragmatic response to the growth of secularism and religious indifference. If your advance is stopped, you move sideways and consolidate! Unfortunately it proved no easy task to abandon the past. Besides, not all were agreed, or committed to the one strategy. Christ's prayer "that they all may be one", like all his teachings, had many interpretations. Did it mean unity of the spirit or the flesh? If of the body, was it to be a limited or comprehensive union, and centralized or federal in nature? Some saw all too clearly what they thought it meant, and they were not prepared to give up their denominational rights and powers. A few were worried about their own prestige and livelihood, though most sincerely believed their denominational way to be the best. As Rev J. D. McCaughey has since remarked: the "act of reunion is not merely a patching-up of the past, even a making-the-most-of-it, it is a leap into the future",(49) and it was from this leap that the churches drew back. So the dream of Christian unity faded!

It was fitting, sixty-seven years after the demise of the union negotiations, that McCaughey, who realized that reunion needed to make definite breaks with the past, should be elected as the first Moderator of the Uniting Church of Australia which was finally formed in 1977 from the three negotiating churches. In honour of Clouston's original vision in 1901, it was also fitting that the first Moderator should be a Presbyterian.

At the very moment when Protestantism was seriously discussing church union, disruptive forces threatened the harmony and unity of the Anglican church. In Australia the debate over the use and abuse of the Anglican liturgy was most prevalent in the Sydney diocese. The low churchmen claimed that the high churchmen and Anglo-Catholics were headed Romeward and that their sacramentalism was a betrayal of the Reformation. The others in turn believed the low churchmen neglected the truth that Anglicanism was "one Catholick and Apostolick Church" and were thus too Protestant. This liturgical controversy further revealed the anxiety within Protestantism, and specifically Anglicanism, at the turn of the century, and the reactions it spawned.

The preface to the Book of Common Prayer stated that "it hath been the wisdom of the Church of England, ever since the first compiling of her Publick Liturgy, to keep the mean between the two extremes of too much stiffness in refusing, and of too much easiness in admitting any variation from it". Some believed that this balance in the correct use of the liturgy was endangered by the English Oxford Movement of the 1840s, which stressed a greater sacramentalism and began a controversy that seethed through the late nineteenth century.

The division between low and high churchmanship rested on two opposed views of Christian life and church order. The greatest rift centred on the ambiguous statements in Article XXVIII of the church concerning what took place during the sacrament of holy communion. The Article explicitly rejected the Roman doctrine of transubstantiation whereby the elements became truly the body and blood of Christ; but did these elements *contain* the spirit and real presence of Christ as the high churchmen maintained, or only *represent* these as the low churchmen would have it? The two also differed in their view of man, because the high-low church split approximated the liberal-evangelical split; the high churchman had an exalted view of men who could by evolution approach God, whereas to the low churchman, mankind was an eternal backslider.(50) The high churchman focused on the communion of God and man through the eucharist, while the low churchman emphasized the atonement of a merciful God and a repentant sinner. Conceptions of church authority and order also separated them. The Oxford Movement reemphasized that Anglicanism was part of the "one Catholick and Apostolick Church" and stressed the "Historic Episcopate" of the apostolic succession of bishops. In simple terms this led the high churchmen to the position of no bishops — no church! The low churchmen, on the other hand, believed that while bishops were traditional and for the good order of Anglicanism, they were not essential to its truth and existence. Thus, disagreement over the nature of authority, the nature of the sacraments and man himself, split low and high Anglicans.

Although only a minority on both sides held extreme views and caused disruption, the controversy was intensified in the late nineteenth century. A number of low churchmen believed that the Anglo-Catholics were attempting to capture Anglicanism for the "church of Rome". This open hatred of the Anglo-Catholics was encouraged in England by the anti-papist views of Queen Victoria, the derision by *Punch* of ritualists, and the publication of Walter Walsh's *The Secret History of the Oxford Movement* in 1897.(51) The controversy exploded into violence as street mobs, led by John Kensit and others, harassed, stoned and disrupted Anglo-Catholic services in London in 1898–99, to a degree reminiscent of the anti-Catholic riots of the early 1850s.(52) On this level, the debate was not over doctrine, but its manifestations, ecclesiastical ornaments and haberdashery.

The current theological debates in Britain set the pattern of theology in the Australian colonies. This was not only because the overworked and undertrained colonial clergy far from the centres of theology produced few ideas themselves, but also because the nexus between the Anglican church in the colonies and in England, meant that the colonial churches were bound by decisions made in the Anglican church in England. If few Australian clergy had a taste for theological debate, even fewer of the laity did so. The Bishop of Tasmania declared that most congregations were thoroughly bored by the custom that a new incumbent would tediously recite the thirty-nine Articles to the congregation in his first sermon.(53) However, while the liturgical controversy may have been the poorer for this lack of theological expertise in New South Wales, it was none the less intense. The form of the debate was not theology, but its manifestations, and so the parties wrangled over chasubles, surpliced choirs, incense, altar lights, genuflexions, prayers for the dead, the eastward position and countless minutiae of Anglican liturgy. The chasuble, symbol of the sacrificing priest and the Real Presence in the sacraments, had deep theological significance, as did some other liturgical requisites. However, minor issues such as surpliced choirs were given equal significance by militant untheological laity. St John's, Parramatta, suffered disruption at a vestry meeting over surpliced choirs. Pectoral crosses worn by the Bishops of Goulburn and New Guinea at St James', Sydney raised evangelical eyebrows,(54) while the following description of the choral eucharist at Christ Church St Laurence probably made many low churchmen livid: "The processions, headed by a jewelled cross with three banners and followed by scarlet cassocks of the bearers and altar servers, was most dignified, stately and effective. In procession the Rev Mr Powell wore a handsome cope, richly embroidered, which was afterwards changed for a white chasuble."(55)

This controversy was centred on the Sydney diocese where the low church party was firmly in command. Fewer than a dozen churches in the suburbs practised high church liturgy and only two churches followed a more extreme Anglo-Catholic liturgy. These two were St James', King Street and Christ Church St Laurence of George Street, both city churches which needed an extreme liturgy to attract a strong congregation. In this context the low church militancy was rather hysterical. In 1907 the Protestant Church of England Union declared that "our churches have become transformed into ecclesiastical music halls and organ recitals . . . while the simple, plain evangelical service was put in the background".(56) This reference was directed to St James' and Christ Church but could not be reasonably applied to more than a handful of churches. However, worried that the whole Anglican world was headed Romeward, extreme low churchmen took on the role of ecclesiastical spies. "Saul" was shocked to report that the celebrant at St James' had used the "eastward position" which indicated the Romish sacrificing mass.(57) D. Ross verified this and listed other illegalities such as the use of altar lights. The temperate Archbishop Smith who received Ross's dossier, coolly replied to him, as he did to others, that it "has been duly noted".(58) The accusations were frequent enough for one correspondent, "Church Guardian", to satirize them, claiming that a knee injury forced his minister to veer eastward while kneeling at the northern end of the table, making him a suspected Jesuit. He concluded that "suspicion is in the air; the churches are full of it . . . we can't think of God, nor of our sins; we are looking for sins in the minister".(59) The ugliness underlying such boyish espionage was revealed by the threatening anonymous letter sent to Rev R M. Turnbull of Cooma, condemning his alleged Romish sympathies.(60) Through the first decade of the twentieth century, a ceaseless flow of editorials, articles, English news and letters to the editor on the liturgical question engulfed the two Anglican papers. The bias of these journals was instantly recognizable by the *Church Commonwealth*'s advertisements for church ornaments and requisites, and the *Australian Churchman*'s advertisements for the Methodist Book Depot and Walsh's *The Secret History of the Oxford Movement.* The amount of newsprint consumed by the controversy was astonishing and at times the debate flowed over into the daily press. Though Anglicans may have been more informed about their church's liturgy than previously, it was a bitter way to get such an education and proved to be a huge waste of Christian energy.

The Sydney diocese, unlike most other dioceses in the colonies, was strongly low church and largely untouched by the Oxford and Ritualist movements, mainly as a result of the influence of Bishop Barker's long incumbency from 1855 to 1882. However, despite the fact that only a few Sydney parishes practised the newly revived ancient Anglican liturgies, tension in the diocese mounted in the late nineteenth century due to both the influence of English events and the introduction of some Anglo-Catholic practises to St James' in 1896.(61) The low church laity in 1886 formed the Church of England Association "to uphold the principles of the Protestant Reformed Church of England"(62) and the smaller high church body, the Churchman's Institute, was formed in 1891. Neither of these was a virile organization, but their formation indicated the growth of party alignments within the diocese. Such disruption had occurred in the synod in the 1880s, and synod more and more became a field of intrigue influenced by militant laymen, especially lawyers and professional men, and controlled by caucus tactics and party tickets.(63) Canon Boyce claimed his election to the canonry of St Andrew's Cathedral in 1900 was the first unanimous election in the chapter,(64) but even this verdict was more expedient than harmonious. It was alleged that, as the tension mounted, some withdrew from synod in disgust or despair.(65) In 1910 twenty-eight high church clergy declared to Archbishop Wright that "we feel in duty bound to enter our earnest protest against the narrow, partisan elections in the Synod, — more accentuated, and having a wider reach, in the recent session than ever before".(66) The Sydney evangelicals became increasingly aggressive because they imagined themselves to be a beseiged low church enclave within a church which was attempting to undo the Reformation.

The most militant low churchmen were organized within the Protestant Church of England Union (P.C.E.U.), established in 1898 "to maintain and extend the efficiency of the Church of England as the origin and representative of Evangelical truth and Apostolic order in our country and as a witness to the principles of the Reformation".(67) Its founder and leading light, Canon Archdall of St Mary's, Balmain, was an Ulsterman and Cambridge M.A. The union held lectures, and published and distributed literature. It attracted several hundred people to its annual picnic and harbour cruise at Flat Rock. A young people's group was formed and the 300 odd members were thoroughly drilled in Protestant principles.(68) The P.C.E.U. denied the title of extremist,(69) but its composition and actions showed otherwise. The membership at its peak in the early 1900s never rose above 600 and was all but totally confined to the Sydney diocese. No more than twenty of the clergy were members, though many others, like Canon Jones, Principal of Moore College, could (with reservations) sympathize with the P.C.E.U.'s aims.(70) A wide range of parishes from St Barnabas's, Broadway, a working man's church, to the more affluent parishes of Coogee and Croydon, formed branches. However, the number of parishes with branches never passed twenty, less than one fifth of the total number in the diocese. The presidency was shared in the 1900s by only three clergy; Canon Archdall, Rev C. C. Dunstan, a Moore Collegeman of Christ Church, Enmore, and Rev W. H. H. Yarrington, a poetry medallist and M.A. of Sydney University, and incumbent of St Luke's, Burwood. As early as 1902, Dunstan expressed regret at the lack of support given to the union by the laity and clergy who "sympathize and speak well of the union, [yet] still hold back".(71) If the P.C.E.U. was small and approaching a lunatic fringe, why then was the ritualist controversy in the Sydney diocese so long and intense?

The fact was that although the P.C.E.U. was a small body, it fed on the wider anti-Catholic and evangelical temperament of Anglicans and the Protestant community generally. Low churchmen were inclined to believe that high churchmen and ritualists were Roman Catholics in disguise, who were attempting to infiltrate and corrupt Anglicanism. The militants voiced these views very frequently and must have sown some suspicion in the popular mind. Dunstan told the congregation at St Philip's, Church Hill that: "Ritualism and lawlessness in the Church had spread like an epidemic. An organized attempt was being made to Romanize the Church of England."(72) The Church of England Association reported that the church was "honeycombed with secret societies, guilds and brotherhoods, some under episcopal patronage, yet all secretly instilling the false doctrine of soul-destroying error that underlies Romish ritualism".(73) Ritualists were "wolves in sheep's clothing", ritualism "Jesuit casuistry and deceit", and therefore unanglican, unenglish, anti-Reformationist and anti-Christ.(74) Dunstan alleged that a third of the Anglican church in England was corrupted by ritualism(75) and even Boyce saw a ritualist take-over as "a tremendous reality".(76) The *Australian Churchman* feared for the Sydney diocese because "the 'conspiracy' has, on the contrary, concentrated its forces here. And if it has not yet altogether captured this fortress of the Gospel in our Church in Australia, it is because there has been and there still is some watchful and strenuous opposition to its aggression."(77)

Added to these fears were those engendered by the different views of man and the world shared by the low and high churchmen. The high churchman who was usually a liberal Protestant, used liturgy to unify and intensify his worship and usually had the security and breadth to accept liturgical change. The low churchman was ascetic in his worship, and being a conservative and disliking change, tended to take a legalistic view of liturgical innovation. As Rev J. S. Hart, later Bishop of Wangaratta, remarked:

> The low churchman is a man of panic. He can only see the danger. Quite rightly he believes that a man must, before all things, be spiritual and he is afraid the outside world may injure his spiritual life. He is afraid that the visible Church, if he thinks much of it, will make him forget the unity of the spirit, and that sacraments, if he makes much of them, will make him undervalue faith and love and penitence, and that outward beauty, if he has much of it will so please his senses that he will not be able to worship in spirit and in truth . . . You may have noticed how easily low churchmen scream with terror, at Rome or at rationalism, or at ritualism. Something terrible is always, they think, just going to happen.(78)

Extreme low churchmen had much in common with the wowsers who decried changes in moral standards, and who were in ascendance at this time.

Thus, the liturgical controversy thrived since the extreme low churchmen were able to paint the high churchmen as law-breakers, innovators and Romish agents, which had great appeal to a community in which anti-Catholicism and wowserism flourished. However, it should not be thought that the movement equalled the violent excesses of the low church mobs in England at this time. The clergy, spear-headed by that thorough gentle-man, Canon Archdall, always remained in control of the movement. Archdall once chastised a low churchman for unchristian and foolish ridicule of high churchmen,(79) and even when he bent the ears of the synod in a seventy-five minute speech on vestments, he did so "in a very self-constrained and reasonable manner".(80)

William Saumarez Smith, Archbishop of Sydney from 1890 to 1909, was the man who had to preside over this wrangling diocese and make many hard decisions during the controversy. Smith was a prizeman at Trinity College, Cambridge, and the only Australian bishop at the time to hold a D.D. by examination. He had been principal of St Aidan's Theolo-gical College, Birkenhead, from 1869 to 1890, and because of this academic background some thought he lacked the pastoral qualities for a bishop. Smith was an able linguist and poet, a lover of astronomy, flowers, tennis and cricket, and was of a modest and retiring disposition. He was acknowledged as a tireless worker and a generous giver, perhaps because he disliked asking for money.(81) He was a strong Protestant and a low churchman, who personally disliked pastoral staves, pectoral crosses and ceremony. However he believed strongly in his church's comprehensiveness which was "by historical development, by constitutional reform, and by authoritative statement of doctrine, Protestant as well as Catholic; and, let me add, Protestant because truly and genuinely Catholic".(82) These, he affirmed, were not party labels but scripturally based views.(83) Above all, Smith was a Prayer Book churchman. He had been alarmed by the ritualist excesses while in England in 1897 and reminded synod on his return that "neither bishop nor clergy should be able to introduce varia-tions in the customary services of the Church, nor additions to them which were opposed to the Articles of Religion, or to the Book of Common Prayer honestly interpreted".(84) Unfortunately, all claimed to interpret honestly. Smith was above all a liberal evangelical, because he tolerated the use of the chasuble at Christ Church, St James' and St Saviour's, Redfern and tried to respect the churchmanship of the individual parish when appointing a new incumbent. His tolerance and retiring disposition were to be tested by the militant low churchmen in the synod.

The battle between the parties was fought in synod on a wide range of issues. The worst excesses of the low churchmen were only prevented by the fact that many of their aims were beyond the local synod's power to legislate. However, the low churchmen did dent the Archbishop's power, which many of them distrusted, and transposed some of it to the synod where a low church majority was assured. They claimed that synod alone had the right to sanction changes to the order of service and only failed narrowly in their attempt to wrestle this right from the Archbishop.(85) One P.C.E.U. member exclaimed in the debate: "This was a democratic country, and the people must rule".(86) The moderates and high church-

men were of course shocked.(87) The low church clique was more successful with its tribunal ordinance of 1904 where it ended the Archbishop's
right to determine whether a clergyman should be tried for liturgical
malpractice or immorality, and transferred this power to a committee to
which the synod elected three members and the Archbishop appointed
only two members.(88) Earlier in 1895, they had determined that if a
parish wanted to choose its new minister and not leave it to the Archbishop to appoint one, this must be done by a committee containing
parishioners and elected synod representatives, and at least one of the
synod representatives had to approve of the committee's choice. Therefore, the low churchman by the 1900s had the power to control the type
of new clergy that came into the diocese, and could also threaten established clergy with malpractice suits (though this would be difficult to
prove). They also claimed the right to determine which liturgy could be
used within the diocese.

Every dispute must have a symbol, and in the liturgical controversy
it was the chasuble which some high churchmen wore while celebrating
holy communion. Low Churchmen claimed this was a "Roman Catholic"
vestment and indicated that high churchmen believed in the "heresy"
that the elements became the very body and blood of Christ in the
communion. Canon Archdall unsuccessfully introduced an ordinance in
the 1899 and 1903 synod to ban its use in the diocese. The ordinance was
blocked by the matter being considered "ultra vires", the Archbishop
ruling that "there is too much doubt about the Synod's power to depart
from the law as exercised in England to justify definite regulations being
made here".(89) A public debate followed between Rev F. J. Albery of
Christ Church St Laurence who wore the chasuble, and Canon Archdall.(90) Low churchmen were dismayed when Archbishop Smith confirmed that he appointed Albery in the knowledge that he wore the
chasuble while a curate at Christ Church, and intended to continue to do
so after his appointment as the priest there.(91)

Canons Archdall, Taylor and Jones drew up a memorial on vestments in
1903 and it was signed by forty-three clergy in the diocese. The document
dramatically claimed that Smith's tolerance of liturgical illegalities in the
diocese was causing laymen to lose their faith and leave the church. It
argued that the diocese had the power to end the lawbreaking that was
undermining Anglicanism, and ban the chasuble "to secure obedience to
the law, and so promote the unity of our Church".(92) Smith replied that
personally he believed the vestments were both " 'illegal' and undesirable",
but that the matter was far from simple, and that it was desirable and
necessary "to wait for further light on what had become a very compli-
cated matter for consideration by those who wished to rule right-
eously".(93) The "further light" was the imminent royal commission on
liturgy in England. Smith himself acknowledged that his view appeared

hesitant and perplexed, while Archdall and his clique referred to it as "weakness".(94) Archdall placed his vestments ordinance on the agenda of the next synod and this evoked a response from a deputation of seventy-five liberal and high churchmen, which waited on the Archbishop. The deputation argued that if the diocese outlawed the chasuble it would cut the clergy off from the rest of the Anglican church and damage the church's comprehensiveness.(95) Archbishop Smith agreed, and in his opening address to the synod called for tolerance, for "self-control, temperance in discussion, largeness of view, patience amid the clash of needed controversy, and a constant desire to be reasonable rather than passionate".(96) Whether Archdall responded to this plea, or more likely believed that Smith would again use his veto and rule the matter out of order to await English developments, he did not introduce his vestments ordinance in this synod. Nor did he do so in subsequent synods, perhaps because the royal commission in England had cut the ground from under his feet by recommending a liberalizing of church liturgy and a toleration for those who used the chasuble.(97) However the liturgical struggle continued outside the synod where it was viewed by the whole community.

Archbishop Smith departed from this world and the troubles of his diocese in April 1909, with the words: "I am in peace with all men, and have no known enemy".(98) He was succeeded by Archdeacon John Wright of Manchester after some furious lobbying by the low church party. Wright was acceptable to this group because he appeared to be a strong evangelical who firmly and publicly opposed the wearing of the chasuble.(99) On his arrival in Sydney Wright stressed his evangelical stance and added that while ever a bishop must be tolerant to all parties within the Church, the introduction of advanced and obscure ritual in parts of the Church had shown that "comprehensiveness has been allowed to degenerate into license".(1) Wright was above all a legalist, because he added: "I regard the Bishop of a diocese as its constitutional administrator, to administer the law and not to make it . . . and when the necessity for action comes . . . he must administer the law as his conscience interprets it."

Only a short time after Wright's arrival the liturgical controversy was revived by the retirement of Rev Carr-Smith which left the St James' incumbency vacant. The St James' parish nominators proposed several clergymen who practised an advanced ritual but these were quickly rejected by the synod nominators on the selection committee. Dean Kite of Hobart was proposed, but he refused on principle the Archbishop's demand for a signed pledge not to wear the chasuble at St James'.(2) Wright rewarded Carr-Smith for his years of dedicated service at St James' by refusing to allow him to return and end the trouble.(3) Wright was determined to eliminate the ritualists and the chasuble from his diocese.

The low churchmen cheered. The controversy dragged on and flowed over into the daily press with partisan comment and letters from both sides.(4) Bishop Stone Wigg of New Guinea devilishly told the congregation of St James' that they "could claim the blessedness of those who are persecuted".(5) In the hope of ending the conflict Wright decided to enter the lion's den and preach at St James'. On 5 June 1910 about 1500 people, 800 of them crammed inside the church, heard the Archbishop preach to the text: "Let all things be done decently and in order". It was an ominous choice, because Wright politely, but firmly, charged the congregation with causing discord in the diocese by what he called the "illegal" use of the mediaeval vestments in the service of Holy Communion. He stressed that he had no desire to end the high church tradition at St James', simply the "illegal" wearing of the chasuble.(6) The congregation responded by declaring in an open letter to the Archbishop that it had "been hated and slandered and boycotted the whole time".(7) The *Australian Churchman* termed Wright's sermon "courageous", while the *Church Commonwealth* summed it up as "tyrannical".(8) The congregation in despair finally allowed the Archbishop to appoint a minister. He chose Rev Wentworth Shields who agreed not to wear the chasuble, and the browbeaten congregation acceded.(9)

Within weeks, a similar though less public crisis arose at Christ Church, St Laurence, when Rev Albery, another wearer of the chasuble, decided to retire because of ill-health. After six months of negotiations and dispute, Rev C. M. Statham agreed under protest to sign the pledge not to wear the chasuble.(10) Thereafter these two city churches had to be content with the splendour of the cope in their services. However, persecution did encourage a larrikin strain, because as the pledge specified that the chasuble could not be worn "in any church", Rev J. Hope, Statham's successor, was known to occasionally wear it at open-air communions.(11) No move was ever made against the eccentric but well-loved Rev A. McLean who wore the chasuble in the slum parish of St Saviour's, Redfern. However, the practice ended with his death in 1943.

The evangelicals believed that Archbishop Smith allowed the chasuble to be worn because he was weak and "lacked energy and force . . . determination and decisiveness".(12) Even in his oration at Smith's funeral, Archbishop Donaldson of Brisbane gave credence to this view by describing Smith's diligence and sympathy as "not necessarily the qualities which the world calls strength".(13) If Smith lacked dynamism in public affairs, he was by no means weak. The fact that Smith failed to ban the chasuble was not due to weakness, but because he believed that the Anglican church was deeply divided over the issue and therefore a decision must await the clearing of the air. Also, he judged that the diocese had to be guided by affairs in England, and could not act independently. Above all, while he personally disliked the chasuble, he had the breadth and tolerance to accept it and as events proved, Anglicanism as a whole was moving towards greater tolerance of new liturgies. Archbishop Wright on the other hand was a legalist who wanted to restore order within the Church, and the vacancies presented him with a unique opportunity to follow his conscience and end what he saw were illegal practices. It can be argued that Smith's hesitation allowed the controversy to drag on for many years, but Wright's seemingly decisive action went no further towards ending the dispute between the two parties in the diocese. Indeed, Wright encouraged the low church party to become more assertive, and increased the level of intolerance in the diocese by capping it with his own. Wright's actions certainly gave the controversy more publicity in one year than it had enjoyed in the previous twenty years under Smith's episcopacy.

What was the upshot of this controversy? The whole low church campaign against the vestments and other liturgical accessories was in a sense pointless, for at base the world view of the high churchmen and even the ritualist was not rooted in outward forms, but in a conception of the sacraments and Christian life. The outlawing of the chasuble would not end belief in the Real Presence of Christ in the elements which it allegedly represented. In thinking that it would, the evangelicals were placing more emphasis on outward forms in worship than the ritualists, whom they accused of doing so, actually did.

It was not only pointless, but disrupted church life to a significant degree. There was little unity and amity among the clergy as a whole, which was revealed by the weakness of the Diocesan Clerical Association. The synod was a source of constant spleen and protracted debate over liturgical questions. The diocese as a whole was unsettled and even the *Australian Churchman*, which did so much to perpetuate the debate, admitted that it "caused friction, spread distrust, alienated sympathy, and led to . . . mean mediocrity".(14) There is little doubt that the attention of the clergy was diverted from the pressing problems of materialism and religious indifference. They appeared to be fiddling while Rome burned. Even church finance suffered because some were reticent in giving donations lest it aid the other side. For instance low churchmen refused to support the deanery fund since they believed a new dean might lead the cathedral in Anglo-Catholic directions. Consequently the cathedral was without a dean for over ten years. Some Anglicans were clearly disgusted with the intolerance and wrangling, and as the P.C.E.U. only had branches in a quarter of the parishes, many clearly refused to become extreme or interested in this question. Others, especially those outside the Church, were bemused or indifferent. The *Church Commonwealth* remarked that the outsider "cannot understand the real points at issue; he only reads that the various parties are squabbling, spending money introducing opponents, and sending spies to try and discover illegalities in the mode of conducting worship".(15)

However, the ongoing nature of the controversy and its prominence in the church press and affairs, revealed a strong lay support. To many who sympathized with the low church point of view it was an effort to protect Anglicanism from inroads by Catholicism, and against those who tried to overturn lawful authority and traditional practice. These views had powerful appeal in a community where the majority valued social control and tribal Protestantism. The smaller group who sympathized with the high church cause supported not only a more Catholic view of Anglicanism, but defended individual freedom of conscience. In many ways it became a conservative/liberal difference of opinion. There was enthusiasm and sincerity of belief on both sides, but little Christian love, and "sincerity without love is not of much value in the sight of Him who is the author of peace and lover of concord", wrote Bishop Barlow to Canon Archdall.(16) There was therefore no reconciliation. The party dispute has dragged on bitterly to this day.

Just how real and cohesive was this entity called Protestantism? Denominationalism did triumph over the forces for unity, and even within each church there was schism, the most prominent and destructive split being found within Anglicanism. Though the Anglicans and other Protestant churches discussed unity in this period, they were not close enough to be able to pray and take communion together. High Anglicans viewed the other Protestants as schismatics who had fallen into error. Even many low church Anglicans acted as if they were a cut above other Protestants. In their turn, the non-episcopal Protestants held mixed feelings towards Anglicans. They resented the snobbishness of Anglicanism, its "sacerdotal arrogance, its assumption of spiritual superiority, its ecclesiastical exclusiveness",(17) and yet they admired its historic nature and fine liturgy and envied its social prestige and vice-regal patronage. Yet these other Protestants did feel much closer to Sydney Anglicans than most other Anglicans, because of the fierce low church and evangelical stance of the Sydney diocese. Therefore at this time, Protestants experienced a tension between their strong evangelical feelings which encouraged unity, and their denominational loyalties. However, on an unofficial level there was little doubt about the existence of strong common views and beliefs. These had induced them to combine together in great evangelistic missions and to consider union, all in the cause of fighting religious indifference. This common Protestant sentiment also encouraged them to unite against the two other dangers which they believed confronted Protestantism in the early twentieth century — the Catholics and rampant immorality.

Federation in 1901 was supposed to herald the unity of the Australian people. The Southern Cross on the new flag symbolized oneness — the speeches, celebrations and the federal compact expressed it. Why, even civic leaders, men from all parties, captains of industry, and trade unionists, all marched together in apparent amity to the inauguration ceremony at Centennial Park. But something was amiss at this moment of unity! The procession had headed off into the heat from Sydney leaving behind Moran, the Catholic cardinal and the heads of the Methodist and Presbyterian churches. The two Protestant churchmen had refused to march because they had been placed far behind the Anglican and Catholic leaders in the order of the procession. After all, they protested, the new constitution guaranteed equality to all religions! Cardinal Moran withdrew, not because he had been refused equality with the Anglican Archbishop Smith, but because he was not given first place over Smith.(1) Instead, he and the children of Catholic schools sang and paid respect to the Commonwealth procession as it moved past the Catholic Cathedral. Archbishop Smith, tolerant Englishman that he was, no doubt brooded over this reminder of the Protestant-Catholic schism as he passed by the Irish cardinal, a distant and rigid figure atop the steps of St Mary's.

Beneath the superficial homogeneity which most contemporary commentators saw in nineteenth century Australian society, lay the reality of Protestant-Catholic animosity. This sectarianism* had been evident since the first years of white settlement in New South Wales. The early colonial administrators distrusted the Irish Catholics because they saw them as potentially rebellious, and some probably believed they belonged to a less developed branch of the human family. Being good Protestant men of their time, the administrators reflected the prejudice of an Anglo-Saxon hegemony that, until 1829, did not concede the right of Catholics to hold public office. On the other hand, the Irish Catholic convicts believed that they were as persecuted by these Protestant, English overseers, as they had been in Ireland. While perhaps not entirely justified, this view was understandable. Certainly early governors had not allowed mass to be said lest it encourage rebellious acts, and instead the Irish Catholics were herded along to Anglican services. The brutishness and coerciveness of convict society reinforced the old world

---

* Sectarian and sectarianism in this work refer to religious animosity, specifically Protestant-Catholic conflict. This is a meaning not only accepted by Australian historians, but one which was common usage at the time.

distrust between Protestants and Catholics, which subsequently continued throughout the nineteenth century.

However, sectarianism in Australia came in waves and its rhythms were often atuned to the political and economic climate of the day, as much as to religious questions. The truism that much of religious tension is not religious at all was supported by the fact that sectarian trouble often surfaced during electoral contests or times of rapid social and economic change. Religious groupings are in reality an aspect of larger and more complex cultural alignments. The religious division is like one facet of a gem-stone. Turn the gem and you see another face, perhaps the social or the political aspect, but all facets are part of the same stone and, without each other, none could exist. Max Weber and Richard Niebuhr were among the first to formalize this view that religious groups were in reality multi dimensional communal groups.(2) Thus sectarianism was not so much religious animosity as part of the power struggle between rival communal groupings. It would also provide a nice means by which one group could scapegoat the other for the ills that beset society at certain times.

In nineteenth century Australia, the Protestants were in the majority, forming three-quarters of the population, yet they were at times paranoic lest this advantage be whittled away. The twenty-five per cent who were Catholics were similarly anxious, but for what they lacked rather than for what they might lose, and their minority status at times induced a persecution complex and claustrophobia. At the end of the nineteenth century, a generation of relative sectarian peace was broken, primarily by the economic and political turmoil of the 1890s which polarized social and economic groups, and, particularly in New South Wales, accelerated the growth of nascent class alignments. This picture is by no means satisfyingly clear, for class groupings in Australia have always been ill-defined, but hazy long-term alignments began to solidify in the 1890s and these had a religious aspect. Throughout the nineteenth century the Protestants, who were solidly Anglo-Saxon, tended to be upwardly mobile and more affluent than the Irish Catholics who experienced slower social mobility and collected more at the bottom of the social heap. The division was by no means neat or total, but Anglo-Saxon Protestants tended to be middle class or to aspire to these values, whereas Irish Catholics were predominantly within the working class or of working class culture.(3) The division was at least firm enough for it to become stereotyped as such during the moments of tension in the three decades after 1890.

Although overt tension re-emerged in the 1890s, sectarian differences always undercut the homogeneity which visionaries claimed for the Australian social fabric. Protestants and Catholics confronted each other with a wariness which reflected a much wider range of differences than the religious. Perhaps most significant of all among Protestants was a suspicion of the hibernianism of the Irish Catholic. There seemed to be a subservience among them to Rome which disturbed many Protestants. The promulgation of the Immaculate Conception in 1854 and Papal Infallibility in 1870 aggravated Protestant suspicions of Catholic subservience to Italian pretenders after Christ's throne. The piousness and ornamentalism of Irish Catholicism worried many Protestants, especially those who ventured into Catholic homes and beheld crucifixes, bleeding hearts, Christs and Marys on the walls. There appeared something shocking about this familiar use of the sacred. The question of heritage, which was a vital one to all Australians at this time, since they had so little of their own, also caused problems between the religious groups, especially as partizan feelings over the Irish Home Rule Question moved to flashpoint. The Irish Catholic bloodline in Australia believed that a long persecuted Ireland must have freedom and independence, while most Anglo-Saxon Protestants saw this as a dagger at the heart of the British Empire. All these cultural and religious differences were symbolized and aggravated by the dual education system which was made irrevocable by the Education Act of 1880. One scholar has remarked of these two systems: "Catholics wanted their children to be taught differently from others, to learn a different history, to read different literature, to owe their loyalty to a different motherland, to be good and true and honest for different reasons . . . As one group of children gazed upon a picture of the Battle of Inkerman, the other looked at a picture of the Immaculate Conception of the Blessed Virgin. And if one group tried to be good because they were British, the other tried to be good because they were Catholic."(4)

As the values of Protestants and Catholics diverged, so did their lives. Though there were many acquaintances and friendships among them, circumstances were against social intercourse. They largely attended different schools and developed different world views. It was little wonder that children easily fell into name-calling. Protestant children chanted: "Publics, Publics, ring the bell, while the Catholics go to hell. Catholics stink!" Catholic youngsters would reverse the rhyme and fling it back; or sing out:

> Salvation Army, free from sin
> All went to Heaven in a kerosene tin.
> The tin caught alight
> And they all caught a fright,
> And they all went to Heaven
> With their tails alight.(5)

It was not unusual that a fusillade of stones or blue metal would follow. Harmless enough perhaps, but this isolation from each other and consequent suspicion could be perpetuated throughout the remainder of their lives. These rhymsters often joined church sporting clubs and leisure societies, or the Hibernians or the Masons, and most of them married their own kind, for only twenty per cent of all marriages were mixed. Indeed, these were the days when a mixed marriage often caused shame or a family bust up, even among those who never darkened the church door.

Thus, members of both groups drank in with their mother's milk a whole world of tribal beliefs and loyalties about themselves and the other group, and saw the world in terms of "us" and "them" — Protestants and Catholics. Protestants alleged that Catholics sinned and lied because they believed the priest could absolve them next week at mass; claimed that they stuck to their own kind beyond all decency; and said that Catholics secretly aimed to take over the country. On the other hand, Catholics were sure Protestants could not get to Heaven; doubted whether they even believed in God; and stated that the Protestants had the best of the running in society to the detriment of Catholics. Both sides claimed that certain businesses and government departments only employed Protestants or Catholics as the case may be. No doubt there was some truth in the matter. It was only due to a servant shortage in the late nineteenth century that such phrases as "no Catholics need apply" or "Catholic preferred", were absent from job advertisements. Therefore, in this fertile soil of mistrust — of Protestant paranoia and Catholic claustrophobia — the political unrest and economic depression of the 1890s created a rapid increase in the number of people who expressed an active, as opposed to a more latent, sectarian prejudice.

It was characteristic of the fighting qualities of Cardinal Moran, the Catholic Primate of Sydney, that he should turn an address on "The Reunion of Christendom" in June 1895 into a chance to have a jib at Protestantism. The theme of his address was that Protestants were lost sheep from the one true Catholic fold, whose continued existence depended on their anti-Catholicism rather than on positive Christian truths. Moran referred to the paucity of their works, and remarked of Protestant foreign missionary enterprises: "We see them equipped with every material resource that unbounded wealth and human energy can supply. Yet from every land the cry is heard that those missions are fruitless, and their best friends and champions are the very first to declare that, humanly speaking, to the divisions and conflicting creeds of rival missionaries this lack of results is due."(6) The Protestants who cherished deeply the heroic deeds of their missionaries were greatly offended by this charge. A packed meeting chaired by Archbishop Smith was held in the Centenary Hall, where Protestants heard Rev G. Brown, an ex-missionary, refute Moran's view with statistic after statistic of the marvellous work accomplished. Many sermons the following Sunday were preached in defence of Protestant missionaries.(7) Moran was not to be silenced, and he launched a fresh attack on Protestant missions in the daily press the following week. The unkindest cut of all in these articles Moran wrote was his reference to the "spiritual cargo" of the *John Williams*, the vessel of the London Missionary Society. This remark stemmed from the fact that the *Sydney Morning Herald* of 20 March 1880, had transposed in its shipping information the alcoholic cargo of an island trader with the goods carried by the *John Williams*.(8) Moran's frequent use of this joke at Catholic functions was not appreciated by temperance-minded Protestants, and he unashamedly used it often to prick Protestant sensibilities. At the succeeding Orange Day celebrations on 12 July 1895, Moran and Catholicism were vigorously attacked by Protestant speakers. Archbishop Smith thought that this controversy had "aroused a true and healthy Protestant feeling, and has been like a bracing breeze for them".(9) However, in the coming years, Moran was to make further aggressive and rash statements, which were to fan Protestant indignation into a hot sectarian wind.

The missionary controversy was revived in mid-1899 when Cardinal Moran spoke at a Catholic bazaar about the recent civil war in Samoa and the related rivalry between the Protestant and Catholic Samoan missionaries. He claimed that the Protestant missionaries had helped overthrow King Mataafa and "went so far as to use their influence with the Commanders of the British Navy to urge them to shell the Catholic Church buildings in which some of the aged and infirm had taken refuge. Owing to the prudence of the officers, no such outrage was perpetrated."(10) Protestant missionary spokesmen fervently denied these charges, and demanded that Moran produce proof.(11) However, his only response was to repeat the *John Williams* joke, which did not amuse the Protestants.

A Protestant protest committee was formed to which some of the churches sent official representatives. Protestant champion Dill Macky, Moderator of the Presbyterian church, orchestrated the decision to send a Presbyterian representative which was opposed only by the liberal conscience of Rev J. Ferguson on the grounds that it would expose "the Cardinal to the mockery of the community, and that was not a beautiful thing for the presbytery to do, especially at this season of Orange demonstration".(12) It was significantly 11 July, the day before the annual celebration of the Protestant triumph of the Battle of the Boyne in far off Ireland as long ago as 1690. The protest committee produced a refutation of the "baseless charges" which was signed by the heads of all churches (except Archbishop Smith), and over one hundred Sydney Protestant clergy. Archbishop Smith, who welcomed the "bracing breeze" of controversy in 1895, now disowned it by declining to sign this document or to attend the protest rally in the Town Hall. Over forty clergy crowded onto the platform at this packed demonstration, which was attended by over 5,000 people. To the delight and applause of the raucous crowd, Archdeacon Langely and the Methodists, Revs L. C. Rodd and P. J.

Stephen, gave fiery speeches in which they condemned Moran and gave enthusiastic support to the Protestant missionaries and the British Navy. With each phrase interlaced with applause, Stephen damned Moran's writing as, "cruel slander — subtle innuendo — cowardly boycotting — and the unscrupulous methods of Jesuitism — ".(13) The *Methodist* reported that "the effect was electrical".(14)

This response might appear to have been a gross overreaction by Protestants, and yet it was a question of honour and prestige to them. As Rev Dunstan said: Protestants saw foreign missionary work as "a sequel to the acts of the Apostles".(15) The *Sydney Morning Herald* appreciated the sensitivity of Protestants on these matters, because it realized that "upon the reputation of these missions depends very largely the reputation of the churches themselves".(16) Certainly, foreign missions were the glamour department of Christian work, and besides, Cardinal Moran had literally accused Protestant missionaries of a willingness to perpetrate cold-blooded murder. Despite all this uproar, Moran was unable to keep quiet and, in a new series of statements in the daily press, he accused Protestant missionaries of inefficiency, of making themselves rich at the expense and degradation of the indigenous population, and concluded that their missions were "manifestly the work of man, and not the work of God".(17) There was a flood of letters in response to these statements, and the *Daily Telegraph* had to paraphrase the correspondence because it was "assuming alarming proportions". Moran had hit a sensitive Protestant nerve. The general indignation was summed up by D. Webster of Ashfield who wrote of Moran: "Every word you utter against the Protestants is nothing but abuse and slander". A "Disgusted Roman Catholic" expressed fears of a Protestant backlash.(18) Most sections of opinion claimed that it was Moran, and not the Catholic community generally, who was creating the sectarian turmoil. This view was given credence by the fact that Moran revived these Samoan allegations three years later and claimed the affair was worse than the recent Armenian massacres. The Evangelical Council responded with a demand for a royal commission to clear the name of the Protestants and the British Navy.(19)

The sectarian wrangels rolled ever on! The *Sydney Morning Herald* of 10 September 1900 reported that Archbishop Redwood of Dunedin had tongue lashed Protestantism while delivering the official address at the dedication of St Mary's Cathedral, despite the presence of the vice-regal party, politicians and leading citizens. Redwood had expounded on the alleged vices of Luther and Calvin and added: "Protestantism   .   .   . covered Europe with blood and ruins in the sixteenth century, and has ever since been the helper and instrument of the worst foes of Christianity. It desecrated the home, it polluted the nuptial bed, it lowered the dignity of womanhood, it devastated the school, and stopped the progress of science."(20) Under the leadership of the Evangelical Council, the

Protestants responded vigorously to these slanders through protest meetings, countless sermons and the newspapers. The daily press as usual gave generously of its newsprint space, since the Protestant invective made exciting reading. For instance Carruthers launched a diatribe on the Catholic crime rate and then passed comment on Catholics in general by saying of Ireland: that he who passes "from a Roman Catholic county, finds that he has passed from a lower to a higher grade of intelligence and prosperity".(21) When some sanity returned to the dispute, it was discovered that Redwood's offending words had not been actually spoken in the Cathedral service, but had only been included in the press release. However, never to be caught out, militant Protestants merely charged that this proved that Redwood was not only a slanderer, but also a coward.

In order to further enrage the Protestants, Cardinal Moran dismissed the whole affair as simply "a storm in a tea cup", and proceeded to elaborate on the Protestant crimes of the Reformation.(22) Subsequently, not all of the 6,000 Protestants who wished to express their indignation could fit into the ensuing Town Hall protest rally. The platform was packed with over forty clergy, and assorted aldermen and opportunist members of parliament. Moran and Redwood's slanders were naturally condemned with great enthusiasm. The daily press believed the meeting was justified and the *Telegraph* claimed that "no political gathering has ever attracted such a great concourse of people".(23) Some of the more liberal Protestants objected to the vulgarity of these Protestant demonstrations, and Archbishop Smith again declined to attend. However, many Protestants were incensed. The *Methodist* passionately wrote that despite the decorum of the huge meeting, "there was in the vast audience suppressed forces which, if the occasion required, could and would assail tyranny and lies to their utter overthrow".(24) Protestant anger was about to boil over.

The sectarian turmoil reached fever pitch in late 1900, with the sensational law suit by bookmaker and cricketer, Arthur Coningham, against Father D. R. O'Haran (Moran's private secretary) for adultery with his wife. After ten days the jury was deadlocked, and hundreds outside the court heard that a new trial had been called. In the succeeding weeks, O'Haran's defence counsel proved to have the best espionage, in discovering collusion between Coningham and his wife to frame O'Haran. A certain Catholic priest who disliked O'Haran had been giving Coningham useful information for his allegations. The whole affair was a sensation, but the significance did not lay in the shabby charges but in the deepening sectarian animosity that it fostered. J. Want, the defence counsel, remarked that "he did not think there was a man, woman or child in the whole community who had not talked the matter over" (25) Certainly, many Protestants fantasized about what might go on behind convent walls, and at times their imaginations ran wild. The fact was that on the one hand, the Catholic Church believed that this was a Protestant conspiracy to degrade Catholicism, and on the other, militant Protestants believed that this was their chance to expose their worst fears about popery. The reality was that it all revolved around a conspirator and his wife, who were attempting to make a killing by demanding £5,000 damages for the alleged defilement of Mrs Coningham. Unfortunately, Rev Dill Macky, Protestant champion and current president of the Evangelical Council, fervently believed with all the blindness and passion of a sincere but bigoted man, that Mrs Coningham had been seduced by this Catholic priest. Dill Macky helped Coningham peruse the jury lists for Catholics, gave him financial aid, and even lent him his own revolver, after Coningham announced to the court that he had received over forty death threats by mail. Dill Macky must have had second thoughts when, as O'Haran's innocence was announced, Coningham threw himself across the court room at O'Haran, sobbing, "I'll kill him! I'll kill Him!" A somewhat chastened Dill Macky declared that he had acted on his own volition, and neither the Presbyterian church, nor the Evangelical Council, had any part in his activities. However, he added with true sectarian panache, that he would do the same thing again.(26) Dill Macky was a fighter. After all, how many clergy owned a pistol?

The reactions to the trial from the Sydney religious world were marked. Of course, the militant Protestants refused to accept the verdict. The *Methodist* ludicrously claimed that ninety per cent of Australians believed Father O'Haran's innocence was "not proven".(27) More liberal Protestants were rather shocked by the whole shabby affair. Catholics who had never doubted O'Haran's innocence (at least publically), demonstrated their faith by raising the enormous sum of £8,537 to cover his legal expenses. Flushed with pride, Cardinal Moran told the Town Hall victory gathering that "a thrill of joy vibrated throughout the whole Catholic community . . . and at no former period of our Australian history has such vigour of unity and such harmony and concord of sentiment been witnessed in the Catholic body as at the present hour".(28) Catholicism had risen phoenix-like from the ashes of imminent scandal, and was reinforced anew in the view that it was persecuted and separated off from the rest of the community. The tension between both religious groups was mounting and the slanders of the sectarian activists were now being listened to by more people than usual.

Obviously in the long term, sectarianism has a circular causation of blow reacting against blow. Thus it is impossible to determine its original impetus. However, in the short term, it can be seen that Cardinal Moran was the explosive element in a society with a long history of sectarian conflict, currently experiencing an atmosphere of tension due to economic strife and political uncertainty. Some other scholars have laid the blame on the Protestants, by pointing to their aggressive reaction to Cardinal Moran's innocent candidature for the federal convention of 1897, and the uproar of the Coningham case in 1901.(29) However, it is clear that the revival of sectarianism in the 1890s did not begin in 1897, but 1895, with the missionary controversy, triggered off by Moran's allegations that Protestant missions were Godless and "fruitless". Certainly, the Protestants were quick to launch into emotional overreactions, but the initial impetus lay with Moran. He was in many ways a fine churchman. He was passionately interested in Australian federation; he doggedly defended the labour movement against the distorted label of revolutionary socialism; and he generally supported the cause of social reform. He was also one of the foremost builders of his church — especially Catholic education.(30) However, while he was all this, and not as aggressive as some of the Catholic hierarchy in the nineteenth century, he was no innocent when it came to sectarian unrest as some have tried to portray him.(31) Eris O'Brien caught the controversialist within Moran when he wrote: "Moreover, he had a dangerous facility of expression, either in the spoken or the written word, a wide fund of knowledge, a ready wit, a slight inclination to impetuosity, and an extraordinary fund of energy."(32) One other historian has stressed that Moran entered controversies with gusto and at times used sources that were not always accurate, or pushed his conclusions beyond the limits of the facts and yet "when his errors were proved he did not have the grace to retract".(33) Cardinal Moran was a fine churchman, but most Protestants could only judge him on what they read in the press, and here he appeared as a fighting Irishman who slandered Protestants with poor jokes and wrong information which he did not have the decency or Britishness to recant when proven wrong.

The initial sense of indignation and passion aroused in religious hearts by these controversies overlay a deeper sense of fear. At the very core of sectarian prejudice lay the fear of being dominated by the other group. The issues of ecclesiastical precedence and the Coronation Oath reflected this problem for many Protestants. Militants argued that the Catholic quarter of the population was trying to run the place. Had not Cardinal Moran refused to march in the procession to celebrate the inauguration of the Commonwealth, because he had not been given first place? Most Protestants abhorred such pretension and believed the Anglican Archbishop should have first place. The more liberal Protestants argued that as all Christian churches were equal, size alone should be the criterion for precedence, while the militants simply stated that Protestants were entitled to and must have first place in the nation. P. R. Waddy, a correspondent to the *Sydney Morning Herald*, argued that "we are a Protestant community — the majority of whom are Protestants — living under a Protestant Queen; and if precedence is to be accorded to the head of any religion first place most undeniably ought to be accorded to the head of the dominant Church of which our Queen is a member".(34) But would the monarch always be Protestant? At that very moment in England Catholics were attempting to delete the clause in the Coronation Oath taken by the sovereign, which declared the invocation of the Virgin Mary and the Catholic mass to be "superstitious and idolatrous". Many people thought that it was time that these offensive words were removed, but militant Protestants argued that this would open the way for a Catholic monarch. Even reasonable Protestants baulked at the thought of this! The *Sydney Morning Herald* declared: "We will not surrender the principle of a Protestant King over a Protestant people; but we will pay reasonable regard to the sincere beliefs of any minority amongst us."(35)

The inevitable monster Town Hall demonstration was held to protect the Protestant throne and Coronation Oath. It was chaired by Dill Macky, who fresh from the Coningham case declared: "The Rev W. Dill Macky had not been brought to his knees yet."(36) The crowd cheered, burst into "Rule Britannia" and resolved that the Coronation Oath should remain unchanged. Dill Macky proposed a similar resolution two months later in the Australian Assembly of the Presbyterian church, but it was defeated by a ratio of almost two to one. However Clouston, who voted against Dill Macky's motion on the grounds of Christian charity, ominously said he accepted Dill Macky's warnings about the papal tyranny that would ensue if the Catholics ever gained control.(37) Truly, the Protestant majority was deeply fearful of the Catholic minority.

However, the important fact was that fear lay on both sides. The Irish Catholics had been persecuted in Ireland, and many of them could not escape this framework of thinking when they came to Australia. Though recent scholarship has disproven the persecution thesis,(38) many Catholics believed they were discriminated against in early colonial Australia. Indeed, Cardinal Moran wrote his *History of The Catholic Church in Australia* (1895) in these terms.(39) Australian Catholicism derived an authoritarian, aggressive and conservative tone from its Irish heritage, and increasingly in the nineteenth century this placed it out of step with the prevailing liberal democratic ethos of colonial society. Catholicism felt alienated and separated from the rest of Australian society. This attitude was accelerated by the creation of a state secular education system, and the subsequent withdrawal of state aid for church schools. In 1909, Father P. Dowling expressed this feeling of alienation when he remarked to the third Catholic Congress: "We are thus surrounded by non-Catholics; we live and work, and take our pleasures among non-Catholics. Non-Catholic ideas permeate the public press, the political parties, the social life of the continent, simply because non-Catholics are dominant, at least in numbers, through the Common-wealth."(40) The Catholic community as a whole was gripped by a ghetto mentality that many non-Catholics were "agin them". This sense of alienation shared by many Catholics induced them to create their own physical world apart from the Protestants and to be at times insufferably triumphalist about the merits of their faith.

To a considerable degree, the Catholic community tried to become self-contained and a separate entity, or at least it appeared that way to those outside. It established Catholic schools, charities, orphanages and institutions for the handicapped, and a whole range of other societies. There were also Catholic sporting and entertainment societies. If perchance Catholics joined a non-denominational movement like the Boy Scouts, more often than not they formed their own subgroups with their own distinctive uniforms. Catholicism even held its own celebration for the Commonwealth inauguration, and a separate official welcome for the arrival of the great United States fleet in 1908. However militant Protestants did not see that this Catholic separateness was based upon claustrophobia and fear for their faith, and instead believed it to be "a deep political design to keep the adherents of the Church in such a state that they can be readily rounded up for action when the interests of Rome demanded their services".(41) Liberals were alarmed that this exclusivism would split the homogeneous Australian community they were trying to foster. The *Sydney Morning Herald* expressed "doubts of the ultimate success or wisdom of forming a State within a State, which is the logical issue of the system which the Cardinal has set up".(42)

This separateness demanded a triumphalism to make it viable. Catholics claimed theirs was the one true church which would eventually reign supreme, and this, quite naturally, galled Protestants. Indeed, anti-Catholic literature often quoted priests who had allegedly made such statements as — "the Catholic Church would be all powerful, and rule this country before 50 years".(43) Liberal Catholics like Bishop Delany of Hobart were able to empathize with Protestant fears to some extent, and he for one admitted that it was natural for those outside his church to "consider her in many ways preposterous, and many of her claims unendurable".(44) However, most Catholics were either unaware, or all too aware, of the enraging effect Catholic triumphalism had on the Protestant mind. So they continued to carry the Host (referred to by some Protestants as the Wafer God) by ferry across Sydney Harbour to celebrate the feast of Corpus Christi, and to have countless public bazaars and stone layings. Of one such event, attended by Cardinal Moran, Catholic bishops and priests, politicians and a large crowd, the *Australian Christian World* commented that: "it appeared as if that Church had reached a very proud eminence, and it was bestriding us like a colossus. It is doubtless a great power in the land, and its influence when concentrated on such occasions as these, is deep, penetrating and extensive."(45) Thus it was that Catholic claustrophobia stimulated an exclusivist and boasting Catholicism, which in turn increased Protestant paranoia.

This fear and distrust that both Catholics and Protestants had tradition-ally held towards each other was increasing around 1900, due to the continuation of unemployment, drought, and a decline in real wages, and also due to the increasing conflict between Labour and Capital (which broadly related to the dispute between Catholicism and Protestantism). As it increased, more moderates on both sides came to accept the views of the extremists – it became self-generating. On the Protestants' side, the extremists maintained that the Catholic church was pursuing a con-spiracy for world domination, masterminded from Rome by the Jesuits. Some believed that the plot was already in danger of succeeding, because "Rome, to a large extent, dominates the social, the commercial and the political life of New South Wales".(46) Some of the charges were ludicrous, but they were given credence by many Protestants at the time. It was alleged that Catholics boycotted Protestant storekeepers, and that nuns by threat of non-payment of their bills, blackmailed Protestant commercial men into donating to Catholic charities. The militants urged defence and exclaimed: "Protestantism arise, and arise in all your strength."(47) A significant number of Protestants, who perhaps were worried about their own economic security, and fearing that the Catholics were about to gain disproportionate power in the community, believed the worst claims of the extremists. Upon the smallest shreds of evidence imaginable, the lunatic fringe on both sides of the sectarian fence created absurd fantasies and myths about the other group, and to many people these myths became reality – but then scapegoats and conspiracies always get a good hearing in hard times. The myths were too numerous to examine all of them, but two of the most persistent were that the Catholics were taking over the public service and the parliament.

It was perhaps natural that one myth the Protestants created was that the Catholics dominated the public service – since not only was the service important in managing the country, but it offered the chance of security of employment in a period when this was not universal. As one journalist remarked: "nearly every second man you meet is, or desires to be, an employé of the Government".(48) Two officers of the Public Service Board stated in 1904 that Catholic schools gave special lessons to coach their pupils for the public service entrance examination.(49) Orange men considered doing the same. Catholics obviously saw the service as a way of escaping their predominance among "the hewers of wood and the drawers of water" of society.

In the late 1890s and early 1900s, the permanent staff of the public service had been expanding at the considerable rate of four per cent per year. However, in 1904 economic retrenchment caused the service to shrink by half a per cent, and one per cent the following year, which made competition for entrance extremely fierce.(50) Militant Protestants claimed that Catholics enjoyed preference in gaining positions and dominated the service; while Catholics alleged that Protestants monopolized the upper ranks of the service. The *Church Commonwealth* commented that "half the usefulness of our civil service is paralysed by the bickerings and plottings of these contending factions".(51) Dill Macky stated that while Catholics formed only twenty-five per cent of the community, they made up ninety per cent of the Customs Department.(52) It was later alleged that Catholic control of this department was the reason for the ban on importing such Protestant works (pornography? slanders?) as Chiniquy's *Maria Monk* and *The Priest, The Woman and the Confessional*. The *Watchman*, a militant Protestant journal, claimed that Catholics also dominated the letter carriers' section of the Post Office, and actually printed lists of names to "prove" this.(53) The *Methodist* argued that sixty per cent of the teachers in the Education Department were Catholics, while the Presbyterian, W. Affleck M.L.A., alleged that it was fifty per cent in his electorate of Yass.(54) This was a popular accusation, because it was argued that Catholic teachers were infiltrating the state education system, to convert innocent Protestant schoolchildren to Catholicism and eventually to undermine the state system and make Catholic education supreme. One bitter Protestant believed that Catholic teachers were "two-faced, double-dealing, unreliable servants — not fit to be instructors of our Australian youth".(55) Several Methodist circuit committees made the point of warning their flock about the proselytizing activities of Catholic teachers.(56)

So persistent were the allegations that in 1902 the See government, which was itself under attack for being dominated by Catholics, issued statistics on the religious affiliation of those in the public service compiled by the Government Statistician. It was an amazing breach of privacy, because the religion of public servants was supposed to be unknown to the Public Service Board itself. It was compiled from the raw census data. The report revealed that, far from controlling the public service, Catholics were in fact under-represented by two per cent in the whole service. More than this, they appeared to be under-represented in the better jobs, because while twenty-six per cent of the population were Catholics, only twenty per cent of school teachers were Catholics. Yet the Catholics had their equitable share of policemen, postmen, transport and construction workers.(57) Ironically, it was the Protestants who were the ones over-represented! Liberal Protestants welcomed the exploding of this myth, while the militants predictably refused to believe these facts. The *Watchman* continued to publish its lists of Catholics in the service, and others made more allegations.

Rev Woolls Rutledge, a prominent Methodist and militant Protestant, was one who had regularly made such accusations, but in 1904 he made the mistake of leaving the safety of vague claims and naming a specific instance of alleged sectarian manipulation. A. Griffith M.L.A., a fierce democrat and liberal Protestant, instantly moved in parliament that an inquiry be made and was alleged to have muttered, "now we will get the slanders".(58) The daily press gave long verbal accounts of the stormy select committee. Griffith's chairmanship was perhaps partisan against Woolls Rutledge who was subsequently humiliated. The accusations proved false and it seems that Woolls Rutledge had unwisely repeated slander told to him by the accused man's vindictive brother-in-law whom he met over "a cuppa" at a church social.(59) The significant fact is that the militant Protestants believed Griffith had covered up the evidence of Catholic influence, a view that was publicized by the *Methodist* at the time, and even by Woolls Rutledge's son-in-law thirty-three years later.(60) No matter what evidence was uncovered, the myths refused to die! Woolls Rutledge was a declared Christian Socialist, a strong social and moral reformer, and supporter of the under-dog. The editor of the *Methodist*, Carruthers, once said that Woolls Rutledge was "chivalrous to an unusual degree, charitable ever in his judgements, constant with the constancy of steel to his friendships, devout in his spirit, beautifully submissive in affliction and suffering, and supremely loyal to the Lord and Saviour of us all".(61) There is curious paradox here of a man who had such a strong sense of justice that he was led into injustice — that within him there was a curious blindness caused by his intense Protestant loyalty — and so sectarianism rolled into madness.

The other persistent myth was that the Catholic church had an undue and direct affect on politics. The Protestant folklore claimed that Catholics voted as a block and therefore, though they were only a minority of the community, they could wield great influence. When asked to point to the force organizing this vote, the shrewd Protestant replied that the Catholic church itself was a political institution. Certainly, there were the usual shreds of evidence to support these assertions, because the Catholic church had tried to influence elections overtly since the withdrawal of state aid to religion. A layman, Dr Kenny, had urged the Catholic Congress of 1900 to form a league to ensure that all Catholics used their vote: "Need I give instances, before a Catholic Congress, in which a full and united Catholic vote would have been at the same time in the best interests of the State and to the advantage of Catholics? If so, let me point to the present State system of Education."(62) However, as the historian of the Catholic church, Patrick O'Farrell, affirms, this Catholic vote never materialized.(63) There was of course some Catholic influence in elections, but so too was there a Protestant presence! J. C. Watson claimed that the 1903 federal election was influenced by sectarianism "to an alarming extent", and Sir William Lyne concurred, alleging that he was defeated by the efforts of some Protestant ministers "who scoured my electorate on bicycles".(64) Thus, although the historian cannot see a strong Catholic vote, militant Protestants at the time were sure it existed, and that was what mattered. They claimed for instance that the introduction of postal votes was a Catholic plot, because the votes of nuns behind convent walls would be mobilized to sway elections. Similarly, the granting of the franchise to women caused some Protestant palpitations, as some argued that priestly influence would mobilize a solid Catholic women's vote.

More specifically, the Protestant claim was that the Catholic church controlled Sir John See's Progressive Party and its partner in government from 1901–1903, the infant Labour Party. Cardinal Moran gave some credence to this when he wrongly hinted while in Rome that twenty-five out of twenty-eight Labour parliamentarians were Catholics.(65) Actually the number was only eight out of twenty-four, but Protestants for once reported him without correction, because he enhanced their accusations. Indeed, only a quarter of the governing coalition and the cabinet were Catholics.(66) Sir John See was himself a Protestant and Mason. However, militant Protestants were obsessed with the belief that the two Irish Catholics, E. W. O'Sullivan, the forceful Minister for Works, and the flamboyant W. P. Crick, the Minister for Lands, controlled the government. Certainly these two were dominant public figures, O'Sullivan for his radicalism and Crick for his larrikin slanders and fisticuffs inside and outside parliament. To politically conservative, militant Protestants, these two were symbolic of the enemy and hysterically seen as a polluting influence in the government, led by See, allegedly an unreliable Protestant who truckled to Catholics for votes. Militant Protestants claimed this was nowhere more obvious than in the St Patrick's Day holiday affair.

This Catholic saint's day was originally proclaimed as a holiday in 1900 in deference to Queen Victoria who wished to acknowledge how well the Irish Brigade had fought in the Transvaal. It was continued in 1901 for the same reason and celebrated with considerable community support. However, in 1902 opposition mounted from the commercial sector which claimed there were too many holidays, and also from the militant Protestants who said that the Catholics were unduly favoured as no Protestant saints were similarly honoured.(67) In 1903, under pressure from these groups, See decided to terminate the holiday. Instantly, Cardinal Moran wrote to O'Sullivan that unless See changed his decision "it must be idle for him I fear, to expect that the men and women of Irish parentage will cast their vote for himself and his friends when the day of trial will come".(68) J. Meagher M.L.C., a son of the Church, told the Bathurst branch of the Hibernian Catholic Guild that although "Catholics had for many years given the See Government their support", the premier had abandoned them.(69) See back peddled and gave public service employees a half day's holiday, but then changed again, and only allowed those who wished, a half day's leave without pay. Militant Protestants were convinced that the affair demonstrated See's subservience to the Catholic vote.

The reality behind the myth of a Catholic political influence was that while Catholics formed twenty-six per cent of the community, only about eighteen per cent of parliamentarians were Catholics. One quarter of the Progressives were Catholics, and one third of the Labour men were Catholics, but not one of the conservative opposition of thirty-seven were Catholic!(70) Therefore, Catholics were slightly over-represented in the governing party, considerably under-represented in the whole House, and had absolutely no voice in the opposition. It is true that Catholics had always voted against Sir Henry Parkes since his anti-Catholic stance over the O'Farrell affair in 1868, and that this had channelled them into support for the Protectionists and later the Progressives and the Labour Party. However, did Catholics support the Progressives and Labour because they were Catholics as such, or because they were workingmen as well? It would be hard to deny that the Irish Catholic penchant for radicalism, as well as their historical working class status, had channelled them away from the conservatives and towards the Progressives and Labour. Sectarian tension only reinforced this tendency. As the recent historian of the Australian Catholic church has stated: "Alignment with the Labour Party was essentially the result not of the operation of Catholic principle (though this played some part), but more importantly of economic logic, and drift — social and intellectual drift."(71) However, because militant Protestants themselves voted along religious rather than economic lines, they were sure that all Catholics did likewise, and therefore, they clung to the myth that a block Catholic vote sought to take over the Labour Party and hence the country.

The other political reality in New South Wales was that the Protestants and the conservatives had been moving together well before the creation of the Catholic-Labour alliance. Indeed, the conservatives did not have any Catholics within their ranks whatsoever in the 1901 parliament! This alliance was historically natural, since the Protestants coalesced with the conservatives because they were basically middle class in sympathy. The Protestant churches overwhelmingly supported individual enterprise and abhorred socialism. When the socialist issue was being heatedly discussed in the early 1900s, most of the Protestant papers took a hard anti-socialist line, some stating bluntly that socialism was anti-Christ and even immoral as they alleged it encouraged free love.(72) The extremists were most adamant. The Australian Protestant Defence Association issued a manifesto declaring its opposition to socialism.(73) The logical extension of these Protestant views was that the Labour Party was socialist and perhaps even anti-Christ. When Cardinal Moran publically defended the Labour Party and Australian-styled socialism,(74) it seemed to all fall into place for quite a few Protestants, who were now certain they were right in opposing Labour and socialism. Even before this, most middle class Protestants had instinctively opposed the strike weapon, party pledges, and caucus direction, all of which they maintained were a negation of the individual Christian conscience.

The relations between Protestantism and Labour, which had never been particularly bright, were finished by 1900. Catholicism was aligned with Labour and the remnants of the Progressives on the one hand, while Protestantism was allied with non-Labour on the other. Thus by 1900, an attack on Catholicism was one means of striking a blow at Labour and the working class. In this way, it can be seen that sectarianism reflected, and also helped to create, the growing tension between classes around 1900. To a large extent, sectarianism was not religious, but political and economic in inspiration. However, sectarianism had other motivations as well, because among other things, it could express a desire for entertainment which could verge on the bizarre, and also could reflect intense patriotism or personal paranoias.

There is little doubt that sectarian controversy provided excitement and perhaps diversion from the economic problems of the day. The daily press highlighted and reported in full all the sectarian gatherings and gave liberal space to sectarian correspondents. It was this type of news that made the daily press interesting and readable. The monster Protestant demonstrations in the Town Hall provided great entertainment for those who attended. It was a little like a vaudeville show, with cries of "shame" for Cardinal Moran, and cheering, foot-stamping and the waving of handkies for the Protestant champions, Dill Macky, Stephen and Woolls Rutledge. It was a rousing experience to hear over 5,000 people singing "Rule Britannia" or "The Protestant Boys". Besides, the speakers argued that they alone were right; that militant Protestants alone knew the truth of the Catholic conspiracy. Many Protestants swaggered home from the meetings warmed by self-righteous indignation.

It is difficult to judge who went to those meetings. Certainly, women were much in evidence, and some reports mention that half the audience were women.(75) This was to be expected in terms of the large degree of female activity in the churches, yet it is notable because it outweighed most of their other public social involvements. Given the leading role the clergy played in the anti-Catholic campaigns, it might be expected that the majority of militants were churchgoers. However, a significant proportion were political Protestants; people who never attended church, but who possessed a strong Protestant group loyalty and a highly developed anti-Catholic prejudice. Several clergy were critical of militant Protestantism which contained too much of the "political" element, as they termed the non religious aspects of Protestant fire.(76) Rev W. A. Charlton felt moved to warn at an annual Orange Day church parade in 1902, that "the Orangeman who puts Orangism before Christ is a thief and a robber".(77) Sydney was obviously a very dishonest town at this time, for while Protestant demonstrations included prayers and sacred songs, sections of the audience always clapped the hymns, cheered and applauded the addresses, and showed little knowledge of church etiquette, much to the chagrin of some of the clergy present.

Extremist anti-Catholic literature which even found its way onto the back pages of some respectable Protestant church papers was generally slanderous and often bizarre. Militant Protestants seemed particularly obsessed by stories of sadism and perversion within convent walls. Ghastly claims were made about foeticide resulting from unholy convent unions. Babies were said to be buried within convent grounds. The Protestant sectarians culled these allegations from their fellow militants from all parts of the world, but local stories occasionally came to light. The *Watchman,* true to its name, claimed that in 1903 alone, there had been seven attempted escapes by nuns from the Good Samaritan Convent in Redfern because of ill-treatment.(78) Some people, who usually claimed to be ex-priests or nuns, made a living out of lecture tours which featured convent and other anti-Catholic scandals. Even Mrs Coningham, who had tried to frame Fr O'Haran for adultery, had the gall to give lectures on alleged convent licentiousness. J. Britten, an irate Catholic, exclaimed that the audience of one such lecture tour by an "ex-religious" couple, the Slatterys, was composed of either "the fanatical bigots whose hatred of the Church blinds them to the dictates of common sense and the larger number of those who love indecency, and whose expectations in that direction are seldom disappointed".(79) The Protestant churches and the press as a whole refused to countenance the Slatterys or their ilk, but unfortunately this did not apply to the extremists. The Australian Protestant Defence Association sponsored a tour by Mrs Shepherd, allegedly an ex-nun, who spoke on convent brutality and immorality, and held "ladies only" meetings to issue special warnings.(80) Protestant minds no doubt were scared and titillated by whispers about the power of priests over ladies in the confessional box and other sexual innuendos. In this prudish society, sectarian allegations provided a mild form of pornographic stimulation; but from the perspective of two generations, sectarianism itself seems nothing short of an obscenity.

Protestant sectarianism also appealed to those who had a highly developed sense of British patriotism. This was inevitable given the divergent ethnic backgrounds of the two religious groups, which clashed bitterly over that running sore — the Irish Question. Protestants believed that the Irish quest for Home Rule was simply a step towards Rome Rule and complete separation from Britain. Militants also believed that Australian Catholics wanted to create a republic of Australia and cut Australia adrift from the Empire. This certainly was the belief of some in the Labour movement, a view which further confirmed in the Protestant mind the existence of a Labour-Catholic alliance. The Protestant fears for the Empire's future were exacerbated by the Irish Catholic tendency to sing the praises of Ireland at Catholic functions. The revival of the St Patrick's Day cult by Cardinal Moran in 1890s was all part of this Irishism. At the separate Catholic welcome to the American fleet in 1908, Moran spoke on the glories of the Irish Rebellion against England in 1798, which emulated the American Revolution. No loyal toast was made, or Union Jack displayed at the dinner, to the added annoyance of Protestants.(81) The other side of the coin to this Irishism, was the burgeoning of Empire loyalty among middle class Protestants, stimulated by patriotic literature such as Rev Fitchett's *Deeds That Won The Empire,* the military escapade in the Transvaal, and the spectre of an Asian invasion. In 1901, a British Empire League was initiated by Canon Boyce (its first president), and he began the movement which established Empire Day celebrations in state schools from 1905.(82)

Lastly, it should be noted that sectarian activists were often motivated by so much zeal that it bordered on obsessiveness and paranoia. But who can say why they saw conspiracies all around them? What desperations or distortions of reality caused Mrs E. Tennant Donaldson (by then married with children), to testify in a sworn statement in 1903, to the harsh conditions she experienced in a Catholic orphanage at Manly six years earlier? She alleged that the children suffered from insufficient food and clothing, unsanitary living conditions, cruel treatment, and endless laundry work and sewing — even of the cardinal's own garments. The See government finally acceded under Protestant pressure to an inquiry, and after breaking six appointments, Mrs Donaldson finally agreed to talk to officers of the State Children's Relief Board, but failed to satisfy them of any malpractice at the orphanage.(83) There were several other similar allegations, which also seemed nonsense, although militant Protestants were sure they were true.(84) Some of these were encouraged by laundry companies, which resented the competition from convent laundry services.(85) These, like the allegations about public service jobs, fed on the economic insecurities of those on the lower rungs of the social ladder, or on those who had a tenuous hold on new-found status or wealth. Sectarianism always seemed strongest at the edge of that blurred line between the working class and the lower middle class.

James Criss, a Baptist, owner of a printing business, and an unfermented wine merchant, was the most prolific Protestant publicist of the period. He wrote anti-Catholic articles of both a moderate and more scurrilous nature under the nom de plume of "James the Less", in the *Australian Christian World* from 1896 to 1918. Cardinal Moran was his special obsession, and every remark that Moran made would be analyzed, ridiculed and countered. One statement on the Apostolic Succession of popes from Peter to the present, launched Criss into an eighty-two part series stretching over two years on the misdeeds of the popes of Rome to prove they could not be a direct spiritual line from St Peter. Like all his articles, these were based on historical and theological knowledge, but written with the tunnel vision and single mindedness which approached the psychotic. Who but the most dedicated sectarian would have the stamina to read them, let alone write them? In all his open letters to Moran, Criss never once considered he might also be at fault when he charged Moran with being "the originator of the religious discord that has disgraced our social life".(86)

One man, Rev William Marcus Dill Macky, minister of historic Scot's Church, Sydney, is vital to an understanding of the sectarian mentality. Dill Macky was the acknowledged Protestant champion of his day. Did dark forces motivate him? Was he a demagogue, or perhaps a sincere, but over-zealous Protestant? One thing is certain: he was an Ulsterman, born in 1849 at Lisfannan, county Donegal, the descendant of sixteenth century Scottish colonists and clerics. He therefore had an impeccable Irish Protestant heritage! One time Anglican minister and pastoralist, Cuthbert Fetherstonhaugh commented that "all Irish Protestants as a rule are extremely low church − narrow to a degree, and puritanical, in fact like St Paul they lived after the most straightest sect of their religion".(87) Was Dill Macky like this? Does this explain much of the sectarian mind?

The fragments we know of young William Dill Macky's life seem to be set very much in this mould. He proudly remembered that as a boy he would often sit astride "Roaring Meg", one of the cannons still on the walls of the town of Derry, that had held off the seige laid by the army of the Catholic, James II, in 1688. The young boy looking out beyond the walls would relive that confrontation, shouting out "no-surrender" as the Derryites had six generations before him. For years Dill Macky was a member of the Apprentice Boys' Club, a sort of junior Orange lodge, where his Protestant principles were further reinforced. History in Ireland was drunk in with the mother's milk.

As he grew older, Dill Macky's adherence to the Protestant folklore developed. He took out an arts degree at Magee College and then followed the family tradition of entering the Presbyterian church. Dill Macky was ordained in 1876. He soon earned a reputation for strident conservative politics at his first pastorate at Draperstown, and had the distinction of being the only minister in the Magherafelt Presbytery to oppose Gladstone's rather liberal Home Rule Bill. Dill Macky claimed Home Rule would mean Rome Rule. Such was the Catholic antipathy to his outspokenness, that on some occasions he travelled armed to the teeth with two six shooters, to ward off imminent trouble. Controversy was so large a part of Dill Macky's life that this fiery man of God continued to carry firearms on and off throughout his life.

When on the verge of middle age and firmly steeped in the Irish Protestant folklore, Dill Macky succumbed to the allure of Australia, as his long lost father had in the golden 1850s. He arrived in Sydney with his wife and three children on board the *Austral* in January 1887. By late April 1887 he had received and accepted a call to Scot's Church, a pastorate he held to his death in 1913.

Dill Macky's strident Protestantism was nourished by the sectarian environment he found in Australia. Within a year he had joined the Orange lodge and in a short time was a leading Protestant publicist. He later claimed that he became an active Orangeman "when I saw the determined effort of Rome to dominate this free country".(88) No doubt the perennial controversy over the education question was an influence in such thinking. However, also of importance was the encouragement he received from his congregation at Scot's. Anti-Catholicism had been a tradition at Scot's Church stretching back to 1820 when the firebrand Rev J. D. Lang first began his fifty-two year pastorate at that church. A religious journalist in 1909 wrote: "Scot's Church with its grim air of old-world Presbyterianism makes the bit of modern Sydney in which it stands look hopelessly unreal . . . It is a living bit of the past, defiantly grafted on to the present and dominating it to extinction. It alone is convincingly real; the rest is painted paper, grotesque stage-scenery".(89)

Strongly evangelical, Dill Macky suited Scot's Church to a tee. He was Pauline in his use of the Scriptures, treating them as literal and a reality of grace, rather than inspired literature and history. God played a very active part in Dill Macky's world. The bubonic plague which threatened Sydney in 1901 was seen as Divine retribution for the community's misdeeds. Somewhat atypically for the 1900s, he firmly believed in the Second Coming of the Lord, preached about it often, and held special services to prepare the ground. In most aspects of theology he was a conservative and certainly refused to consider the Higher Criticism of the Bible.(90) This led in 1907 to a revolt by the final year theology students at St Andrew's college where Dill Macky taught Systematic and Biblical Theology. The students claimed that his lectures were merely verbatim readings from Hodge's *Systematic Theology,* and that these ill-prepared them to assess modern critical biblical scholarship. Dill Macky's reply is illuminating. In a typical self-righteous, evangelical response to these student complaints, he declared there was a "flood of rationalism that is sweeping into our church" even into the theological college.(91) This Irish Protestant, true to his folklore, saw most changes or challenges to the established order of things as conspiracies. The Higher Criticism of the Bible was a conspiracy; so too was High Anglicanism; and of course Sin itself which was eating into the very vitals of society. The greatest conspiracy of them all was Catholicism.

Yet there was another side to this fiery Protestant. He was also a man of God. Those who heard Dill Macky preach claimed that his biblical exposition was of a high calibre. It could be both impassioned and quietly sensitive; always straight-forward, yet warm and brotherly. He was genial yet candid, and his manner "tingling with a certain quick relish and sharp gusto". Dill Macky, summed up a religious journalist from the *Australian Christian World*, was "one of the most salient and popular figures in the religious world of Sydney".(92) More accurately, the statement should have read, the Protestant religious world.

Dill Macky's pastoral and administrative record matched his preaching. Besides ministering to his own congregation, he was Presbyterian chaplain to the forces for over a decade, Presbyterian chaplain to Sydney Hospital, a lecturer at St Andrew's College, a councillor of Scot's College, and Presbyterian Scripture teacher each week to the young men and ladies of the Fort Street schools. Dill Macky was elected Moderator of the state Presbyterian Assembly in 1899, from which he developed the penchant for wearing knee breeches. The Moderatorship also brought with it an honorary Doctorate of Divinity conferred by the Theological Faculty of Ireland. For the next five years he served on a third of his church's standing committees. He was President of the Evangelical Council in 1900, Christian Endeavour in 1898, on the executive of five different mission boards, the Temperance Alliance, several welfare societies and other Christian bodies. In the early 1900s he edited the Christian Endeavour's *Roll Call* and the Protestant journal *The Watchman*. Not surprisingly he was also Grand Chaplain of the Orange Lodge. All this together with nine children!(93) Was it any wonder that he ate "Force" breakfast food and testified that "it is palatable, strengthening and has good staying qualities". Dill Macky was a sincere, hardworking clergyman as well as being a militant Protestant.

Even his Protestantism had complexities. He always claimed to have Catholic friends though on one occasion confessed that he "found it very difficult to make his Roman Catholic friends understand that it was not against them, personally, that he had any ill-will".(94) Indeed, he maintained amiable relations with the neighbouring Catholic priest, Father Rentoul, who, it is claimed, warned Dill Macky of several attempts on his life.(95) Dill Macky liked to believe he was opposed to principles not people — but could the two be separated? How did his fellow Presbyterian and former friend, Rev John Ferguson, feel, when Dill Macky moved a censure motion against him because Ferguson had innocently visited the Pope while visiting Rome.(96)

How did a man like Dill Macky who had so many admirable qualities get mixed up in sectarian bigotry? The key lies in his Irishness. One religious journalist rightly remarked that Dill Macky "is a controversialist only by accident of nationality: by genius and grace he is a pastor".(97) Both Moran and Dill Macky held to their convictions tenaciously and perceived conspiracies everywhere, because they had grown up in a post-famine Ireland wracked by decades of trouble, poverty and oppression.

Here, two religious subcultures had eyed each other venomously for generations. Each individual was compelled to take sides, since group loyalty was a fact of life and sectarian Myth and Folklore the educators of every child. It was natural, if regrettable, that when these two arrived in New South Wales in the 1880s and sensed the underlying sectarian animosity, they, like many others of their kind, believed that here was another Ireland and acted accordingly. The fact was that Australia was not like Ireland, though their bigotry threatened to make it so. Despite their being great individualists, the sectarian views of Dill Macky and Moran were only the feelings writ large of a great number of Protestants and Catholics. At the core of the sectarian mentality was its Irishness!

But was this sectarian animosity after all healthy conviction or madness? The Catholic, Bishop Delaney of Hobart, in 1900 pleaded for the former when he stated that "men must really detest what they believe to be detestable, and they will in spite of their better selves – or rather not in spite, but because of their very goodness – wish and strive to prevent the advance of what to them appears fraught with so much evil consequence".(98) Yet there was a point at which conviction became a madness. Dill Macky, Cardinal Moran and other sectarian activists must be seen as men whose sincerity, loyalty and sense of justice was so distorted by obsessiveness over the sectarian issue, that they verged on paranoia.

Two mutually suspicious and fearful religious groups had been thrown into open discord in the 1890s by the folly of the controversial Catholic cardinal of Sydney and a too willing Protestant backlash, all set against a background of economic difficulty and growing class alignments. This Protestant militancy which surged until after the 1904 state elections, was led by the Australian Protestant Defence Association (A.P.D.A.) which was formed in June 1901 by none other than Rev Dill Macky. This body was created to protect the common interests of Protestants and ensure they had equal opportunity in social, economic and political life.(99) Dill Macky believed that Catholicism was conspiring to usurp Protestantism's rightful place in society. He was duly elected president of this association, which took as its motto, "For Christ, Crown and Covenant". All Protestants over eighteen of either sex were eligible to join. By encouraging women and a moderate image, the new president was attempting to attract the many Protestants who thought that all the male Orange lodges were too closed and too fanatical. Dill Macky was hoping for a huge membership.

The A.P.D.A. got off to a reasonable start. It launched a journal early in 1902, called the *Watchman*, which described itself as a "weekly journal of social, political and religious progress".(1) However, this initial claim soon proved false, as the articles became narrowly anti-Catholic and slanderous. Still, it fulfilled a need, because the first issue of 5,000 increased to 20,000 within two years.(2) The A.P.D.A. itself grew more slowly, because within its first year of existence only twenty-two branches were formed, numbering about 1,000 members in all. Most of these branches were in the Sydney area, with one in both Newcastle and Picton. The first and strongest branches were formed in the lower middle class suburbs on the edge of the inner city, namely Newtown, Chippendale, Leichhardt, Annandale, Botany and Balmain. Sectarianism was most virile here, where the lower middle class and upper working class either clung to respectability, or aspired to it. Either way, they were susceptible to believing in plots and conspiracies. However, some branches were being formed in the more salubrious and less socially tense outer suburbs.

Dill Macky was not satisfied with the progress being made, since he had predicted at the outset that one branch a week would be formed. Therefore, in September 1902, the A.P.D.A. launched a new offensive, to establish a branch in every suburb and town in the state and build up strength before the next state election. Branch number one, known to those on the outside as Scot's Church, gave Dill Macky six months leave of absence to stump the country in the cause of the A.P.D.A. The campaign was opened at a packed Town Hall meeting complete with the usual parliamentarians looking for votes, and indignant clergy. A Protestant manifesto was presented and approved with great enthusiasm. It alluded to "the secret tactics and open aggressiveness of Roman Catholicism as an element of danger to the civil and religious liberties of the people of this State", and proceeded to list twelve areas of Catholic "espionage" which were by now very predictable.(3) The daily press reported it all in full, and although the editorial comment advised tolerance of Catholics, it suggested that the Protestant backlash was understandable and perhaps reasonable in the face of the recent and persistent Catholic demands for state aid to Catholic education. Moreover, the *Sydney Morning Herald* did not reject the conspiracy theory outright, preferring to say that only future events would confirm or disprove it.(4) Of course, the Protestant journals were firmly convinced that the conspiracies were true, and many moderate Protestants were beginning to give them some credence. After all, they had always had their suspicions about Catholics.

In November 1902, Dill Macky began a vigorous five months tour of rural areas. Upon arrival in a town, he would hold a church service and attempt to get the local clergy and Protestants on his side. Then the following day, supported by the clergy and the local civil and business leaders who were game enough to attend, he addressed a Protestant meeting on some aspect of Protestant folklore. "The Seige of Derry" was one of his favourite and best topics. After his fiery bursts which would often last more than an hour, Dill Macky would ask all those in sympathy with the A.P.D.A. to rise, and invariably the great bulk of the now indignant audience would jump to their feet. It was a little like the revivalism of the tent mission which was also touring the country areas at this time, and similarly owed some of its successes to the rural recession and drought which currently gripped the state. An A.P.D.A. branch would be formed and members enrolled. Three hundred did so at Newcastle, 283 at Goulburn and 93 at Wagga, 60 of these alone being secured by one zealous Protestant. Dill Macky alleged that more would have attended the meetings, but Catholics threatened Protestant businessmen with a boycott if they dared go.(5)

Meanwhile, back in Sydney, the Congregationalist, Rev H. Gainford, and W. M. Madgwick, an evangelical Anglican layman, and owner of a printing business, formed many new branches and enrolled hundreds of members. The Burwood branch enrolled 90 members at its first meeting, while at Paddington there were 100, Manly 102, Gladesville 180 and Glebe 240 inaugural members.(6) By the end of 1903, there were 135 A.P.D.A. branches throughout the state, with over 22,000 members.(7) Thus the aim of a branch for every significant centre in the state was almost achieved, while the membership itself approximated four per cent of all Protestants over the age of eighteen.

Catholic indignation mounted in the face of such Protestant activity, and there were rumours of trouble brewing. Interjectors disrupted the meetings at Mullumbimby and Casino, and Dill Macky was escorted into Coraki by a mounted detachment of Orangemen because a skirmish was expected.(8) At Murrurundi he was refused the use of the Oddfellows Hall, allegedly because of Catholic influence. He was pelted with rotten eggs four times, but boasted: "not once have I received a smutch".(9) However, more than hisses and eggs awaited him at the mining and pastoral towns of Wyalong and Temora. Barely had Dill Macky begun his address to 600 people at the Excelsior Hall in Wyalong on 27 March 1903, when there was a rush at the side door and an attempt to capture the platform by the hostile crowd outside. When the attack was repulsed, the hall was subjected to a fusillade of sticks, stones and bottles, slingshots were freely used and several shots were fired. The pandemonium among the audience inside was only quelled by the singing of "Rule Britannia", which provoked a fresh barrage of missiles from outside. Order was only restored after the police magistrate took the extraordinary step of reading the Riot Act.(10) Two nights later, a similar disturbance occurred at nearby Temora and crowds roamed the streets after the meeting seeking Dill Macky.(11) The magistrate fined twenty-five people at Wyalong for the disturbance. Throughout each barrage, Dill Macky upheld the "no surrender" motto of his own town Derry, by continuing his speech and forming an A.P.D.A. branch. The *Watchman* cried that this attack was premeditated "Papal hoodlumism", while Dill Macky claimed that respectable Catholic shopkeepers were involved, and that the whole thing had been engineered by the Jesuits.(12) He made great capital out of the incident, producing some Wyalong stones at Protestant rallies, and likening his adventures to the stoning of the martyr, St Stephen. The Catholics of Temora in turn named a local renegade dingo, "Dill Macky".

Despite all the years of sectarian controversy, physical violence was rare. However, the state was at this time still in the grip of its worst drought, which had cut production and jobs by over a third in many places, so it was not surprising that the gradual build-up of tension during Dill Macky's successful tour had exploded in violence at Wyalong and again at Temora. The Catholic communities in both these towns were very strong, because they formed two-fifths of the population, fully fifty per cent above the Catholic state average.(13) Not only were Catholics numerous, but many of them were miners and railway navvies who were not adverse to a little show of strength to put Dill Macky in his place. The miners were singled out in descriptions of the riot,(14) and it is significant that the 700 strong protest meeting, held after the disturbance to complain about Dill Macky's activities, took place at the pit-head of the Golden Fleece mine.(15) Within three months of the affair, the Wyalong A.P.D.A. was 132 strong, almost a third of the adult Protestants in the town. Dill Macky's tour had enflamed parts of an already tense rural community, and if the word "defence" in the association's name had ever had any justification, it was now nothing but a farce. Dill Macky had become much more irresponsible than Moran had ever been; but that is how sectarianism feeds and grows. Undaunted, Dill Macky promoted his anti-Catholic campaign in Melbourne and Adelaide in late 1903, but was disappointed at the poor Protestant response.(16) It seems that the harsh economic conditions and greater gulf between Labour and anti-Labour, which was peculiar to New South Wales at this time, contributed greatly to the more intense sectarianism in this state.

Though the A.P.D.A. was largely a layman's response to the alleged Catholic menace, the clergy did play a considerable part in the association. The founder and life president was a clergyman, and most of the association's leading publicists were clerics. The great bulk of the clergy initially sympathized with the aims of the movement, out of indignation at Cardinal Moran's slanders, and the pretensions of Catholicism when it called itself the "one true church". Even clergy who were generally moderate or liberal, initially supported the A.P.D.A.'s stand. Rev J. Cosh, for one, admitted that he rolled up to the Drummoyne A.P.D.A. meeting somewhat dubious about the association's merits, but was soon convinced by the various speakers that the A.P.D.A. was necessary for the defence of Protestantism.(17) It seems that the clergy were often among the first to believe the conspiracy theory. Liberal churchman, Dr Roseby, remarked with indignation regarding the speeches of Moran and Archbishop

Redwood: "Who can listen to such slanders without anger?"(18) Their love of Protestant truth, and the belief that they were protecting civil and British liberties, made many of them active sectarians. There is clear evidence that at least one third of the 800 clergy in the state actively supported the A.P.D.A. around 1903. Over 40 clerics were presidents of their local branches, 64 were committee members and at least 150 chaired, addressed or attended A.P.D.A. rallies.(19) The number of active supporters among the clergy must have been many more, with the majority at least sympathetic to the cause. While on tour, Dill Macky wrote this of his support among the clergy: "Presbyterian ministers generally with me; Congregational ministers generally with me; Baptist ministers generally with me; Methodist ministers always with me; Anglican ministers seldom with me — with rare exceptions this body is opposed to the movement; Salvation Army always with me".(20) The Anglican reticence was a handicap, but some of the most prominent clergy of the day were among his active supporters. However, as the association became more fanatical and as violence broke out, clerical support dwindled. The St Andrew's Theology faculty disapproved of Dill Macky's presidency of the A.P.D.A. while still a member of the lecturing staff, and the Methodist church publicly expressed anxiety at the involvement of clergy in politics through the A.P.D.A.(21)

In the years 1902 to 1904, Protestantism was truly aroused, and this was not confined to the A.P.D.A., because the Orange lodges experienced a new period of growth. New branches of Orangemen were formed and membership began to climb back to the 20,000 peak in the sectarian interlude of the 1880s.(22) Once again large crowds attended the 12 July Orange Day demonstrations in both city and suburbs. The number of Protestants who processed in the regalia of sashes and aprons through the streets of Sydney and later lunched at the Clontarf picnic grounds doubled in these years. In 1903, a special train brought south-coast Protestants to Sydney to swell the marchers to 4,000 that year and the picnickers at Clontarf to 15,000 people.

However, by early 1904, some of the Protestant fervour was beginning to wane. Militants wondered how the enthusiasm could be maintained. On the local A.P.D.A. branch level, this often devolved to the attempt to entertain by parlour games, pound nights and musical entertainments. There were also debates, discussions and mock elections to hold the troops in readiness. A handful of clergy and laymen gave regular lectures to the branches on Protestantism and the errors of Catholicism. Yet still the future gave cause for concern. Membership was in decline and fifteen branches had become defunct, thirteen of them in the country, where the stimulation of lectures and the press rarely reached. An essay competition was initiated on the subject of how to renew interest. The winner, Mr P. D. McCormick, known more widely for penning "Advance Australia Fair", suggested more lectures, regular readings of Protestant history, and the establishment of an A.P.D.A. benefits fund and a youth group.(23) McCormick obviously believed that Catholicism must be beaten if Australia was to remain "young and free". The runner up, who by the sound of it was unlucky not to win, argued that "we must always be ready to present a united and bold front both to the insidious and open attempts of the R.C. hierarchy to bring a free people into the thraldom of Popery".(24)

The needed revival came from the imminent 1904 state elections which promised to be a tight struggle. In 1903, J. H. Carruthers captured the leadership of the Liberal and Reform Association (L.R.A.) Party, which was a creation of both a grass roots movement and the *Sydney Morning Herald*'s posturing, to oppose parliamentary mismanagement and the rise of the Labour Party. Those on the Right not only believed the See ministry was mismanaging the economy, but that its alliance with the Labour Party was "a subversion of the principles of free government".(25) Labour was at this time a political ogre to the conservatives, who were attempting to form an anti-Labour coalition. However, because this anti-Labour alliance was in danger of fragmenting on the eve of the election, Carruthers and the Liberals accepted the support of militant Protestants and also the temperance movement, to make every vote count in what promised to be a close election. Not that Carruthers had to woo the Protestants very much at all, because they were already solidly anti-Labour. The Liberals in the 1901 parliament had been Protestant to a man, and the continual Protestant claim by 1904 was that the See ministry and the Labour Party were dominated by the Catholic church. Thus it all added up, and it was little wonder that Dill Macky could declare at this time to an Orange gathering: "In politics, Orangemen as we are, or A.P.D.A. men as we are, we know no fiscal party. But the providence of things compels us at the present time to choose one party, because Protection at the present time, and Labour as it is manipulated at the present time spells one word, and that in big letters, R-O-M-E."(26) The party militant Protestants opted for was Carruthers's Liberal and Reform Party.

A great deal of subsequent Protestant influence made itself felt in the L.R.A.'s preselection battles to ensure the choice of reliable Protestants or block the unlikely chance of a Catholic candidate. In several ballots, namely those in the Balmain, Leichhardt and Phillip electorates, the local A.P.D.A. branch members reversed the previous L.R.A. committee choice of a candidate simply by flooding the subsequent meeting. Madgwick, the state secretary of the A.P.D.A., declared at the Phillip preselection ballot that the electorate had returned too many Catholics and it was time they had a Protestant member.(27) The Parramatta L.R.A. preselection was deadlocked for two months, due to the influence of the local A.P.D.A. branch. Even Carruthers was unable to settle the dispute, and finally the

A.P.D.A. candidate, T. R. Moxham, a teetotaller, Mason and Orangeman, gained the preselection. In a number of other electorates the Protestants caused disruption. The A.P.D.A.–L.O.L. (Loyal Orange Lodge) political committee selected R. Booth, an A.P.D.A. and Orange lodge member, and it was reported "that practically the same body a few nights later, with a few additions formed itself into a local branch of the Liberal and Reform Association".(28) On the whole, these struggles were atypical. The anti-Labour-Protestant alignment was so complete and now so solid, that there was little chance of Catholic preselections and thus little need for fights. Of the seventy-eight candidates selected by the A.P.D.A.-L.O.L. central political committee, all but five were also L.R.A. candidates.(29) The temperance-L.R.A. alliance was almost as solid, because of the eighty-four candidates chosen by the Temperance Alliance, sixty were also L.R.A. candidates.(30)

The election was closely fought as expected. The Catholic press supported Labour, while the Protestant press solidly supported the anti-Labour, L.R.A. Party. A few clergy on both sides openly entered the fray, but usually support was given in an oblique manner. Cardinal Moran allegedly said at a Catholic function that "they had a friendly Government which he felt sure would be returned again, particularly his friend, Mr O'Sullivan".(31) Sectarian friction was overt in some electorates where belligerent Orangemen and A.P.D.A. men stood, notably the marginal inner city candidatures of T. Jessep, S. Law and R. Booth. William Affleck M.L.A., who gained a handsome Protestant victory in 1901 as a spin-off from the Coningham affair, claimed his defeat in 1904 was due to the three priests and two nuns who canvassed the electorate to "down Affleck".(32) In most electorates, sectarianism was not overt, but simply very pervasive beneath the surface, helping to influence crucial votes. It is not unreasonable to say that militant Protestants and the Protestant temperance vote won the narrow two seat victory for Carruthers. Certainly, the nine L.R.A. parliamentarians who appeared on the platform of the post-election A.P.D.A. victory rally believed in showing their gratitude to Protestantism.(33) The Protestant-anti-Labour alliance was perpetuated, because only one of the Carruthers men in the House was a Catholic. The much talked about Catholic-Labour alliance was feeble compared to this.

The 1904 election only momentarily arrested the decline of sectarianism, and with it the A.P.D.A. Perhaps the actual election result accelerated this decline, because the Protestant victory made many Protestants feel safe and complacent about Catholic threats. The A.P.D.A. membership shrank and only the strongest branches, usually those on the edge of the inner city, remained active. One of these, the Alexandria branch, whose minute book has survived, revealed that even the stronger branches soon became the social clubs of a small hard core of Protestants.(34) The great

Protestant demonstrations were now few and far between, and the attendance was usually small. The *Watchman* continued to be published, but it was taken over by the Orange lodge, because the A.P.D.A. had all but ceased to exist by 1910. Just as active sectarianism had arisen from a Protestant over-reaction to some unwise statements by Cardinal Moran within the rather tense atmosphere of an economic downturn and Labour and socialist scares, it melted away with the return of economic prosperity by 1907, the growing acceptance of Labour, and the ageing and weariness of the main protagonists.

In his final years, Dill Macky moved across the harbour to Manly in the hope of improving his health. At times he and Cardinal Moran caught the same ferry to Sydney, but they would never speak to, or acknowledge one another. This religious division, which they claimed at times was only over principles, certainly came to divide men and a whole society. These old warriors passed away within two years of each other, Dill Macky surviving the longer till 1913. Thousands of Protestants lined the streets of Sydney to pay their last respects to Dill Macky, who was escorted by several hundred Orangemen in regalia. Over 2,000 people continued on to the graveside at Rookwood cemetery. Rev Morgan in his funeral oration said of Dill Macky: "He believed with all his might the religion of his fore-fathers, of his youth and early manhood, and that religion ever became dearer and dearer to his heart. In my opinion, the intense love of our brother made him a son of thunder, and yet with all his contention for the faith there was no hatred, no malice, no bitterness in his soul."(35) Morgan recognized that Dill Macky never escaped the anti-Catholic passion of his boyhood, when he would sit astride "Roaring Meg" and re-enact the battles between the Orangemen and Catholics of 1688. Dill Macky was enmeshed in a web of Irish suspicion and intrigue, and so too was Cardinal Moran and many other sectarians.

In these years of political and economic flux, the actions of the militants on both sides activated the latent suspicions that Protestants and Catholics had always held about each other. Thus this social gulf was perpetuated, as Catholic and Protestant kept to their own. Even when this gulf was bridged by a mixed marriage which most thought unwise, often the only religious dialogue it produced was the agreement that the boys would be Protestant and the girls would be Catholic. Most of society, even most of the sectarian extremists, claimed to decry sectarian animosity, as people who fight decry war. Archbishop Kelly once stated that "religion as a virtue is based on reason and faith conjointly. Its essence consists of faith, hope and charity and the greatest of these is charity. Sectarianism is poison to charity and must needs be fatal to religion."(36) Yet he and others often failed to be good Samaritans, due to the blind rigidness with which they held their principles — principles which after all taught that all men were brothers and children of God.

An outsider landing in the midst of all this religious controversy could have been forgiven if he initially believed that it revealed that New South Wales was a strongly religious society. However, the reality was that much of this sectarian tension was non-religious in inspiration. Yet this was not the first, nor the last time, that the things of God became debased by the pursuits of man. Similarly, the crusade to reform the morals of society, which was the final response of a concerned Protestantism to remedy its supposed decline, became entangled with the hegemonic aspirations of middle class culture.

To some people, the chance to drink, gamble and taste the delights of the flesh are the spice and the diversions that make life tolerable, while to others, these are cancerous forces sapping the very vitals of individual and national life. This eternal debate over how man should conduct himself received new vigour in the wake of the Methodist and evangelical revivals in Victorian England. These moral reform impulses flowed to the colonies in the nineteenth century and came to have special pertinence in a rough and tumble frontier society. The early governors, the clergy, Mrs Caroline Chisholm, the founders of the Mechanics' Institute Movement, and many others, tried to erase barbarism and the convict stain from New South Wales. Generally they fought a losing battle, because this brutalizing penal experience was reinforced by the pastoral and gold eras which bred tough and rowdy men who liked to drink, swear and gamble when they were not working. What else was there to do in a masculine society of little culture and few traditions? However, as women and bourgeois culture slowly made their presence felt, home and family life developed, society became more orderly, the colonies became more urbanized, and respectability gained a foothold. After all, moral and thrifty behaviour was the ethos of a developing, upwardly mobile, self-improving immigrant society. Barbarism was pushed back upon itself and now only thrived in the inner city and the bush areas outside country towns. But it was a slow process, and by the latter years of the nineteenth century, the "respectable" sections of society believed that there were still far too many hotels selling too much liquor; that there was too much vice; and that gambling was unfortunately enshrined as the national pastime, at least among many parts of the community. It was this belief that formed the basis for a moral reform crusade in the early 1900s.

Reformism was the hallmark of politics in the generation after 1890. Overseas influence was important in this, but more crucial was the effect of the great strikes and depression of the 1890s which accelerated long term indigenous reform impulses. However, various sections of the community differed on the shape that reform was to take. The liberals and radicals favoured major social reconstruction in the form of pensions and other social welfare initiatives, while those on the Right professed less radical and less "socialistic" changes.

Where did Protestantism stand on the reform question? From the outset it should be plainly stated that the great force of moral reformism came from Protestantism and the middle class. J. D. Bollen has sought to argue that Protestantism was deeply influenced by the new theology of the social gospel which emphasized social rather than moralist solutions to change, and that the old style evangelical moralism was somewhat on the fringe of Protestantism by 1900. He believes the latter was only dragged to the centre again after 1904 by political entanglements and sectarian tension. However, after a close examination of the early 1900s and the class composition and leanings of Protestantism, the evidence suggests the reverse; that moral reformism was central and the social gospel only a new and moderate influence.(1)

When the Protestant clergy debated the need for reform, they overwhelmingly meant moral reform. Even when they did use the words "social reform", more often than not they spoke of moral issues, not social programmes. It is true that the younger clergy and the more liberal and flexible of the older clergy advocated social reconstruction and welfare which Bollen has admirably shown, but the bulk of the clergy still adhered to moral solutions to social evils. If individuals experienced moral regeneration through a life in Christ, the world would automatically be a reformed place. As Rev H. T. Burgess put it epigrammatically: "the soul of reform is the reform of the soul".(2) A survey of the fifteen years after 1900 reveals the churches' concern for moral reform, but their neglect of wider social reform. They sent literally hundreds of petitions to parliament on moral issues, but only a handful relating to questions of social justice. A few clergy did advocate social welfare reforms, but even some of these were more in the hope of influencing the working class to return to the Christian fold, rather than in support of a principle per se. This is a fact, not an accusation! The clergy were men of their class and of their time, who were too overworked and undertrained to grasp the complexities of social reconstruction and readjust their theology to match.

It is not surprising to note, given the interrelationships between Protestantism and the middle class, that this Protestant view of reformism was also shared by much of the middle class, and those who liked to think of themselves as the " decent people". The bourgeoisie valued individualism and moral rectitude, and believed that the way to reform lay in moral regeneration, perhaps assisted by minor social tinkering, rather than in any major social reconstruction. These two natural allies publicly and politically embraced each other in the 1904 state election campaign (as outlined in the previous chapter and by Bollen).(3) This political alliance, which lasted to 1910, resulted in major moral reforms but only minor social readjustments.

The strength of this Protestant-bourgeois alignment depended on a unique convergence of historical circumstances around 1900. The steady ascendance in the late nineteenth century of the indigenous moral reform impulse, which was really a variant of Victorian respectability, was intersected around the 1890s by the movement for women's suffrage. The suffrage impulse in general, and not simply the Women's Christian Temperance Union arm of it, gave a great fillip to moral reformism, because its claim for the franchise was partly based on the premise that the women's vote would highlight moral issues and thus clean up and civilize society.(4) Certainly it was the women who carried the greatest burden of the moral evils which many complained about. It was only the woman who was battered by a drunken spouse and perhaps then deserted by him; it was the woman who had to make ends meet when drink and gambling ate into the family income; it was the woman who had to sell her body if necessary, or suffer her partner's amorous adventures with others. It was no coincidence that the moral reformers' greatest victories were made possible by their 1904 election win; the first time that women in New South Wales were allowed to vote in a state contest!

The third force which combined with the moral reform impulse and the suffrage movement to create a militant moral reformism was the feeling of insecurity which permeated Protestantism around 1900. This anxiety spurred ministers to constantly pray and beg for a moral resurgence in the hope that this would bring back the lost sheep to the Church. Sermons on wickedness and vice were the hallmark of the period and possibly overshadowed those on the Christian verities of the love and mercy of God — at least in some churches and among some clergy. Civic leaders and politicians, who held the contemporary belief that "the churches are the pillars of Christian States", gave the churches solid support in this quest for a moral revival. The Governor of New South Wales, Sir Harry Rawson, argued that there "was not a case in history where a nation had continued great after its religion had gone down to a low ebb".(5) It was also the common belief that religion and morality were inextricably related — if one was lost, so was the other, and with the loss of both went national greatness. Thus the reformers argued that both the Church and the State would benefit from a moral reformation.

However, of greatest importance to the sudden growth of moral reformism as a social force, were the difficult economic conditions and class tensions that prevailed around the turn of the twentieth century. The long boom that existed with few exceptions from the 1850s was ended abruptly by strikes and economic depression in the early 1890s.(6) Unemployment rose to forty per cent and this position was slow to improve under the influence of an uncertain London money market, and the devastation caused by the record seven year drought from 1895. In the early 1900s, unemployment was still at six per cent of the workforce, and real wages were depressed.(7) Political life was similarly under stress and polarized by the industrial events of the 1890s and the rise of the labour movement, whose policies and whole existence was anathema to those on the Right. "Capital versus Labour" was by 1900 a well established journalistic turn of phrase to describe the confrontation, as politics took on an overt class basis. Unionism had recovered from the debacle of the great strikes by the turn of the century, while employers were similarly strengthening their own associations. In the political arena the alignments were forming into the now familiar labour, non-labour mould, and these were solidified on the state and federal level in the years between 1904 and 1910.

The importance of the economic and political environment to the rise of moral reformism is highlighted by George Bernard Shaw's comment that "the degree of tolerance attainable at any moment depends on the strain under which society is maintaining its cohesion".(8) In the tense social atmosphere of New South Wales around 1900, there was very little tolerance of others' moral habits and social manners. Moral failings were seen by the respectable as cancers on the social fabric. Not only were drinkers and gamblers scapegoated over social ills, but moral reformers saw their proposals as panaceas for poverty and other social difficulties. It was also predictable that moral questions would flow into class questions, because of the political and religious alignments which were solidified by 1904. Since the moral reformers became identified with Carruthers's Liberal Party, the liquor trade and the gambling fraternity gravitated to the Labour Party. Therefore, an attack on vice became a means of attacking Labour, and a moral reform victory gave added social prestige and hegemony to Protestant values and middle class culture.

However, although the moral reform movement was solidly Protestant, Protestants were not unanimous in the view of what should be reformed and to what extent. The split is neatly summarized in two views on the use of leisure found in the *Methodist* in 1907.

One was the view shared by liberal Protestants and reflected in a letter written by W.J. Wiseman who argued that billiards was not a sinful game and should be accepted by Christians, because "if a Christian's love for his Saviour is so weak that any amusement can take it away what use is his faith at all? I am forced to ask what use is a soldier who cannot stand the test of battle, or a Christian who is afraid of every puff of temptation."(9) The liberal Protestant view held that games and pastimes were not inherently evil, and as long as they were kept in perspective, could be instruments of "joy and refreshment" to man. Liberal clergy such as H. Bryant and E. H. Webber of St Paul's Burwood condoned dancing, although not of the modern fast and rowdy sort, yet they declined to dance themselves, for "a 'dancing parson' is scarcely the man to whom souls would naturally turn in their hour of need".(10) A little more adventurous was Rev Cowling who advocated church dances and theatre to keep abreast of "the spirit of the age".(11) Most liberals thought him a little too advanced when he married a couple on the back of Alice the

Elephant at Wonderland City. Still, the liberal Protestant outlook held that given the right environment, mankind would choose the right over the wrong, and could develop to moral and spiritual excellence. The liberals had two great insights that the more zealous conservative Protestants could have benefited from, and which would have saved the people of New South Wales from a lot of needless irritation. Firstly, the liberals saw that it was unwise to call every little thing a vice, because this would depreciate the awfulness of real vices. Secondly, they believed that in the long run it was futile to hope that coercive legislation would produce a morally regenerated people, because a true and lasting reformation could only come from the conscious and free decision of each individual to lead a new life.

The other view expressed in the this issue of the *Methodist* was that of the evangelical Protestant. Exhibiting the tenseness and asceticism which marked the evangelical, a "Methodist" who reported with dismay that his new minister had just joined the church cricket club, wrote: "The word of God is plain enough, that we are to come out from the world. If you love the world you must hate God, and if you love God you must hate the world. What is of the world is of the devil."(12) This was a puritan perception of reality that only encompassed blacks and whites and no greys. All amusements and temporal things were sinful. While the liberals saw mankind in an aura of hopefulness, the evangelical was pessimistic and panicked in the fear that man was eternally falling into temptation. Typically, the Baptist Rev J. A. Soper lamented that "the Church today is largely made up of backsliders. There surely was never a time when prayer was more needed."(13) Similarly, hymn 957 in the *Methodist Hymnal* cried out in anguish:

Far and wide around us,
See on every hand,
Through the mighty city,
Satan's strongholds stand:
Selfish greed and grinding
Lust, and drink and hate —
These his chains which bind men
With their iron weight.

The evangelical mind envisaged two eternally conflicting forces; the heavenly and the temporal. The *Messenger* remarked: "Whatsoever is not of the faith is sin. The doubtful is the dangerous."(14) In any case, as the Baptist Rev C. T. Bryant argued, if Christian men went about their work properly there would be no time for doubtful amusements.(15) Even those who countenanced some recreation saw it in ascetic terms. Rev Allen advised young Christians that "play is intended to fit us for a better discharge of life's work. If any play hinders our work, we have not carried our religion into our play — which must not take up too much time, too much thought, or too much money."(16) Unfortunately for personal freedom this evangelical view of moral questions was the dominant mode of Protestant thought at this time.

Whereas, within reason, the liberal Protestants left morality in the hands of individual conscience, the evangelicals who feared the worst rather than the best, conversely, put what they believed to be social obligation and religious duty above individual freedom and conscience. The evangelicals' view of moral questions was often harsh, because as Rev E. J. Prescott, speaking particularly for Methodists, stated: they "would rather err, if they are to err at all, on the side of over-strictness than of over-laxity".(17) This tendency for "over-kill" was married to a penchant for coercion within the evangelical breast. Mr W. H. Judkins, a celebrated Melbourne Methodist moral crusader, told a Methodist rally in Sydney that:

> Social reform could not be brought about by moral suasion alone. It had been tried for years, and was unavailing without legislative assistance, which would help people to do right and make it hard for them to do wrong. Laws were the expression of the sentiment of the people, and were absolutely necessary if moral suasion were to be made effective.(18)

The willingness of Judkins and the bulk of Protestant moral reformers to use legislation to attain righteousness was, as he plainly stated, due to the failure of "moral suasion", and the feeling among Protestant reformers that perhaps they no longer represented majority social opinion, but only the largest and most important single minority view.(19) Nowhere is this problem so clearly seen as in the fight for Sunday.

Sunday was a symbolic issue because it was the focal point of religious worship, and the deference afforded it by the community signified the respect paid generally to the Christian religion. The Catholic church to the chagrin of the Protestants held a liberal view of Sunday observance, and believed that as long as Catholics went to mass they could spend the rest of the day as they choose. Most Protestants held a more ascetic view. They stated that there should be no work of a Sunday, nor any picnicking and travelling, but rather it should be a day of rest in the home, devoted to religious or refined reading in between the two visits to church. Of course the liberal Protestants were less adamant in their attitude and more closely resembled the Catholic view. Therefore, the activity to keep Sunday quiet and dull was basically an evangelical Protestant battle. Indeed, rabid Protestants who were prone to see conspiracy everywhere, claimed that the Catholic tolerance of Sunday dancing, parties and excursions was "one of the primary methods by which Romanism hopes and attempts to undermine Protestant Christianity"(20) which is based on the quiet observance of Sunday.

Though Sundays around 1900 were deadly quiet in comparison with today, they were changing from what they had been a generation earlier. Since the 1850s the public library, art gallery and parks were open of a Sunday and the government tourist bureau offered such Sunday attractions as harbour and beach excursions, and trips to the Jenolan Caves and the Blue Mountains. The Manly and Coogee piers contained fair grounds that operated on Sundays and at the Clontarf picnic grounds ju-jitsu displays and balloon ascents entertained onlookers. Many people played sport, although as yet most official fixtures were confined to Saturday afternoon. Shops and organized entertainments were generally closed, and trading was carried out illegally only by the adventurous few. However in the country, Sunday shopping was quite a regular feature as distance often meant that many were unable to get to town during the week-days. Sunday sport also flourished in the bush — as Steele Rudd sardonically remarked: "we always looked forward to Sunday. It was our day of sport".(21) Rev Morgan, an outback parson, despaired that in the far west of the state "sticking wild pigs, duck and turkey shooting, hunting and such like are the only Sunday services many know . . . or care for . . . the only difference between Sunday and any other day in the week is that trade is brisker, drunkenness is more general and gambling is crowned king".(22)

Therefore, while Sunday was still relatively sacred, there were deep secular inroads into its observance and the clergy believed the situation was deteriorating. The ministers who assumed that "unbelief, indifference and a lax view of the Sunday generally go together",(23) predicted that unless a stand was made "with the Rest Day will go to a very large extent the Christian Religion".(24) Following their logic further, along with Christianity would go national power and virility. Many clergy seriously alleged that the Christian Sunday was the basis of the British Empire.(25)

In May 1900 the Protestant clergy decided it was time to act against those who would secularize and desecrate the Christian Sunday. They led several deputations to Premier Lyne to point out the illicit Sunday trading carried out by hotels and also the vendors of soft drinks, fruit and tobacco. It appeared that these activities were carried out largely in the inner city and the working class areas. The police superintendent of the inner metropolitan area estimated that eighty per cent of all hotels traded illegally from the side door by the clever use of touts.(26) Refreshment shops near the harbour and park areas also traded illegally and received only token fines when caught. The premier agreed to end the illicit Sunday liquor trading and this was done with the best ability of the force. However, he insisted that shops in the city and harbour areas must be allowed to supply Sunday excursionists with refreshments.(27)

While the clergy fumed over this decision and predicted disaster, the daily press expressing the tide of opinion thought it a wise decision by the premier.(28) However, Lyne and successive premiers for the next fifteen years avoided the sticky question of legislation, which revealed just how delicate the Sunday question was in the minds of the electors. Instead they left it to the police to make the difficult decisions. The police only allowed those on the harbour front and near parks to trade, but many others in the inner city, feeling discriminated against, stayed open by being as cunning as the illicit Sunday traders in grog. The police naturally became impatient with all this. Superintendent Larkin testily complained that the police have "more important matters to attend to in the preservation of good order, the supervision of licensed public houses and the protection of life and property".(29) The public also became irritated by the arbitrary nature of where refreshments were available or not.

It was merely the recognition of a long term secular trend, and not a deference to the anti-Christ as some claimed,(30) which led the first Labour administration of New South Wales in 1910 to recommend that the police should not be too zealous in prosecuting refreshment sellers.(31) By 1915, the Labour Chief Secretary decided by executive action to allow trading everywhere in the state on Sundays between eight and ten in the morning, though doors were only to be ajar during church hours.(32) In the following year an act was passed which allowed trading in refreshments on Sundays except within the morning and evening church hours. The restriction on trading in the evening service hours was subsequently dropped by executive direction and the strict Protestant Sunday dwindled to two hours on Sunday morning.(33) It was this decline in deference to Christian values which prompted Protestant moral reformers to adopt pressure group and coercive tactics in the 1900s, in their bid clean up the state of New South Wales.

Those who attempted to coerce others to abandon alleged immoral ways became known in this period as "wowsers". It was a term whose origin is obscure, but which was elevated in a short time from slang to become acceptable usage for premiers and cardinals alike. Some winced when it was applied to them, while others wore it as a badge of righteousness. John Norton the humble editor of the scandalous Truth, once claimed:

I invented the word myself . . . when I applied it to A . . . house, whom I referred to as the white, woolly, weary, wasting wowser from Waverley. I am proud of my invention . . . stroke of genius . . . To my humble self – to me, . . . belongs the sole undivided glory and renown of . . . single, simple word, that does at once describe, . . . that numerous, noxious, pestilent, puritanical . . . whole blasphemous, wire-whiskered brood.(34)

The Oxford Dictionary preferred to list its origin as unknown. If he was not the inventor of the word, Norton was certainly one of its popularizers. So too was Norman Lindsay who represented them in pen and ink and helped form the popular image of the wowser in the *Bulletin*. He portrayed them as sourfaced, thin, unattractive, black-garbed men and bird-like women, who always carried umbrellas, no doubt with which to lash out and hit innocent citizens. Those who were dubbed wowsers had a highly developed and often warped sense of moral outrage, that could be inflamed by the sight of a bottle, ladies' underwear in shop windows, a pack of cards, a french novel or the half clad figure of a bicycle-rider on Parramatta Road. They forgot the biblical injunction to "judge not, that ye be not judged", and after condemning others, proceeded to try and stop their pleasures and reform them. The hallmark of the wowser was his willingness to coerce others.

Who were the wowsers? One thing was clear, Catholics made poor wowsers because they specialized too much and neglected other evils. As one Catholic doctor reminisced: "Ten Commandments there were, but only one sin really mattered — the sin of the flesh. The priests were always declaiming against it. It was an age when hell-fire still had its uses as a figure of speech. Alcoholic over-indulgence was therefore deplored, more as a minor error of conduct."(35) As every good Protestant was told, priests drank, and gambling was carried out at every Catholic church fete. Thus the wowsers' strength lay amongst the evangelical Protestants and the middle class. It was also stronger among women than men, because women attended church more regularly and were generally more receptive to the moral message of the need to protect home life. The archetypal wowser was the Methodist, whose church laws both written and unwritten forbad the use of alcohol, gambling, dancing and other ungodly pursuits such as cosmetics, flash dressing and racy conversation — all of which some other people called simple pleasures.

Yet not all who acted in the guise of wowsers were sincerely concerned to clean up the moral life of the community. Reform movements always attracted their share of "ratbags" or opportunists. One particular wowser, Mr A. C. O. Lane, wrote such wild letters to the Chief Secretary regarding the government's lax view of Sunday trading and indecent advertising, that he was eventually investigated by the police. It appeared that he was the owner of a small soap manufacturing business and was described by one police officer as a quiet man who received few visitors and appeared to suffer "from religious mania and writes the letters when in that condition".(36) However on closer inspection it can be seen that Lane's letters only briefly stuck to the point of moral evil, for they quickly launched into long and strong tirades against the government's economic policy.(37) Given the fact that the bulk of his letters were written in the difficult economic climate of 1902 and 1903, when the See administration was being accused of economic irresponsibility, and also that his earnings were described as a modest £500 per annum, Lane's wowserism probably expressed economic insecurity as much as moral rectitude.

Lane also denounced Italian shopkeepers (who he pointed out were Roman Catholics) as the worst offenders against the quiet "British Sunday".(38) This racism was a feature of many complaints about Sunday trading. A Mr E. Hawes, who made frequent allegations, admitted that he disliked "dagoes" (as he called Italians), and added: "Why are a few foreigners allowed to rule the roost at the expense of the Britisher".(39) It was no coincidence that Hawes was also a shopkeeper who obviously feared the economic competition of these industrious Italians. While police surveillances clearly showed that two-thirds of the offending shop-keepers were British, more Italians were convicted than Britishers, and the fines imposed on the Italians were much higher.(40) J. Hurley M.L.A. suggested that the Italians were being victimized.(41) He was probably right, because G. S. Golder, the Newcastle Police Inspector, claimed that Italian shopkeepers were the worst offenders, and revealing his narrow ethnocentric bias he added: "By their conduct in broadly and openly selling goods for which there is no need on Sundays, and in brilliantly illuminating their shops on Sunday nights, [they] appeared to think they had greater privileges than our own countrymen, and [were] entitled to conduct their business on lines repugnant to British ideas on the subject."(42) Even some of the clergy indulged in such cultural chauvinism. They grouped the Italians with socialists, brewers, publicans, Roman Catholics and other "persons whose opinions are of no value to the community" as the enemies of the British Protestant Sunday.(43) Therefore, moral reformism was not only the sincere expression of a concern for moral values but also, for some, the means by which they could legitimize otherwise irrational attacks on those they wished to scapegoat for their own or society's ills. Unfortunately, we may never find the means to discover precisely how many used wowserism as a vehicle for other prejudices.

The whole crux of the moral reform movement to discourage vice, drunkenness and gambling was the protection of family life. One of the popular images of the day was that the Christian home was the Christian state in microcosm, and it was claimed that it "is the nation that is a nation of homes that is a great nation. The nation that is a nation of families, that is a strong nation."(44) It is the conception of the home which revealed most clearly the relationship between class, religion and moral values. The home and family symbolized the middle class emphasis on the ownership of private property, and the bourgeois division of sex roles with the man as provider and the woman as housewife and mother. It was also the vehicle of moral and spiritual nurturing of the young so far as the churches and the state were both concerned. The future fathers and mothers of the Empire were formed in the home. The churches stressed that Christianity must form the basis of every home. The 1906 Methodist Church Pastoral appealed to its flock: "Let religion in all its cheerfulness, considerateness, prayerfulness and purity, be the atmosphere of the home, an atmosphere on which evil cannot live, but in which good can find its greatest encouragement."(45) Rev J. G. Greenhough, delivering an address on "The Making of a Home" identified the bourgeois nature of Protestantism by remarking that the ideal home was one of unassuming affluence and respectability, "a modest dwelling, sufficiently furnished, not too large, but large enough for a variety of interests and occupations, and lifted above the perpetual grinding anxiety about ways and means".(46) This was certainly not a description of a rented worker's cottage in an inner city suburb! Respectability, security and Christianity were the hallmarks of the Protestant conception of the home.

At the focal point of the home was Christian marriage and motherhood, which was epitomized by that virtuous mother of the Empire, Queen Victoria. Marriage was not to be taken lightly or selfishly, as it had religious and patriotic implications. A female journalist in the *Australian Christian World* epitomized the view of a class and a generation, which placed social duty and moral obligation above individual aspirations, when she wrote: "The great end of marriage is the preparation and development of the spiritual life of the race. The good of society demands that we consider marriage a permanent bond. The individual's happiness is not of as much concern as the welfare of the race . . . It must not be said the individual is sacrificed to a social end. The individual achieves his own highest good here as elsewhere in serving the social good."(47) It is interesting that the doctrine was put forward somewhat self-consciously, but it remained sound for years to come, certainly long enough to cause the nourishing of Flanders fields with a flow of Australian blood.

However, around the turn of the century, the clergy became concerned about the stability of home life. The warnings were endless and this one by the *Australian Churchman* was merely one of the more colourful.

Scores of our children are roving and roaming the streets, lanes, dark alleys, dark parks, dark places with many a conversation, many a thought, many an action leading on to many a fall and many a sad and early death because the home has lost its good influence, its homely ties, its spiritual aspirations and its future hopes . . . Parents beware! The devil still goes about seeking whom he may devour and his agents are legion. Children beware! Swerve not away from home, leave not the right path, stick to the teachings of your teachers in holy and scriptural lessons.(48)

One new development which sparked off this concern was the liberalization of the New South Wales Divorce Act in 1892 to include divorce on the grounds of desertion, habitual drunkenness, assault, imprisonment for more than three years and judicial separation over two years. Previously the grounds had only covered adultery and cruelty. The new provisions markedly increased the divorce rate. In the period from 1873 (when the New South Wales Supreme Court first handled divorces) to 1900, there had been 3,529 petitions for divorce, 2,871 of these since the 1892 amendments.(49) This gave New South Wales the third highest divorce rate in the world, behind the United States and Sweden, in an era when the "decent people" believed divorce was socially scandalous. The *Australian Christian World* in typical clerical fashion remarked that "among ourselves divorces are becoming more and more frequent and so the degradation of women, of the home, and of children goes on apace . . . terrible retribution is sure to come on nations that are lax in morals and that think lightly of marriage".(50) The clergy saw a relationship between divorce and civil marriage. The statistics certainly appeared to support this interpretation because, although civil marriages formed less than three per cent of all marriages, such unions formed ten per cent of divorce cases. Special criticism was levelled against "marriage shops" which arranged quick, cheap and unchristian unions. Even some clergy performed quick marriages, often at the rate of one a day. The Congregational Union had to warn several of its clergy against solemnizing such hasty unions, and was forced to advise the Registrar-General to revoke matrimonial powers from several clergy.(51) However, these were rare instances and one of the ministers in question, who ran a renegade Congregational group, probably performed these marriages due to financial necessity as much as liberal thinking.

The clergy and reformers believed that Christian marriage was endangered not only by divorce reform, but by modern attitudes and contraceptive methods which were undermining the great unstated sexual assumptions they held about Christian marriage, namely, a virgin beginning and a chaste, restrained practice. It is unclear how far the clergy and others were aware of the extent of these trends, but the figures were available from the government statistician for whoever wished to read them. It must have been disturbing knowledge to the more informed to learn that in New South Wales in the years around 1900, seven per cent of all births were illegitimate, and at least 27 marriages in every 100 *followed* the conception of a child.(52) Therefore, the rate of premarital coition in this supposed age of Victorian respectability was well over thirty per cent of newly married couples — how much higher no-one can know.

The problem for the churches was that the sex question was the great social unmentionable of this period. However, enough innuendo and euphemism can be gleaned to reveal their thoughts on "social impurity" as they called the unsanctioned expression of sexuality. Despite the handicap of their having to use subtle and indirect approaches due to the delicacy of the matter, the churches won some small but notable victories in the area of sexual morality.

In the 1900s the reformers lobbied through press and parliament on a number of open or more veiled sexual matters, in an endeavour to expunge sexuality from the public life of the state. These efforts were moderately successful. In 1901 the government passed the Obscene and Indecent Publications Act which strengthened earlier legislation, and also prevented contraceptives from being furtively advertised as cures for nervous debility and female irregularities. The judiciary also helped. Justice Walker in 1905 ordered that the lurid details of adultery in divorce proceedings should be withheld from press reports. Protestant, temperance and women's groups lobbied vigorously for the protection of the young. One fruit of this concern was the Neglected Children's and Juvenile Offenders' Act of 1905. These groups were also appalled that a girl of fourteen "cannot dispose of her property, cannot marry, but can consent to the loss of her virtue while yet a mere child, and thus become a social outcast".(53) Their activity meant that after 1910 the honour of girls under seventeen was protected. The reformers also urged clamp downs on brothels and opium dens which were begun under the amended Police Offences Act of 1908.(54)

However, on a more harmless and indirect sexual level, Protestants lobbied less successfully. The evangelically minded believed that modern dances such as the tango and the bunny-hug were fast and, by implication, sexually dangerous. Indeed, Methodists were forbidden to dance at all. It was alleged that dancing broke down the physical barrier between the sexes, and scanty evening wear, stuffy rooms and late nights, not only endangered health and industrial efficiency, but also chastity.(55) Alderman T. Jessep M.L.A., a strong Methodist, in 1899 persuaded the Sydney City Council to regulate dancing and music halls, and similar action followed in other councils.(56) The Evangelical Council and the Public Morals Association lobbied for legislation in 1906 and 1907 to regulate these "dancing hells", which Rev E. Price maintained started young people on a life of degradation.(57) The Theatres and Public Halls Act (1908) passed by the Liberal Ministry, provided for the Sunday closure and general regulation of these previously unlicensed entertainments. However they were never closed, only supervised, and the young continued to be lured by the fascination of the dance.

Yet even if legislation existed there were problems. First, could it be policed? Despite the passing of the Juvenile Smoking Suppression Act in 1903, which made it an offence for those under sixteen years of age to smoke, little boys in a timeless fashion still lurked in laneways or behind the back shed trying their first or one hundred and forty-first smoke. Second, legislation could easily be revoked if public opinion swayed in the other direction. Many respectable people were alarmed when the prohibition on public sea-bathing after 8.00 am was revoked at Coogee in 1902, and elsewhere from 1905, provided that swimmers were clad in "neck to knees". This meant that young men and women could frolic in the surf together and one religious columnist was so alarmed by this prospect that he warned that the swimmers would be exposed to "a moral undertow which may prove more dangerous than that met with in the breakers".(58) However, the wowsers' attempts to prevent this mixed baring of bodies was unable to overcome the public joy for the new surfing craze. Indeed, Victorian morality may well have been ultimately dumped by the Sydney surf as much as by any other force! Similarly, the wowsers were unable to ban "Deadwood Dick" comics, racy French novels, cards, billiards and countless other "sins" they saw around them, although they doubtlessly banned these from their own households.

Although indecent literature was kept from young eyes, the wowsers believed that there were always evil thoughts and voices ready to corrupt the young. One school of moralist thought believed that to be forewarned was to be forearmed, and so they argued that basic sexual information should be imparted in a Christian context. The White Cross League which had been formed in the 1880s by Bishop Barry of Sydney, after 1901 became an interdenominational Christian sex education group which had the support of most of the churches. It gave addresses to youth groups and private schools. In 1906 the Governor, Sir Harry Rawson, unsuccessfully pressed Premier Carruthers to allow the league access to state schools.(59) It is perhaps surprising that few opposed its activities on the ground of placing indelicate topics before the minds of innocent children. Yet it was a Christian organization with church support. Besides, the league's approach was so delicate that the facts of life were taught through the analogy of the pollination of flowers, which no doubt left many young listeners none the wiser about sexuality.(60) Again, the league probably ruffled few churchgoers and clergy because its message, though seemingly enlightened, still basically relied on fear to prevent premarital sexual activity. It claimed that unchaste actions and even thoughts caused heart and brain disease, consumption, epilepsy and insanity, while self-abuse (masturbation) caused insanity, stunted growth and general lassitude. Young girls were warned that premarital intercourse induced the red plague (venereal disease) and pregnancy resulted in social ostracization and thus loneliness.(61) So much did they fear their own impulses that most evangelicals preached that sexuality was purely for procreation, and that the precious life fluid must not be wasted on lust and enjoyment. Mrs V. Cooper Mathison, speaking for the league from her soap box in the Sydney Domain, declared that sex — "this cancerous sore, spreading like a filthy leprosy" — was not for pleasure but procreation, and she demanded of her male audience that they curb their "wilfil, ungovernable passions;

keep them in leash as you would a vicious and ravenous dog".(62) Freud would have had a field day with such a personality! The advice the league gave to young people who were confused and tempted by their sexuality was contained in a pamphlet entitled, *Helps to Purity of Life*. It suggested that unchaste desires could be warded off by avoiding an idle mind, lounging in bed, rich food, alcohol, bad company, and instead by using hard beds and plenty of cold water. It sounded like a joke, but it was far from it for those whose lives became dogged by sexual guilt and frustration.

In 1903 Sir Timothy Coghlan, the Government Statistician, emerged from his mountain of figures to proclaim that the New South Wales birth rate was in decline.(63) Immediately the conservative press and business circles showed great alarm, since this news could endanger national productivity and strength. A royal commission was established in August 1903, headed by Dr C. Mackellar M.L.C., Anglican, company director, and head of the State Children's Relief Board. It was filled out from among his confreres in the medical and business fields. It appears that the commissioners were intent on "proving" that the decline was due to community selfishness and moral laxity.(64) Their questions often tried to lead witnesses and they blatantly ignored evidence which revealed that the 1890s depression, declining real wages, unemployment, and modern social trends also deterred people from early marriage and large families. The royal commission "found" that the decline was due to the use of contraceptives by couples who selfishly wished to avoid the strain and economic responsibility of raising children, while still enjoying their lust and pleasure. Fortunately the report acknowledged the need for child health facilities, but one of the main proposals was that the churches should lead a crusade against contraception.(65)

The churches responded to the best of their ability within the limits of propriety. They were shocked by the alleged prevalence of contraceptives, which the commissioners had probably exaggerated. However, one was still too many, because these devices catered to lustful desires and obstructed God's design for creation. Indeed, the clergy were distressed that so many people did not see that this practice was blasphemous. They were also dismayed that some of the large correspondence in the press on this matter overlooked the all important moral aspect, and centred on the question of wages and family finances. Yet the clergy themselves argued in non-religious terms, by appealing for a higher morality to ensure national greatness. One fifth of the Anglican Encyclical of 1905 was devoted to the question of contraception, and it warned that this practice, and the consequent declining birth rate, endangered the Anglo-Saxon race and the social fabric.(66) Other clergy called for a revived "racial pride" to end this "racial suicide", otherwise the Anglo-Saxon race would be "swamped by the feeble, but more fecund races of central and eastern Europe".(67)

The *Australian Christian World* by giving health and fitness advice to promote the birth rate seemed to be treating young Australians like stud animals.(68)

The issue seethed for some years. The campaign against contraception revealed Protestantism's commitment to two things besides personal purity — Australia's imperialistic future and middle class hegemony. Regarding the first, here as elsewhere the clergy threatened to outpace others with their patriotic appeals over the birth rate. Unless this "rottenness" was stopped, declared Bishop Anderson of the Riverina in 1909, there would be no men to use the artillery, the airships and the dreadnoughts which Australia needed.(69) Concerning the second, Protestant clergy revealed an uneasiness about the growing size and power of the working class. As the Presbyterian Pastoral stated in its case against contraception and in support of an increased birth rate: "If the frugal, and thrifty, and educated among our population allow the fear of poverty to pervert their lives in this fashion, then the continuance of our race must depend on the thrift-less, the reckless and the uneducated."(70) In similar but plainer terms the City Coroner, Mr S. Murphy, concurred: "It would seem that the humbler the walk of life the more prolific are the parents. If the present practices continue the whole political control of the State must eventually fall into the hands of the working class."(71) To put it bluntly, many conservatives saw that national greatness and the middle class (which in their minds were interrelated) might be defeated by the condom and the prophylactic sponge. The wowsers also saw decency and greatness threatened by the bottle — and because unlike sex it could be openly discussed, temperance became *the* moral reform issue of this period.

The late nineteenth century saw the increasing dominance of the bourgeois notion of respectability over barbarism, and with this came a decline in the use and availability of alcohol. The 1882 Liquor Act was one phase in this middle class ascendance. This Act cleaned up some of the worst abuses of the trade, made Sunday trading illegal, and introduced the concept of local option by which electors in local municipal elections could vote on whether they wanted to reduce or maintain hotel licences in their local municipality. In 1890, temperance became part of civics lessons in the primary schools. Thus, most children at some stage were confronted with the wisdom of Dr Richardson's *Temperance Lesson Book*. By the 1900s, the liquor statistics should have been a great satisfaction to the temperance movement. In 1882 there was one hotel to every 225 persons in the metropolitan area and one to every 271 in country areas, whereas in 1905 there was only one hotel to every 663 persons in the metropolitan area and one to every 408 persons in the country.(72) The slower improvement in the country ratio from the temperance point of view, was due to the special need for the existence of hotels in the bush to provide accommodation. This overall improvement was due not so much to local option, which only prevented the introduction of more licences, but to the strict licensing provisions which culled out dilapidated and disreputable hotels. In 1882 there had been thirty-nine arrests per thousand population for drunkenness, while in 1900 it had dropped to twenty-three per thousand.(73) The great bulk of these were men. Finally, while five guineas per head was spent on liquor in 1882, this had dropped to three guineas by 1899.(74)

Given these advances, why should temperance become such an issue in the 1900s? Of utmost importance was the conjunction of economic recession, middle class insecurity and Protestant anxiety outlined earlier. Yet the ardour of the ever vigilant temperance movement should not be underestimated as a cause of this temperance revival. The wowsers saw that there were still battles to be fought. Sunday trading was still carried out almost at will, and the several hundred convictions each year for this offence gave no indication of the incidence. The metropolitan police superintendent in 1900 estimated that eighty per cent of hotels traded illegally on Sundays, while the police report of 1904 stated that under the "present state of the law the police are in a great measure powerless".(75) Also, although the number of hotel licences had slightly decreased since 1882, the number of wine shop licences had increased from 490 in 1891 to 675 in 1900, and this probably applied to spirit merchants as well.(76) Further, although the ratio of people to hotels was declining, certain working class areas had too many hotels, while there were few in many middle class areas. In 1900 in the city of Sydney area itself, there were 112,000 people and 424 hotels or one to every 264 persons, whereas in the suburbs there were 376,000 people and 423 hotels, or one to every 888 persons.(77) While there needed to be more hotels in the city to service the daily requirements of the city workers who were attracted by free counter lunches with their liquor, there were clearly a great number of hotels to tempt the inner city working class.

The temperance forces believed that there were too many hotels. Licencees backed by the breweries could afford to run attractive, brightly lit hotels on the best sites in town or suburb. One Christian journal remarked:

No trade is carried on under more extravagant conditions . . . Palatial structures are erected, and fitted both without and within with all the latest scientific improvements to ensure the comfort, and almost the luxury of the guest. Gorgeous draperies and magnificent pictures, frequently bordering upon the indecent, are to be seen under the most favourable circumstances, while all that can minister to the appetites of men is freely supplied with no unsparing hand.(78)

In a sense the hotel was a secular version of the church, because in its own way it offered spiritual refreshment from the real world. Some clergy obviously saw it in this manner and thus as competition. Rev Campbell sarcastically remarked that while there was only one clergyman to every 1,149 persons in the state, and that churches were always in debt, "the brewer and the distiller can easily supply a temple for every 336 of the people: salary priests and hire vestal virgins to minister at the alter – the Bar!"(79) His view mirrored the image of Satan's "churches" in the Methodist hymn number 958:

> Hell builds her palaces of state,
> Makes bright her walls and wide her gate,
> And thousands press within to share
> The cup of madness and despair.

The clergy and other temperance reformers abhorred "strong drink" for many reasons. The more liberal accepted moderate drinking, but the bulk of the movement came to define the aim of temperance, not as moderation, but as total abstinence. Indeed, the hardliners saw the moderate drinker as the most evil, because he allowed the drink trade to highlight his sensible attitude and gloss over the gross evils of over-indulgence and addiction. The clergy as the main spokesman of the move-ment, argued that over-indulgence and drunkenness abrogated Christian conscience and freewill. They believed that the use of alcohol led invari-ably to lust, profanity and general moral laxity. They maintained that this was increased by the unprincipled use of women as barmaids, who at best merely tempted men to have another glass, and at worst could lure them into greater sins. Certainly prostitution appeared to be connected with some of the most disreputable pubs. Reformers also claimed alcohol destroyed Christian home life. Those who ignored this fact, remarked Rev Campbell, "obviously cannot hear the shriek of the drunkard's wife under the cruel blows of his brutal hand: nor the bitter cry of the children for bread, the earnings for which have gone into the publican's till! Nor do they hear the wail of broken-hearted parents over their ruined sons and daughters!"(80) Most temperance reformers also claimed that alcohol caused poverty, despite the fact that social investigators were beginning to see that intemperance was a complex part of a wider social problem which largely stemmed from unjust social conditions. Canon Boyce, president of the New South Wales Temperance Alliance, was a social reformer who had been active in slum clearance in Sydney and in the introduction of the old age pension. However, even Boyce claimed that drink caused poverty when he argued that "were it not for the curse of alcohol and certain other evils, we should soon be rid of the last vestiges of slumdom".(81) The indomitable Rev Hammond who edited the temperance journal *Grit*, alleged that money invested in the liquor industry provided far fewer jobs than if invested elsewhere, and said liquor production used grain that should be eaten by the poor.(82)

The drink trade was seen as a conspiracy which aimed at undermining national efficiency. This image of the trade as an octopus was fed by the knowledge that ninety per cent of all hotels were tied to the breweries by financial shackles.(83) Rev Fordyce in an address to the Congregational Union quoted Lord Roseby to the effect that if the state did not control the liquor trade, the trade would control the state.(84) Some claimed that the British Empire was gripped by the vice of intemperance far more than other nations, and thus would ultimately lose the race for commercial supremacy to fitter and healthier races. Another popular image used to fit the conspiracy theory was that the drink trade was a cancer. The 1903 Methodist Conference Pastoral warned that "there is no greater enemy to the progress of religion than the Liquor Traffic, which is a moral canker continually sapping the vitals of the body politic".(85) Above all, the existence of intemperance was seen as evidence of communal religious and moral indifference. To the reformers, temperance was a panacea for a myriad of troubles. George Clark M.L.A., a good templar and editor of the *Australian Temperance World* since 1883, wrote in retrospect in 1928: "Prohibition means prosperity. It means happier domestic relations, improved public morality, a purer civilization, increased avenues of employment, higher wages for operatives, easier conditions of life and an immense advance in all that makes for individual contentment and for national progress."(86) It was this vision that gave the temperance movement such zeal and power.

The movement had considerable strength of numbers to sustain this fervour. Numerous organizations advanced the cause of temperance, the major ones being the Masonic lodges, the Rechabite Orders, the Good Templar lodges, the Sons and Daughters of Temperance and, most notably, the Protestant churches, the W.C.T.U. and the New South Wales Temperance Alliance. The alliance president, Canon Boyce, stated in 1900 that there were 600 alliance lodges throughout the state, and by 1905, he claimed that the alliance had 50,000 members.(87) These groups were strongest in the middle class suburbs and had the patronage of many social and civic leaders. The executive of the alliance at this time comprised a solicitor, an estate agent, a builder, an accountant, a merchant, a publisher and a person of independent means.

Temperance reform was at heart a Protestant reform! Canon Boyce's leadership of the alliance for twenty-four years from 1890 is indicative of the church support that lay at the centre of the temperance movement. The clergy almost to a man welcomed reform and the majority of them were enthusiastic supporters. The annual meetings of all the churches invariably passed resolutions which encouraged temperance.

However, the movement was strongest among Methodists. One of the laws of the Methodist church stated that members were "required to discountenance the Drinking and other customs of Society which foster the vice of intemperance, and to promote such legislation as aims at the restraint or extinction of the liquor traffic".(88) One of the unwritten prerequisites for the Methodist clergy was that the candidate was a total abstainer. Methodist minister R. Sellors rejoiced that among his flock "seldom had he seen on any table of the houses he had visited intoxicating liquors of any kind".(89) Perhaps the bottles had been whisked away upon his arrival, but generally Methodists did abstain. By 1900, Methodists on principle celebrated the Lord's Supper with unfermented grape juice. Over twenty-five per cent of Methodist Sunday school children were enrolled in temperance Bands of Hope and over twenty per cent had pledged themselves to be total abstainers.

While the Methodists were out in front, the other Protestants were not too far behind. Although the Presbyterian church rejected a suggestion to substitute grape juice for wine in the Lord's Supper, most Presbyterian churches also had Bands of Hope which sought pledges from their wide-eyed and innocent members. The Baptists were also fierce on the question of temperance, although the Congregationalists and Anglicans were not so extreme. Indeed, the Anglicans at times showed what only amounted to a lack of zeal. The Church of England Temperance Society was only able to form branches at ten per cent of city parishes and less than this in the country. The evangelical wing of Anglicanism provided some of the movement's greatest publicists such as Boyce and Hammond, but its liberal and high church segments believed that the temperance movement's "intemperate aggressiveness and unctuous rectitude are not the methods by which to fight a national evil".(90) Still, even the Anglicans closed ranks somewhat once the fight was on.

Although it was not always recognized, the Catholic church did sympathize with the aims of temperance, but was kept apart from this movement, largely for two reasons — the first being the overwhelming Protestant flavour of temperance and the second being due to a certain lack of zeal over temperance. Herbert Moran, a Catholic doctor, wrote of this period that alcoholic over-indulgence was deplored by Catholicism as only "a minor error of conduct. The priests themselves were much given to it. Everyone felt sorry for them — was it not part of the price of their celibacy?"(91) Thus it was that temperance reform and the moral crusade generally remained a Protestant affair. Only once in 1914 did the Protestants and Catholics try to come together on a public morals committee, but the attempt ended in sectarian suspicion and failure.(92)

Therefore, a temperance reform impulse was abroad. But how was reform to be achieved? The temperance movement was divided between moderates and hard-liners who could not always agree on means and ends. For instance, although most supported gradual reform, the liberal suggestion that the liquor trade be placed under state control met with fierce conservative opposition. The alliance and possibly the bulk of the movement rejected this on the grounds that "our business is to fight it [the liquor trade] and suppress it, and not enter into it with the hope that we will be able to regulate it out of existence".(93) The bulk of the temperance movement was not temperate but coercive, and aimed at the ultimate end, rather than the regulation of, the liquor trade. However, new strategies had to be found by 1900. Firstly, it was realized by this time that the local option provisions of the 1882 Liquor Act were unsatisfactory. Only about twenty per cent of electors bothered to vote because the liquor question was asked at the low-keyed municipal polls, and besides, the Act itself was too weak.(94) Secondly, the emergence of political parties in the 1890s had made the old temperance strategy of gaining pledges for reformism from individual members rather futile. The temperance movement, headed by the New South Wales Temperance Alliance, saw that there was a need for a political party as a whole to be pledged to temperance reform, if the movement was to succeed.(95)

It was here that historical forces proved propitious for the movement. In 1903 Joseph Hector Carruthers succeeded to the leadership of the Liberal and Reform Party which was bent on changing the economic policy of the allegedly Labour dominated Progressive Ministry of Sir John See. The Liberal party had the support of the conservative press and an almost populist styled middle class enthusiasm. It called for an administrative clean-up and espoused the virtues of individualism and free enterprise. These were platforms and principles which were quite akin to moral reformism. Yet Carruthers was no wowser! Indeed, he was a divorcee, led a bright social life and was a director of the Associated Racing Clubs. However, he had a Methodist upbringing, was the brother of prominent cleric J. E. Carruthers and appeared to be sympathetic to moderate moral reforms. In the heat of the ensuing August 1904 elections which promised to be desperately close, a vote-hunting Carruthers appeared at an alliance meeting supporting its platform of "local option without compensation" to any publicans who lost their licences in the voting.(96) The shadow Attorney General, C. G. Wade, had already made a similar pledge some months earlier.(97) Yet it was not really surprising that these middle class politicians should seek the temperance vote; nor that the movement should give them its support. As outlined in the previous chapter, Carruthers won a slender victory, largely due to the Protestant and temperance vote, which gave an official reality to the Protestant-Liberal alliance. Indeed, thirty-eight per cent of Carruthers's party were Methodists and Presbyterians, twice their proportion in the population, and only one of his party of forty-six was Catholic.(98) These new men elected in 1904 contained many zealous Protestants and things augured well for moral reformism.

In 1905 a temperance victory seemed imminent. The government was pledged to amend the liquor legislation and Protestants from the pulpit and in the press hammered the issue. The *Sydney Morning Herald* remarked that "when he [Carruthers] or the Chief Secretary is not being approached by deputations he is instructed daily in the correspondence columns of newspapers by the representatives of different kinds of organizations which have to do with the reform of the liquor trade".(99) A ground swell of support came from outside the temperance movement. For instance, the recent defeat of Russia by Japan threw many Australians, notably Billy Hughes M.H.R. and the *Bulletin* school into a panic about national defence. The *Bulletin* claimed that drinking and gambling were destroying Australia's manhood.(1) Thus, the concern for national strength aided moral reform. The leader of the federal opposition, Alfred Deakin, told an alliance rally that intemperance caused "a decrease of industry, a decrease of efficiency, a decrease of thrift, a decrease of prosperity".(2) In this atmosphere, both Wade and Chief Secretary Hogue reaffirmed the government's support for "local option without compensation" before church gatherings. By May 1905, Wade was busy drafting a liquor bill, based on English legislation, and the writings of Boyce and the English temperance reformers, Rowntree and Sherwell.(3)

Wade introduced the Liquor Amendment Bill into the lower chamber on 10 August 1905. In a 15,000 word speech, later supported by Premier Carruthers, Wade made it perfectly clear that the government would not grant money compensation to publicans who lost their licences under local option voting, and at best they would be offered time compensation. The bill also had teeth, because licensing provisions were tightened. Clubs hitherto unregulated were to be licensed, and trading out of hours or on Sundays was to be more effectively policed. This was to be achieved by the provision that persons found on licensed premises out of hours had to prove lawful intent, whereas formerly the police had to prove unlawful purpose, which was difficult when the glasses could be whisked off the bar in a flash as the police came bounding in. This clause went against the whole tenor of British law that one was innocent until proven guilty. The main feature of the bill was the revised local option provisions, which allowed for a vote every three years, but now during the state, not the municipal elections. This accorded the vote more status and enabled the temperance cause to mount a simultaneous state wide campaign instead of a lot of small, discontinuous efforts. Under the provision, each electorate decided whether it wanted to maintain the current number of hotel licences, reduce them, or abolish them altogether. Fifty per cent of the electorate had to cast a vote to validate any decision and "no-license" required a two-thirds majority before it could be implemented. Disqualified licencees were to be given a three year period of grace, but no other compensation.(4) The bill was almost all the reformers had asked for!

The daily press applauded the bill which they claimed had the support of the community as a whole.(5) The churches and temperance organizations were delighted and submitted 117 petitions in support containing a few suggested amendments.(6) However, the liquor trade retaliated with a huge petition containing 44,000 signatures, but which only demanded one thing — money compensation.(7) It is indicative of the strength of temperance that the trade did not feel strong enough to make any more demands.

The debate on the bill was long and tedious and lasted three full days. It was only made interesting by attacks on parsons, ludicrous interpretations of various national drinking statistics, and the revelations made by politicians of their own drinking habits. Many in the House supported moderate liquor reform. The major opposition came from the Labour Party, which was so split over the issue, that a free vote was allowed. Labour leader, J. S. McGowen was absent — allegedly sick — but obviously as he was a committed Anglican and teetotaller, his "illness" may have been really due to an irreconcilable conflict of principle. Therefore W. A. Holman led the Labour assault. Holman maintained that poverty and misery caused intemperance and claimed therefore that the bill and the temperance cause both attacked the problem at the wrong end. He stated that the liquor trade could only be regulated by nationalization. The fact that clubs were to be free from the local option decisions was branded by him as class hypocrisy. Holman suggested (with some truth) that the whole temperance movement was simply a middle class attempt to suppress the workingman's club and haven — the pub. His speech reached a crescendo with a denunciation of the middle class view that "the working man must be protected; the man who goes into a bar to get a drink must be fenced around with safeguards to protect his morals and his manners, but the member of the club or the man who can keep his own sideboard need not be interfered with".(8) Holman added perceptively that local option voting would only succeed in middle class areas where reform was least needed. The other Labour members, sensing a good argument, roused themselves and pressed the attack further for the sake of their friends in the liquor trade. They demanded that if licences were revoked, money compensation must be given. Ironically, the liberals who were the traditional champions of the rights of private ownership and vested interests, continued to oppose financial compensation.

The temperance men were not inactive during the debate. It was reported that the Methodists, Woolls Rutledge and Beale, who were seated in the gallery, "lent valuable assistance by their counsel and suggestions to the friends of reform on the Government benches — and were in frequent consultation with those in charge of the bill as to the effect and purport of the various resolutions submitted".(9) How much closer could the churches get to politics?

As usual in the clash of interest groups, compromises were made, but the temperance party fared the better. Clubs were now liable to have their licences revoked by local option voting. The cause of reform was also aided by the change in the proportion of votes cast needed to validate a local option decision, from fifty to thirty per cent of the electorate, and by the reduction of the proportion of votes needed to achieve "no-license" from two-thirds to sixty per cent. On the other hand, the three year time compensation given to disqualified licencees was extended to a long eight year period of grace. It was a fitting finish to this temperance campaign that Premier Carruthers and Attorney-General Wade should be the guests of honour at the alliance's victory rally to celebrate the passing of the 1905 Liquor Act.

As the first local option vote was not until 1907, the jubilant reformers in late 1905 looked around for other evils to slay. Gambling, the third in the Protestant trinity of sins, soon felt the full force of the reform challenge. The Presbyterian *Messenger*, in early 1906, declared that the gambling mania was fast becoming a greater evil than strong drink.(10) Gambling was opposed for much the same reasons and with the same intensity as the use of alcohol. The Anglican bishops in 1905 summed up the major view by stating that gambling "is the cause of unhappiness and estrangement in the family, it frequently drives to crime and suicide; and upon the individual character it leaves the mark of selfishness, hardness and heartless cruelty".(11) The clergy's prime concern was that gambling threatened the economic stability of the family unit. But they also believed it debased the value of hard work, because some money was gained by no effort at all. The individual Christian was supposed to use what God had given him wisely and with charity, and not squander it away on games of chance. Ministers also claimed patriotically that gambling was a waste of national resources. Rev Stephen, the Methodist crusader, lamented that £3 million was gambled annually in Sydney alone.(12) The perennial attempt by the racing fraternity to introduce the Totalizator met with relentless clerical opposition. The Methodists argued typically that it would further increase gambling and "give countenance to the withdrawal from industrial pursuits of valuable time, energy and capital, thus weakening the fibre of national life and sanctioning practices that minister to unhealthy excitement and illegal speculation".(13) Needless to say, the clergy never considered that playing the stock exchange was gambling!

These Protestant middle class arguments revealed little empathy with the need of the working class to risk a bob in the hope of winning a few more. In that little read Australian novel *Jonah*, Louis Stone outlined this necessity through the larrikin Chook, who "was always in a shilling sweep, a sixpenny raffle, a hundred to one double on the Cup. He marked pak-a-pu tickets, took the kip at two-up, and staked his last shilling more readily than the first. It was always the last shilling that was going to turn the scale and make his fortune."(14) Besides, "unhealthy excitement" (as the Methodists saw gambling), was one of the few pleasures of those at the bottom of the social heap! The Protestant view was also divorced from the Catholic position which condoned small bets, especially in the cause of the Church. Archbishop Kelly claimed that Catholics gambled at church bazaars to lose, not win,(15) but this did not impress Protestants who likened Catholic bazaars to "gambling hells".

It is alleged that Australians will gamble on two flies traversing a wall. Certainly, the deepest silence in Australia is not reserved for fallen diggers, but for the three minutes during the running of the Melbourne Cup. Perhaps gambling was not endemic in 1900, but it did permeate all aspects of life. Foot racing, horse racing, cycling, boating, boxing, football or anything else which involved sporting competition was gambled on. The working class backed thoroughbreds illegally in houses, pubs or the streets, while the genteel placed bets legally at the Turf. Why even the governor patronized the Turf, for after all, it was the sport of kings, and he the monarch's representative! In the city and working class areas Chinese gambling shops were quite the vogue at this time. Rightfully or not, the reformers claimed that there was too much gambling. They alleged that even ladies held sweeps in their homes and children placed threepenny wagers in betting shops.

Because of the strength of the gambling instinct, it took several gambling misadventures for the reformers to gain the support of a wider section of the community. On the third of April 1905, M. Slattery M.L.C., a solicitor and former Minister of Justice, was convicted of fraudulently using about £7,000 of a widow's money to cover financial difficulties allegedly created by gambling debts. The presiding judge, Justice Pring, was shocked that such a bad example should be set by one so high, and declared in his summation: "I hope that one of the results of this case will be to send a shock throughout the community that this vice will die out. If it does not I do no know what will happen to Australia. It is sapping the whole community. Week after week we read of bankers' clerks and others purloining money to pay these wretched debts of honour — as they are called."(16) The inevitable indignant letters appeared in the morning press condemning gambling. In true authoritarian reformist style, some suggested the instant dismissal of staff who gambled, while others proposed vigilante raids on gambling establishments. Even Rev S. S. Tovey, an erstwhile moderate, urged the formation of an anti-gambling league, because even "good living men and women" gambled.(17) The Evangelical Council and the Amateur Sports Clubs sent deputations to the chief secretary.(18) A ground swell of indignation began to mount.

The Carruthers government reacted with some spectacular raids on working class gambling haunts, which caught the imagination of the "more respectable" in the community. The clergy were delighted, and held rallies and formed deputations in support. In May 1905, large police raids were carried out on two-up schools in Engine Street, the Haymarket. Several thousand locals and passersby jeered at the police who hauled away those unfortunate enough to be found inside. Those prosecuted, reportedly from the "labouring class", were given the maximum penalty of a £5 fine.(19) Other raids followed. Ten months later, another raid surprised thirty-three men inside the Engine Street school. Panic reigned, because for most, capture would mean arrest, a night in the lock-up, a stiff fine and a lecture from the magistrate. But as Louis Stone said: "To some it meant more. To the bank clerk it meant the sack; to the cashier who was twenty pounds short in his cash, an examination of the books and discovery; to the speiler who was wanted by the police, scrutiny by a hundred pair of official eyes."(20) Many of the players escaped, while others fought desperately with "the Johns", until revolvers were drawn and the police restored order. A crowd of 10,000 soon gathered to heckle the police. Someone fired a shot at the police, and then a fusilade of blue metal descended upon the officers from a section of the crowd. It turned into a simple display of working class dislike for police authority. A record 169 men were arrested and fined £4 or two months' hard labour.(21) Similar raids were carried out on S.P. bookies and the Chinese gambling shops. The latter had mushroomed after a High Court ruling invalidated sections of the existing Gaming Act. However, the 104 pak-a-pu and 19 fan-tan haunts were quickly closed by a new act which was rushed through parliament in two days with the consent of all sections of the House. Apart from those members who disliked gambling, most parliamentarians shuddered in fine Australian fashion, at the thought of "women and children dodging in and out of these Chinese shops" to place wagers.(22)

As far as the reformers were concerned, the final straw came in July 1906 when D. McLeod, a Melbourne bookmaker, was punched to the ground and kicked to death on the flat at Flemington, by an inflamed crowd of punters who accused McLeod of welshing on his debts. There was now no doubt in their minds that gambling caused damnation.(23) Even the public at large was alarmed that such a thing could take place. The *Sydney Morning Herald* called upon the churches to lead a scheme for gambling reform, because the time was now ripe — "they have the country behind them in this attempt. They could do anything they like in the present state of public opinion."(24)

In late July 1906, the Carruthers ministry responded to this reform impulse with two bills, one to curb gaming and betting, and the other to stop the growing incidence of raffles and lotteries. Attorney-General Wade who introduced the Gaming and Betting (Amendment) Bill into the lower house, alleged that the number of embezzlements to cover gambling debts was increasing, and that gambling saloons generally corrupted the young. A gambling suppression measure was a necessity! He pointed out that thousands of people a week visited "Bank Lane", the centre of illicit gambling in the city, to bet on the ten race meetings held each week. Wade claimed that while it was not possible to end gambling on horses, the bill would reduce the number of race meetings to be held, and aimed to ban all off-course betting. What the bill in effect proposed was the sanctioning of gambling at racecourses where theoretically it could have been suppressed most easily, and the suppression of betting in any one of a thousand and one pubs, houses and back lanes in the inner city where it flourished. The disturbing added powers of entry and right of search given to the police under the bill were supposedly to achieve this feat.(25)

The Labour opposition criticized the bill as blatant class legislation. It certainly appeared as if there was one law for the rich and one for the poor. What was legal at the course for those who had the time and money to be there, was illegal in "Bank Lane" or the Haymarket. The working class who wanted to indulge in a flutter, and who most needed a windfall, were to be denied the chance. The bill appeared to be aimed at the working class rather than gambling as such. The reformers might have wanted to end all gambling, but the government seemed more concerned with wanting to clean up the surface of things by removing gambling from the streets, and driving it underground. It might thrive at the race-course, but as Wade candidly admitted in the House, it would at least be out of sight. Labour member, T. H. Thrower, retorted that "the Bill is only a piece of make-believe to please a section of the community who want gambling prohibited".(26) Fellow Labour member, J. R. Dacey, was most scathing when he hissed that "the whole attention of the Government — not only this Government, but all Governments, appears to be concentrated on the poorer classes who assemble at the tote shops. Special provision is made at the police station for running in large batches of these unfortunates . . . people who are driven through the streets like cattle, while their more wealthy compatriots are allowed to bet as they please."(27)

Support for the bill was running strong outside the House. Both morning dailies had for some time stated at considerable length that gambling was excessive in the community. The *Sydney Morning Herald* regretted Labour's opposition to the bill, because it considered that gambling was "an open moral sore, sapping the steadiness, if not the honesty of the younger section of the community".(28) The *Daily Telegraph* condemned illicit betting and yet ridiculed the suggestion that the bill was class legislation because it allowed on-course betting.(29) Just as the Liberal politicians had been careful not to attack the Australian

Jockey Club, both dailies avoided any condemnation of on-course betting. A great deal of their livelihood depended on turf news, forecasts and results. Besides, any enterprise supported by the governor, the present premier and the moneyed section of society could not be too vicious. It only became so on the level of the street, where money passed between the horny-handed. Church and women's groups held meetings and drew up petitions in support of the bill. Sermons against gambling were the order of the day. The word "crusade" came into vogue to describe the reformers' efforts. Activists from the concurrent Melbourne reform movement spoke at packed meetings of anti-gambling enthusiasts. At the eleventh hour the churches even gained an amendment that betting odds were not to be published in the press before the meetings, which again hit hardest at off-course betting by the common man. With the numbers in the House and wide public support, it was now merely a formality that the Gaming and Betting Bill became law.

This was not the case with the Lotteries Bill introduced into the Upper House three weeks before the Gaming and Betting Bill. Originally introduced in July 1906 to prohibit all lotteries, raffles and art unions with "no exception and no exemption", this bill was still in the committee stage by December. By this time, Premier Carruthers was claiming that it was aimed only at lotteries for money, and should not be pushed too far in other directions.(30) Why was there such a delay and such a reversal of policy?

It seemed that this bill ran headlong into the direct interests of both the labour movement and the Catholic church. The Trades Hall Council had built and financed its offices from a yearly Eight Hour Day Art Union, and therefore it presented a petition of 35,000 signatures to parliament to support its case for an exemption from the legislation.(31) Similarly, the Catholic church also financed some of its enterprises from raffles and other games of chance. Thus, Cardinal Moran launched a stinging public attack on the government, saying: "The scheme against raffles was based on bigotry, with a view to oppose those humble Catholic works of charity which were being carried on. Such law-making was based on envy of the works of beneficience, generosity, and charity which Catholics maintained "(32) Opposition from both the Trades Hall Council and the Catholic church caused Carruthers to seek a compromise — he was not going to create a storm over a few raffles especially as his ministry was under a cloud due to the recently tabled royal commission on scandals in the Lands Department. Similarly, popular support for this bill was less than that for the other anti-gambling bill, simply because raffles were not seen to be as vicious as betting on the horses or two-up. In the end, the government allowed the Lotteries Bill to lapse.

Immediately the sale of raffle and sweep tickets boomed; as many as 90,000 tickets were sold on big horseraces.(33) Under the pressure of renewed Protestant lobbying, these sweeps were finally suppressed by the Police Offences (Amendment) Act of 1908. However, the Catholic raffles and the Eight Hour Day Art Union flourished unhindered. The fact that the prize for the 1908 Eight Hour Art Union was a diamond tiara, ironically revealed that the working class had at least some of the aspirations to respectability that the reformers wished to inculcate in this class. The upshot of this anti-gambling crusade was that the reformers had forced gambling off the streets, although it continued to flourish underground. Still they were satisfied — at least New South Wales had the appearance of being purified, and their cherished aims had largely been given the legitimacy and prestige of law.

With the approach of the 1907 state elections, the forces of moral reform had to confront a new challenge. Not only was the first local option voting to take place under the new and strengthened provisions of the 1905 Liquor Act, but the Protestant-Liberal nexus was to be tested at the polls. The temperance alliance was well prepared, having established a fighting fund, planned methods and styles of propaganda, and distributed 25,000 copies of its president's latest pamphlet, *Shall I Vote for No-License?* In this pamphlet Canon Boyce urged a "no-license" vote because, under the 1905 Act, if "no-license" was not carried, these votes became automatically "reduction" votes, so that a "no-license" vote had two chances of success for the temperance cause. A large section of church opinion favoured a hard line "no-license" vote. The annual meetings of the Methodist, Presbyterian and Baptist churches advocated this prohibitionist stance. While the official Congregational and Anglican view opted for the more moderate "reduction" option. However, the "no-license" stance of the Anglican *Australian Churchman*, the Church of England Temperance Society, Canon Boyce, and a manifesto signed by sixty-eight Sydney Anglican clergymen, probably carried more weight than the official Anglican view.(34)

While the Protestants were girding their loins for the contest, Premier Carruthers was trying to refurbish his own support, which of late had begun to wane. His popularity had been damaged by the great Australian tradition of land scandals. Also some commentators claimed that the state's economic recovery was due to international price movements and monetary trends, rather than Carruthers's own efforts, which were described as piecemeal, deflationary and disappointing.(35) The *Sydney Morning Herald*, which had formerly been a supporter of the government, complained of a lack of educational and financial reform and criticized Carruthers's "lack of fibre, lack of statemanship [and] initiative".(36) With the Carruthers ministry facing a tough fight against such criticism and

Labour's growing strength, Attorney-General Wade called on the Protestant and moral reform lobby to form a united front for "social reform" against the forces opposing the liquor and gambling legislation.(37) Similarly, Carruthers tried to ensure the solidarity of the reform forces with the claim: "It is manifest that the Labour Socialist vote will this time have the assistance of an organised liquor trade vote, and of the so-called Sporting League, which aims at opening all sports to gambling on and off the courses and grounds."(38)

So, as in 1904, the Protestant-Liberal Party campaigns went hand in hand. Carruthers and the Liberals tried a catch-all "bag of bogies". He raised the anti-Socialist, anti-Labour banner; depicted the liquor trade as the financial base of the Labour Party; found a "state's rights" cause on the eve of the election in a dispute with the Commonwealth government over import duties on fencing wire; and in true evangelical style which must have harked back to his Methodist childhood, pointed to the "better and happier homes, more money and less temptations" created by his liquor and anti-gambling legislation.(39) The alignments were even more solid than in 1904. An official of the Liquor Trade Defence Union confirmed this from the other side, when he declared: "The new Liquor Act, passed by the Carruthers' Government, was an iniquitous measure and a stab at the Labour Party. The only friends the liquor trade had in the Assembly were the Labour Party, who fought tooth and nail so that they might get something like a reasonable measure."(40) The temperance aspect of the Liberal-Protestant campaign fared the best. The dailies strongly supported a reduction in the number of liquor licences. Even the Liquor Trade Defence Union, which circulated 40,000 copies of Rev Carr-Smith's appeal to vote for the more moderate "reduction" rather than the extreme of "no-license", seemed to have accepted a "reduction" majority as inevitable. This is another strong indication of the dominance of the mood for moral reform. The alliance's campaign ended with an emotive march by 12,000 toddlers and children through the streets of Sydney under the glorious banner of temperance.

The Carruthers ministry was narrowly returned, but with a reduced majority, which the *Methodist* claimed was due to the combined forces of "Rum, Romanism, Socialism and Gambling".(41) The Liberal-Protestant alliance had held, but it had lost some of the impetus of 1904. No doubt Carruthers's deflationary fiscal policy and his piecemeal reformism had lost votes, and on the other hand Labour was becoming more of a viable alternative. Even the *Sydney Morning Herald* admitted after the election that the suspicion and dislike of Labour was disappearing and "it is gaining the allegiance and the help of temperate, thoughtful men".(42) Also the Liquor Trade Defence Union and the Sporting League, which both supported Labour and virulently opposed Carruthers and the wowsers, had fought hard in some electorates. These two groups claimed to have caused the defeat of some of the militant Protestant Liberals, namely, Booth, Law, Jessep, Anderson and Bruntnell, who had been voted into the previous parliament by temperance and Protestant support. An exhausted E. C. V. Broughton, who narrowly escaped defeat, wrote to Carruthers: "With a few exceptions, the whole of the liquor trade was against me, and the Gaming and Betting Bill, Childrens' and Protection Act and Second Hand Dealers' Bill also lost me hundreds of votes. However, should I determine to stand again I trust that time will soften the resentment engendered by these measures."(43) Carruthers himself intimated that the alliance with temperance had hindered him, because he claimed that in some electorates the temperance issue had overshadowed the contest between "Liberalism and Socialism". It is certainly true that the temperance issue was at times dominant, because 20,000 (or five per cent) more votes were cast in the local option vote, than in the state election itself.(44) However, it is doubtful that Carruthers was harmed by the temperance cause, which itself won a strong victory in the contest.

In the local option polling of 1907, the combined "no-license" and "reduction" vote exceeded that of "continuance". "Reduction" was carried in sixty-five of the ninety electorates. While "reducation" was carried in only one of the seven inner city working class electorates, every one of the twenty-six suburban electorates, and thirty-eight of the fifty-seven country electorates voted for "reduction". The temperance movement was understandably pleased, though a little disappointed that "no-license" had not been carried in any electorate. However, in eleven suburban and eighteen country electorates, the "no-license" vote had exceeded fifty per cent of the vote, just short of the sixty per cent needed under the Act to carry complete abolition of licenses. Indeed, the drinkers in the Gloucester electorate on the Upper Manning River retained their right to enjoy a beer by only four-tenths of one per cent of the votes.(45) The figures revealed that the majority of the voting community had been convinced by the temperance reformers that there was too much drinking and too many pubs. It also revealed clearly that the hard core of the temperance support lay in the blue ribbon Liberal areas of the affluent southern and south-western suburbs, where the Protestants were at their strongest.

What were the implications of the local option poll? The Liquor Trades Union forecast gloomily that the results would mean that 400 or 500 liquor licences would be disqualified.(46) The Act specified that if "reduction" was passed, up to twenty-five per cent of all licences in the electorate could be disqualified. Surprisingly, only 293 licences were eventually cancelled by the Licensing Court.(47) This fact is explained by an ironic twist within the local option temperance strategy. The movement was largely directed towards suppressing intemperance within the working class, and encouraging the adoption of middle class morals and manners.

But as voting on temperance in each electorate only determined what happened in that particular electorate, it was likely that the reformers would be unable to control the vote in working class electorates. This is precisely what happened! Those of the working class who in general did not consider that they were drunken or debased, voted for "continuance". Only one inner city working class electorate out of seven voted for a reduction in the number of hotels. This provides the explanation as to why only half the expected number of licences were disqualified. H. J. Hughes, the Metropolitan District Licensing Inspector perceived the irony when he reported: "It seems anomalous that where the hotels are the most numerous, and reduction of licences could be carried out without any public inconvenience, continuance was carried, and where a small number of licences existed in sparsely populated electorates, reduction of licences was carried."(48) Holman had predicted this when the Liquor Act was before the House in 1904 and social researchers Rowntree and Sherwell had discovered this empirically in Europe, Canada and the United States.(49) However, the bulk of the temperance advocates in New South Wales seemed either unaware of these opinions and findings, or were convinced that they could be more successful in persuading the working class to vote for liquor reform. Besides, a decline in the number of hotels was seen as a blessing to temperance advocates, wherever this may occur.

The 1907 local option vote marked the pinnacle of the moral reform movement's achievement; but this very success created considerable opposition. When Judkins, the Melbourne Methodist, called E. W. O'Sullivan M.L.A. of the Sporting League a "social bandit", he was denounced in return as a puritan and an anti-democrat.(50) The charge of corrupter of public morals was wearing a little thin by 1907, whereas the retort that the moral reformers were coercive found increasing sympathy in a community which adhered to a democratic ethos. The wowsers were seen to be trying to kill too many simple joys — for instance, disapproval of mixed sea-bathing was by this time running against the tide of popular sentiment. So was the attempt to keep Sunday free from play, recreation and travel. Again, the moralists miscalculated when they tried to prevent the staging of the world heavyweight title fight between brash negro Jack Johnson and the abrasive Canadian Tommy Burns, to be held at the Sydney Stadium on Boxing Day 1908.(51) The sporting instinct was sufficiently embedded in the Australian breast for this attempt not only to fail, but to come in for some savage criticism. One correspondent, "Freedom", condemned "the wild vapourings and frothings of a certain class of religious professors and professional platform denizens, who seize the opportunity of a prize fight, or even a dog fight, to fill the air and the press with declamations as to the wickedness of the 'other People' and the righteousness of the speakers and their ilk".(52) "An Australian" similarly denounced the hysterical pulpiteers and appealed for an end to the restrictive moral legislation, adding: "Mr Wade and our clergy are certainly laying the foundation for a bloody revolution. They will find that bigotry, intolerance, and oppression have their limits [for they] will be swept into oblivion."(53)

This anti-wowser sentiment was fostered further by the campaign of the Liquor Trade Defence Union before the 1910 local option vote. The union allegedly spent £90,000 on the campaign, but whatever the sum, its financial resources outmatched the temperance movement's funds. Through its journal, *Fairplay*, and other channels, the union promoted the view that the "no-license" temperance campaign was a denial of British freedom and the forerunner to total prohibition. This was enough to scare the wits out of the drinking public, and alarm all Australian democrats. The union appealed for "sane, state-regulated trade in wholesome liquor", free from the evils of home consumption and sly grog that prohibition would bring.(54) The union's appeal for moderation and free access to liquor for consenting adults, completely overwhelmed the temperance movement's home-spun campaign, which was led by such quaint devices as this clerically composed song:

> When the ballot-box, you reach,
> You must vote Drink out,
> As you can, by deed and speech
> You must vote Drink out.(55)

The local option campaign of 1910 polarized the community on the drink question. This was symbolized not only by the heat generated, but the consolidation of forces on both sides. The Congregational and Anglican churches decided to officially support the "no-license" campaign instead of the more moderate "reduction" option as in 1907. The upshot of the campaign was a vote in 1910 which completely reversed the balance of forces existing in 1907. This trend continued in the 1913 vote. It is true that the absolute percentages of the vote gained by each option did not change as dramatically as this reversal might imply. The actual percentages are shown in the table.(56)

	Continuance	Reduction	No-license
1907	45	16	39
1910	56	7	37
1913	57	7	37

However, the shift just tipped the percentage of absolute votes in favour of "continuance", and because the voting was on an electorate basis the impact on the final outcome was enormous. While "continuance" was carried in only twenty-five electorates out of ninety in 1907, the number leapt to seventy-five out of ninety in 1910, and seventy-six in 1913.(57)

It is important to note that the voting changes (perhaps predictably) were only among the middle group who proved to be swinging voters. The "no-license" percentage changed only fractionally! It appeared that those with moderate views towards the use and abuse of alcohol had been persuaded by the reform crusade carried out from 1900 that a reduction in the number of hotels was necessary, but by 1910 they were no longer convinced that this was needed. As the temperance campaign became less temperate and more coercive, and was also made to appear so by the liquor trade's propaganda, the moderates in society drew back from reformism and voted for "continuance". Some were shocked by the growing orientation of the reform movement towards prohibition; some thought enough reform had been achieved; while others simply were wearied by the wowsers' continual cries of wolf. The Chief Secretary, W. Wood, commenting on the latter said in the House as early as 1906: "I am prepared to give every assistance, but I am getting into this position: that I am not going to turn Parliament into a sausage machine, a chaff cutting concern, to turn out legislation which they say has only to be put into operation and the moral tone of the community will be purified and elevated."(58) In the end, many hard-headed Australians lost faith in moral reformist panaceas.

Despite the reverses of 1910 and 1913, the temperance (by now prohibition) phalanx stood firm at a formidable thirty-eight per cent of the voting community. Time was to chip at the size and strength of this group, but for years it remained solid. The moral reformists were not a majority of the community, but they were certainly the largest minority! This group had at important times in this period persuaded a sufficient proportion of the remainder of the community to go along with them in the cause of moral reform. On the liquor question alone, they not only tightened up control of hotels, but strengthened the right of the community to express an opinion as to the number of hotels that should exist. Due to the 1907 poll, 293 licences or ten per cent of the state's total were eventually disqualified, although in 1910 the number had plummeted to twenty-eight disqualifications or only one per cent of the total number.(59) Ironically, as has already been explained above, it was largely the middle class suburbs that became drier and the frontiers of alcoholic barbarism in the bush and the inner city slum areas remained very wet. To this day, party-goers in Sydney and Melbourne look in vain for a pub to get supplies as they drive through some of the older "respectable" suburbs.

What were the forces behind the rise of moral reformism? Anne Summers has written perceptively that: "In the early years of this century a rampant puritanism descended upon Australian society. It was the product of a family-oriented petty bourgeois mentality and its object was to promote and protect family life and, particularly, to enforce its morality on single women." She adds: "Its prevalence was a class pheno- menon, an indication that the middle-class had achieved political and economic power and had ousted the last remnants of the pre-capitalist squattocracy."(60) Summers is right to stress the middle class nature of this movement and the conjunction of it with the women's suffrage move- ment and the apotheosis of motherhood. However, as outlined at the beginning of this chapter the perspectives must be wider still! Two other social phenomena intersected with these abovementioned forces and com- pounded them. First, an acute anxiety within Protestantism around 1900 dramatically heightened the moral concerns of Protestants who were, in any case, the ones that were leading the puritan sweep at this period. Only a knowledge of this deep Protestant anxiety over the place of religion in society can explain the rampant nature of this puritan outburst. Again, this movement can only be understood when it is seen against the pre- vailing climate of considerable economic insecurity and the growth of political alignments along more overt class lines which existed till 1910.

Summers may be right in seeing moral reformism as the triumph of the middle class over the last remnants of the pre-capitalist squattocracy, but the final shots of old battles are not as important as the opening sallies in new ones. Moral reformism, apart from being a genuine reformist move- ment, also expressed the new-found concern of the bourgeoisie with the growth of the newly conscious working class. The Protestant middle class reformers castigated the morals and manners of Catholic and working class culture in the name of national strength and survival. But behind this rhetoric for individual and national regeneration lay quite a deal of bashing of the working class per se. Moral reformism was on this symbolic level a clash between middle and working class culture and values. By persuasion and coercion, much of bourgeois morals and manners became legislatively enshrined in the early 1900s which increased the power and prestige of the Protestant middle class. Even those who objected to these laws were forced to acknowledge their power when they chose to oppose or contra- vene them. Thus the law supported the bourgeois view of the world!

Why then did the actual moral reform crusade falter by the outbreak of the Great War? Certainly, the end of the Protestant-Liberal alliance in 1910 due to the return of a Labour government (the first in the state's history), played a part in the demise of moral reformism. Indeed, Labour set a legislative trend in the opposite direction by liberalizing Sunday trading and legalizing the Totalizator in 1916, which allowed off-course betting. However, there was much more to the decline of moral reformism than this electoral result. For one thing, the churches' opposition to the Totalizator was surprisingly small and lethargic in comparison to earlier protests.(61) The reform movement appeared to have lost its drive! Exhaustion no doubt played a part in this. Canon Boyce, who retired in

1915 after twenty-four years at the helm of the New South Wales Temperance Alliance, referred to his fatigue due to years of constant reformist activism.(62) Similarly, that great agent for moral reform in the period, the New South Wales Evangelical Council, was now all but defunct.

Not only had the zeal of the reformers flagged, but the context in which they moved had changed because social and class tensions were generally in decline by 1910. Economic recovery was achieved by 1907, industrial relations were more harmonious with the rise of conciliation and arbitration, and there was a greater acceptance of Labour and unionism after 1910. This growing calm was shown by the fact that sectarianism, an accurate barometer of social tension in Australia had waned after 1905. This greater social stability created less anxiety among Protestant churchmen generally, who were less inclined to preach religious doom after 1910 than they had been around 1900. It was also clear that the achievements of a decade had calmed their nervousness! The *Methodist* in 1910 summed up the Protestant satisfaction with reformism which induced this attitude of calm: "New South Wales is to-day a cleaner and better place to live in because of the so-called 'blue laws' of the past six years. It behoves us to watch vigilantly that none of these laws be repealed or amended out of all effective power of usefulness."(63)

Calm vigilance, not anxious activism was the Protestant mood around 1910. Even the hard core of the reformers, the wowsers, who would always remain tense and anxious in this secular world, drew back from public activity, comforted and absorbed by their own righteousness. After the disappointing results of the 1913 local option poll, the *Roll Call*, organ of the Christian Endeavour movement, commented: "As we pass by these wretched drink shops that have brought so much sin and suffering and sorrow to our fair land, we can say 'Thank God, I gave my vote against this place of temptation that degrades men, and women, and drives them to destruction'."(64)

One final problem is the historical assessment of the wowsers who energized the moral reform crusade which for several years significantly affected public life in New South Wales. Certainly they were products of social forces that even they did not always comprehend. The wowsers were idealists whose vision of reform aimed to make Australia a better place. In this sense they were great patriots, prepared to give time and energy to the cause of national righteousness. Their intensity has to be admired. Yet there was an emptiness at the heart of their vision. There was little love, knowledge or understanding of their fellow man in their actions — only the desire to change and to coerce.

8. Conclusion

Martin Luther once stated that "the world and the masses are and always will be unchristian, although they are baptized and nominally Christian. Hence a man who would venture to govern an entire community or the world with the gospel would be like a shepherd who should place in one fold wolves, lions, eagles and sheep. The sheep would keep the peace, but they would not last long. The world cannot be ruled with a rosary."(1) This belief may place him among the realists in Christian history, but it was not the view which was shared by the bulk of Protestant churchmen of the nineteenth century. This century was a time of great religious movements, revivals and expansions, and most who witnessed these believed that Christianity appeared destined to spread across the face of the earth in train with Western civilization. But Australian Protestants of the nineteenth century were not only optimists because they were men of that century, but also because they were Australians and, like many of their countrymen, held utopian visions of the future state of the Antipodes. Their particular utopia was for a Christian Australia.

However, the 1890s — a time of social upheaval in Australia — was a decade of reassessment. Also, at the end of the 1890s, churchmen took stock of their position because this period marked the end of a century. With the death of their beloved Queen in 1902 it also marked the end of an era. To their great despair, when they looked about them they saw that the bulk of the community was not at prayer on a Sunday. Christian Australia appeared to be a fading dream, and it was this disjunction between their ideal and the reality which caused the outburst of Messianic Protestant energy of the ensuing fifteen years, before the outbreak of world war threw up other needs and perspectives.

If the daily press had cared to sum up the results of church extension over these fifteen years, the headlines, in typically compressed journalese, might have read "more reached, more preached"! Certainly the growth rate of church building and additional clergy in this period was thirty per cent, which exceeded the state population growth of twenty-two per cent. There was no doubt that the churches had responded vigorously and managed to enlarge their physical presence in the community! This increased activity was aimed at the problem areas of religious practice, notably the slums and the backblocks of the state. However, too often the churches settled for true and tried methods. It was largely the Anglicans and Methodists who showed a flexibility and willingness to experiment in pastoral care among the working class. Here they drew on their English experiences. Overall, too many Protestant clergymen knew too little about the condition of the inner city working class to minister to them effectively. In this they were prisoners of their own class perceptions. Certainly, the adoption of interdenominational, large-scale evangelism did reveal a creative spirit among the churches. These efforts were fruitful in some respects and won a few new souls for the Church. However, they largely served to cheer the committed troops rather than gain new enlistments. Similarly, the efforts to dismantle church barriers and form a united Protestant church was a creative act, but it was frustrated by Christian power-brokers, parochial jealousies and traditional loyalties. The Protestant churches were really attempting to wrestle with the problems of indifference, and they showed great strength and energy in doing so, but always the efforts drew back from the radical means necessary.

Although the Christian presence was more dominant by 1914, there is considerable doubt as to whether more of the indifferent were brought into the Church. The evidence from their pastoral and evangelistic work and from the church statistics which exist(2) suggests that religious practice was stagnant in this period — that by 1915 the churches were still attended regularly by thirty per cent of adults and forty per cent of children. The churches had simply kept pace with the tide of indifference and secularism against which they rowed. This was in itself an achievement! But it brought them no closer to a Christian Australia. Yet, while there were still those who were anxious about the position of the Church, the cries were less numerous than in 1900 and had merely the ring of perennial clerical laments rather than anything more insistent.

Why had the note of urgency gone? The sense of satisfaction with their position in society had partly resulted from the strenuous efforts of the churches over the last fifteen years. Also, the calm was to some extent due to exhaustion. Similarly, strident evangelicalism had reached a plateau by 1915. The best days of the Evangelical Council had long since passed, and even that evangelical star, Christian Endeavour, had reached the end of its growth by the outbreak of the war.

However, there was also the sense that more clergy were taking a subtler view of the place of the Church in society. The importance of the churches could not always be gauged by the number of people in the pews, but in the more general recognition of religion and the social punch the churches could deliver. In 1907 Archbishop Donaldson of Brisbane enunciated this view of Christian presence when he said that despite the existence of sin, secularism and religious indifference "the Church still remains the paramount power in Australia . . . The sincere Christian man, whatever his faults, does command everywhere a sincere respect. The Christian ideal is cherished in a thousand homes where there is no outward profession, and the heart of the nation remains sound."(3) This was a Christian Australia in another style, not one hundred per cent church attendance, but a pluralist society in which Christianity was only one force – but certainly the dominant force and a permeating one. Christianity was still the basis of social morality in early twentieth century Australia. The success of the moral reform crusade attested to that. Indeed, forty per cent of the population alone continued to support the prohibition of alcohol from their local area. Protestantism which formed three-quarters of the Christian phalanx had the greatest social prestige.

There is no doubt that the social power of Protestantism was expressed in the 1900s at some cost to the cause of Christianity. This was because the public image of Protestantism came too often to be associated with wowsers, bigots and the bourgeoisie. These were certainly stereotypes and care should be taken not to paint a caricature of Protestantism, but these were also powerful Protestant traits as seen then and now, and were very firmly rooted in and produced by the reality of a society in flux. There was much charity, understanding and love within Protestantism, but these were overlaid in this period of anxiety and tension. Thus when moral reformism ran to excess the coercive image of Protestantism prevailed in a large proportion of the public mind. When the sincere but rigid antediluvial low church Anglicans carried out a witch hunt against high church ritualists, the rest of the community looked on intrigued, but aghast. Similarly, when Protestants and Catholics hammered each other in the age old Australian tradition of sectarian bigotry, the prestige of Christianity was dented. Finally, when the Protestant churches formed an open unholy alliance with the conservative party, Catholics, the working class, secularists and the indifferent alike were no doubt soured. Thus Protestantism, supposedly a branch of the universalist Christian religion, found itself within narrow class limits and linked in unsavoury alliances.

The only other assessment of Protestantism in this period has been by J. D. Bollen in his *Protestantism and Social Reform in New South Wales 1890–1910*. He has concentrated on the relationship suggested in the title and the new theological developments within Protestantism. However, my reading of the evidence suggests Bollen has exaggerated the Protestant interest in social reconstruction and the extent to which the new social gospel permeated the churches in the pre-1914 period. Certainly it is true that theological reassessments were under way at this time. But they were only gathering force late in the period and then largely among the liberal and younger clergy. The subject matter of the encyclicals of the five yearly Anglican General Synods symbolize the change. In 1905 the encyclical dwelt on moral issues such as intemperance, gambling and the evils of contraception, while that of 1911 (perhaps surprisingly) took up social reformist issues such as the cause of the Australian Aborigines. Throughout the period the dominant Protestant view of reform was not social reform but more narrowly, moral reform.

The outbreak of war in 1914 reinforced some of the trends of the previous fifteen years and cut across others. A lot of the old bogies were trotted out. The alleged evils of popery were symbolized in the person of Cardinal Mannix, and Catholicism was charged with threatening the very war effort. Again, gambling and alcohol were said to be undermining national strength and the chance of an allied victory. Religion once more became *overtly* allied with class. While Catholicism sided largely with Labour and the working class in the conscription referenda, Protestantism overwhelmingly aligned itself with Capital and the Right. Many clerics placed their patriotism above their religion in a Protestant chorus of support for the war. Indeed, many claimed it would herald a religious revival! The few Protestant voices which expressed the pacifism of the Prince of Peace of the New Testament were drowned out by the jingoistic din. Yet those who saw the war as a just cause and a religiously purifying experience were not so much displaying a corruption of ideals, as a continuing (if misguided) Messianic concern to create a more godly Australia.

The desire to Christianize Australia was the goal that Protestant churchmen had always followed. They lit their path with what St Paul had described to the Corinthians as "the light of the knowledge of the glory of God in the face of Jesus Christ". Overall, Protestant churchmen brought more benefits to New South Wales society than evils, though the balance did not always dip so clearly in the direction of good during the days of sectarian uproar and wowserism. However, their failings — and they were numerous — existed because the treasure of the teachings of Christ has to exist in this world within the hearts and minds of such wonderfully frail earthen vessels as men and women.

Appendix 1

Percentage of Each Religion to the Total Population of New South Wales at Censuses 1891–1921.

Denomination	1871	1881	1891	1901	1911	1921
Church of England	46.04	46.41	45.32	46.58	45.45	48.91
Methodist	7.94	8.72	10.13	10.29	9.32	8.66
Presbyterian	9.86	9.83	9.86	9.91	11.33	10.47
Congregational	1.86	1.94	2.17	1.86	1.40	1.06
Baptist	0.83	0.99	1.18	1.24	1.27	1.18
Roman Catholic	29.64	28.14	25.85	25.96	23.24	22.97
Greek Catholic	—	—	0.02	0.04	0.07	—
Protestant Undefined	1.44	1.35	0.87	0.97	2.29	0.97
Catholic Undefined	—	—	—	—	2.27	0.96
Salvation Army	—	—	0.93	0.72	0.46	0.45
Seventh Day Adventist	—	—	—	0.10	0.12	0.20
Lutheran	—	0.66	0.72	0.55	0.44	0.24
Free Thinkers, Agnostics)	0.23	0.14	0.56	0.26	0.12	—
No denom., No religion)			0.73	0.47	0.24	0.32
Object to state	—	—	0.90	0.97	0.20	0.62
Church of Christ	—	—	—	0.20	0.40	0.38
Total Christian	97.80	98.15	97.17	98.18	98.67	97.26

APPENDIX 2

PERCENTAGE DISTRIBUTION OF RELIGIONS IN EACH SUBURB OF THE SYDNEY METROPOLITAN AREA AT CENSUS OF NEW SOUTH WALES, 1901

Suburb	Population of each suburb	Church of England	Roman Catholic	Methodist	Presbyterian	Congregational	Baptist
City of Sydney	112,137	43.5	34.9	4.3	6.6	1.5	0.7
Alexandria	9,341	48.8	25.4	7.7	6.2	3.8	0.9
Annandale	8,349	49.2	20.9	9.4	10.3	3.0	1.6
Ashfield	14,329	50.1	13.8	10.9	9.4	6.2	4.7
Balmain	30,076	46.4	22.6	8.9	13.5	3.2	0.9
Bexley	3,079	49.1	11.5	11.0	10.1	9.2	3.9
Botany	3,383	54.2	15.9	10.8	9.9	0.8	0.9
Botany North	3,772	48.4	22.9	14.6	5.8	1.7	0.3
Burwood	7,521	51.8	14.7	7.7	10.5	8.6	2.2
Camperdown	7,931	48.8	26.0	7.2	8.7	2.7	1.6
Canterbury	4,226	45.9	16.2	14.6	9.4	6.4	2.0
Concord	2,818	52.5	27.3	4.5	4.4	6.5	1.7
Darlington	3,784	51.2	26.3	5.5	8.7	2.2	1.6
Drummoyne	2,843	50.8	18.3	9.0	11.6	3.2	0.6
Enfield	2,497	54.6	12.9	13.0	8.0	5.0	1.9
Erskineville	6,059	52.3	24.2	8.6	7.2	2.1	1.2
Five Dock	1,401	60.9	16.1	8.4	5.1	4.8	2.1
Glebe	19,220	50.2	25.6	6.7	9.1	2.3	0.7
Hunters Hill	4,232	47.9	32.4	4.2	8.1	3.4	0.5

APPENDIX 2 (cont'd)

Suburb	Population of each suburb	Church of England	Roman Catholic	Methodist	Presbyterian	Congre-gational	Baptist
Hurstville	4,019	55.5	11.6	9.4	12.1	3.2	2.3
Kogarah	3,892	51.9	15.5	8.0	8.5	10.2	1.4
Lane Cove	1,918	38.2	30.1	6.4	9.2	7.9	2.3
Leichhardt	17,454	45.9	19.1	10.7	10.7	4.5	2.1
Manly	5,035	52.3	18.9	7.1	11.3	5.1	0.6
Marrickville	18,775	48.2	14.1	11.7	8.1	7.2	3.1
Marsfield	713	50.8	16.0	24.2	0.8	1.1	3.9
Mosman	5,691	57.6	13.5	5.5	11.5	3.6	0.6
Newtown	22,598	50.7	18.4	9.9	8.3	3.2	2.1
North Sydney	22,040	53.8	20.7	5.6	10.7	2.9	1.4
Paddington	21,984	46.8	27.6	5.9	8.9	3.3	1.4
Petersham	15,307	46.5	14.8	10.4	8.4	7.0	5.7
Randwick	9,753	48.0	27.5	5.7	10.9	2.0	1.3
Redfern	24,219	44.7	31.4	7.9	6.5	2.4	0.7
Rockdale	7,857	49.9	12.8	15.2	7.2	5.4	1.2
Ryde	3,222	53.8	22.1	8.2	8.0	0.6	3.2
St Peters	5,906	52.7	17.0	14.7	5.4	2.1	0.9
Strathfield	2,991	52.7	12.3	8.6	8.2	12.4	1.3
Vaucluse	1,152	51.3	29.3	3.1	6.4	7.5	—
Waterloo	9,609	46.0	31.8	6.9	5.8	3.9	0.7
Waverley	12,342	45.9	23.2	9.3	11.4	2.5	0.9
Willoughby	6,004	48.9	18.3	9.8	9.7	5.9	0.9
Woollahra	12,351	49.2	22.5	5.1	10.0	5.1	1.0
All Suburbs	369,693	49.0	21.4	8.7	9.2	4.1	1.7
Shipping	6,070	26.0	12.9	3.2	6.0	0.4	0.5
Total Metropolis	487,900	47.5	24.4	7.6	8.6	3.5	1.5

Abbreviations

The following abbreviations are used in the Notes to the Text.

A.C.W.	*Australian Christian World*
A.G.J.	Attorney-General's and Justice Department
C.S.	Colonial Secretary's Department
M.L.	Mitchell Library
N.S.W.P.D.	*New South Wales Parliamentary Debates*
N.S.W.P.P.	*New South Wales Parliamentary Papers*
S.M.H.	*Sydney Morning Herald*

Notes to the Text

INTRODUCTION

1. K. S. Inglis, *Churches and the Working Classes in Victorian England* (London: Routledge and Kegan Paul, 1963); W. W. Phillips, "Christianity and its Defence in New South Wales 1880 to 1890" (Ph.D. thesis, A.N.U., 1969).
2. Rev R. W. Dale, *Impressions of Australia* (London: Hodder and Stoughton, 1889), pp. 225–26.
3. *N.S.W. Statistical Register* (1910), p. 937.
4. *Census of New South Wales* (1901), p. 233. See also appendix 1.
5. R. Broome, "Protestantism in New South Wales Society 1900–1914" (Ph.D. thesis, University of Sydney, 1974), appendixes 11–13. My calculations differ only slightly from those found in W. W. Phillips, "Religious Profession and Practice in New South Wales 1850–1901; The Statistical Evidences", *Historical Studies* 15, no. 59 (October 1972): 378–400.
6. R. Mudie Smith, ed., *The Religious Life of London* (London: Hodder and Stoughton, 1904), pp. 15–18. *Methodist* (13 February 1904).
7. Phillips, "Christianity and its Defence", chap. 3.
8. R. V. Jackson, "Owner-Occupation of Houses in Sydney, 1871–1891", *Australian Economic History Review* 10, no. 2 (September 1970): 138–54.
9. See appendixes 2 and 3.
10. While Catholics formed 25.96 per cent of the total population of New South Wales in 1901, Catholic males formed 12.7 per cent of those "engaged in Finance and Property", 17.9 per cent of those "engaged in Government, Defence, Law and Protection", 19.1 per cent of "persons of independent means" and 28.9 per cent of those "supplying Board and Lodging and rendering Personal Service". *Census of New South Wales* (1901), pp. 786–93.
11. P. J. O'Farrell, *Documents in Australian Catholic History,* vol. 2, (London: Geoffrey Chapman, 1969), p. 21.
12. The unemployment rate among Catholic males in New South Wales in 1921 was 6.18 per cent. The percentages for the other religions were Church of England 4.83; Methodist 3.44; Presbyterian 4.03; Congregationalist 3.12 and Baptist 4.11. The percentage of male Catholics who were employers was 3.20. The percentages for the other religions were Church of England 3.89; Methodist 5.03; Presbyterian 5.93; Congregationalist 6.20 and Baptist 4.46. *Census of the Commonwealth of Australia* (1921), vol. 1, table 33, pp. 400–401.
13. T. A. Coghlan, *The Wealth and Progress of New South Wales 1900–1901* (Sydney: Government Printer, 1902), p. 200.

1 THE PROBLEM OF RELIGIOUS INDIFFERENCE

1. *Presbyterian* (5 July 1900).

2. *Baptist* (1 January 1901).
3. Rev W. H. Beale, *Souvenir of the Official Year of the Rev W. H. Beale: President of the New South Wales Conference 1900–1901* (Sydney: Epworth, 1901); also, *Church Standard* (1 September 1900).
4. *Official Report of Proceedings of the Australian Church Congress* (1898), p. 24.
5. *Diocesan News* (Grafton-Armidale Diocese, 13 July 1904).
6. Rev R. Bavin, *Official Address and Ordination Charge 1903–04* (Sydney: Epworth, n.d.), p. 4.
7. Rev J. Fordyce, *Some Spiritual Ideals and Aspirations of the New Century* (Sydney: Christian World Publishing House, 1900).
8. *Methodist* (30 May 1903).
9. *Church Standard* (30 March 1901).
10. *Church Commonwealth* (27 February 1902).
11. *Church Standard* (5 May 1900).
12. Rev J. Fordyce, *A.C.W.* (23 May 1902).
13. "H", *Methodist* (11 June 1904).
14. Rev J. Macauley, *Modern Religious Life* (Sydney: H. J. Dunn and Co., 1908), p. 10.
15. *A.C.W.* (9 March 1900).
16. O. Chadwick, *The Victorian Church*, Part 2 (London: Adam and Charles Black, 1970), pp. 423–25; R. Lloyd, *The Church of England 1900–1965* (London: SCM Press Ltd, 1966), pp. 68–82.
17. *A.C.W.* (24 August 1900).
18. *Australasian Independent* (15 May 1902); *Methodist* (27 April 1901).
19. *Presbyterian* (6 July 1899).
20. *Presbyterian* (July–August 1900).
21. *Messenger* (16 January 1903).
22. Rev J. Walker, *Some Urgent Church Problems* (Sydney: Angus and Robertson, 1902), p. 28.
23. *Church Commonwealth* (31 January 1907).
24. *Australasian Independent* (18 November 1899).
25. *Australasian Independent* (1 December 1906).
26. *N.S.W. Methodist Conference* (1903), statistical returns.
27. "Methodist Papers" (M.L.), item 477, "Singleton Circuit Minute Book 1895–1916" (9 January 1902).
28. *N.S.W. Methodist Conference* (1903), p. 205.
29. *N.S.W. Methodist Conference* (1904), pp. 139–40.
30. *Australasian Methodist Conference* (1904), p. 60.
31. *Methodist* (25 June and 24 September 1904).
32. *Daily Telegraph* (7 July 1900). The articles are reprinted in "Anglicanus", *The Anglican Church in New South Wales: Its Position and Prospects* (Sydney: William Brooks and Co., 1900).
33. *Messenger* (17 April 1903); *A.C.W.* (6 June 1902).
34. *Messenger* (24 August 1906).
35. *A.C.W.* (26 April 1901).
36. *Messenger* (29 June 1906).
37. It is my view that J. D. Bollen, who admirably traced the influence of the social gospel in his *Protestantism and Social Reform in New South Wales 1890–1910* (Melbourne: Melbourne University Press, 1972), has overestimated the impact of this new thought at this time in New South Wales; see chapter 7.
38. *Daily Telegraph* (20 October 1899).
39. Beale, *Souvenir of the Official Year*, pp. 9–11.

40.   Rev W. G. Taylor, *Methodist* (2 March 1907); Rev J. Paynter, *Baptist* (1 November 1904).

41.   Canon (later Archdeacon) F. B. Boyce, *Fourscore Years and Seven: The Memoirs of Archdeacon Boyce* (Sydney: Angus and Robertson, 1934), pp. 80 –81; Rev J. E. Carruthers, "A Half-Century's Retrospect", newspaper extracts in M.L.

42.   *Methodist* (29 April 1899).

43.   *N.S.W. Presbyterian Assembly* (1904), pp. 164–67.

44.   *Church Standard* (3 November 1900).

45.   "Report of the Synod Committee on Sydney Church Extension", *Sydney Synod* (1901), p. 97.

46.   Ibid., pp. 97–102.

47.   Rev J. E. Carruthers, *Suburban Methodism* (Sydney: Epworth, 1901), for private circulation only.

48.   *Report of the Sustentation and Home Mission Society of the Methodist Church of Australasia in New South Wales 1904*, p. 7.

49.   *Newcastle Synod* (1904), p. 16.

50.   "Congregational Papers" (M.L.) Box 10, "Home Mission Board Superintendent's Reports" (May 1904), pp. 40–41.

51.   *New South Wales Bush Missionary Society Messenger* (17 August 1909).

52.   H. E. Cooper, "Obstacles to Religion in Australia Arising from the Conditions of Australian Life in the Country", *Australian Church Congress* (1906), pp. 52–54.

53.   Rev W. Robertson, *Outwest for Thirty Years. Notes of a Ministry in the Real Australia* (Sydney: W. C. Penfold and Co. Ltd., 1920), p. 60.

54.   J. Roe, "Challenge and Response: Religious Life in Melbourne in 1876–1886", *Journal of Religious History* 5 no. 2 (December 1968): 149–66.

55.   *Baptist* (1 November 1901).

56.   *Australasian Independent* (16 November 1901).

57.   Quoted by Rev D. Smith, *Presbyterian* (3 January 1906).

58.   *Australian Churchman* (19 April 1902).

59.   *Presbyterian* (17 April 1902).

60.   *S.M.H.* (14 April 1903).

61.   *S.M.H.* (25 April 1903).

62.   *Methodist* (25 April 1903).

63.   Canon M. Archdall, *The Analytical Higher Criticism of the Old Testament* (Sydney: W. M. Madgwick and Sons, 1903).

64.   *Messenger* (22 May 1903).

65.   *Australian Churchman* (2 May 1903).

66.   A. M. Ramsey, *From Gore to Temple: The Development of Anglican Theology, Between Lux Mundi and the Second World War 1889–1939* (London: Longmans, Green and Co. Ltd., 1961).

67.   *S.M.H.* (22 April 1905).

68.   *Daily Telegraph* (28 April 1905).

69.   *S.M.H.* (1 and 20 May 1905).

70.   *Daily Telegraph* (28 April 1905).

71.   *Sydney Synod* (1905), p. 37.

72.   *S.M.H.* (5 May 1905).

73.   *Australasian Independent* (1 July 1905).

74.   *S.M.H.* (8 May 1905); also *Messenger* (28 April and 5 May 1905).

75.   *Methodist* (6 May 1905).

76.   *Daily Telegraph* (6 to 25 May 1905); *S.M.H.* (May 1905).

77.   *Daily Telegraph* (20 May 1905).

78. *S.M.H.* (20 May 1905).
79. "Congregational Papers" (M.L.) Box 12, "Home Mission Board Superinten-dent's Letter Book 1912–1914" (3 and 26 April, 2 May 1912), pp. 36, 59 and 66 respectively.
80. J. Watsford, *Glorious Gospel Triumphs as Seen in My Life and Work in Fiji and Australasia* (London: Charles H. Kelly, 1901), p. 322.
81. *S.M.H.* (20 May 1905).
82. S. N. Hogg, "Balmain, Past and Present" (typescript, 1924, M.L.), p. 260.
83. Rev H. Kelly, *Messenger* (28 April 1905).
84. See the controversy *S.M.H.* (9 May to 12 June 1907).
85. "Methodist Papers", item 593, "Minutes of Examining Committee 1905–1913" (28 May 1908), pp. 138–39.
86. J. H. Trevarthen, letter to editor, *Methodist* (27 May 1905).
87. *Church of England Outlook* (24 October 1903).
88. *Methodist* (29 February 1908).
89. *Census of New South Wales* (1901), p. 233; *Census of the Commonwealth of Australia* (1911), vol. 1, p. 201.
90. *Australian Churchman* (8 March 1902).
91. *Messenger* (13 April 1906).
92. *Messenger* (23 February 1906).

2 THE QUEST FOR MEN AND MONEY

1. Compiled from *Census of New South Wales* (1901), p. 253 and *N.S.W. Statistical Register* (1901), pp. 878–85.
2. See church year books and *Moore's Australian Almanac and Country Directory*, Sydney.
3. R. Lloyd, *The Church of England 1900–1965* (London: SCM Press Ltd, 1966), pp. 75–77.
4. Compiled from the relevant church year books from 1900 to 1930 and *The Methodist Ministerial Index for Australasia* (1903, 1914, 1926 and 1936). For percentage of Australian born see *N.S.W. Statistical Register* (1902), p. 690.
5. *Church Commonwealth* (13 March 1903).
6. *Presbyterian* (7 September 1899).
7. Rev C. A. White, *Presbyterian* (21 June 1900); *Methodist* (10 August 1901).
8. *Messenger* (3 April 1903).
9. *S.M.H.* (30 September 1907).
10. *New South Wales Public Service List* (1908), especially pp. 112–13, 126–29.
11. Rev J. Walker, *The King's Business: Pastoral Addresses on the Work of the Ministry* (Sydney: Angus and Robertson, 1908), p. 155.
12. Ibid., pp. 24–25.
13. Ibid., p. 194.
14. See the images in Steele Rudd's *On Our Selection*, W. T. Goodge, "The Bush Missionary", Thomas Spencer, "Rum and Water", and others.
15. Rev C. H. S. Matthews, *A Parson in the Australian Bush* (London: Arnold, 1908), p. 198.
16. *Australian Churchman* (10 August 1901).
17. *Australian Churchman* (29 September 1906).
18. *Methodist* (19 May 1906).
19. For changes in theological training see especially: Archbishop M. Loane, *A Centenary History of Moore Theological College* (Sydney: Angus and Robert-

son, 1955); L. W. Farr and J. Garrett, *Camden College. A Centenary History* (Sydney: Camden College, 1964); Rev J. Cameron, *Centenary History of the Presbyterian Church in New South Wales* (Sydney: Angus and Robertson, 1905); A. C. Prior, *Some Fell on Good Ground. A History of the beginnings and development of the Baptist Church in New South Wales, Australia 1835– 1965* (Sydney: Baptist Union of New South Wales, 1966).

20. Compiled from the relevant church year books from 1900 to 1930 and *The Methodist Ministerial Index for Australasia* (1903, 1914, 1926 and 1936). For fuller details see appendix 14 in R. Broome "Protestantism in New South Wales Society 1900–1914", (Ph.D. thesis, University of Sydney 1974).

21. *Methodist* (24 October 1903, 15 April 1905).

22. Rev J. Colwell, "The Church Sustentation and Extension Society" (typescript, n.d., M.L.), p. 16.

23. *Methodist* (3 June 1905).

24. *Church Standard* (23 September 1899).

25. *S.M.H.* (2 March 1908); *Messenger* (3 November 1905).

26. A. Trollope, *Australia and New Zealand* 1873, (London: Dawsons of Pall Mall, 1968 reprint), p. 225.

27. Cameron, *Centenary History* p. 190.

28. Rev J. E. Carruthers, *Memories of an Australian Ministry 1868 to 1921* (London: The Epworth Press, 1922), p. 117.

29. Rev R. W. Dale, *Impressions of Australia* (London: Hodder and Stoughton, 1889), p. 241.

30. *Church Commonwealth* (11 April 1901).

31. *Australian Churchman* (6 September 1902); see also *Church of England Outlook* (16 September 1902); *Australian Churchman* (3 June 1905, 7 April 1906).

32. *Australian Baptist* (28 October 1913) and Archdeacon Greer, "Home Missions", *Australian Church Congress* (1906), p. 183, respectively.

33. *Diocesan News* (13 September 1902).

34. *General Synod* (1905), pp. 185–87; *N.S.W. Presbyterian Assembly* (1907), pp. 120–21; *Methodist* (9 and 15 May 1902); *N.S.W. Congregational Year Book* (1904), p. 99; *N.S.W. Baptist Year Book* (1901–02), pp. 17, 39.

35. Cameron, *Centenary History*, pp. 143–44.

36. Rev J. Colwell, "The Passing of a Great Philanthropist" (typescript, M.L.). His assets in 1902 were in excess of £800,000 – *Memorandum and Articles of Association, E. Vickery and Sons Ltd.* (Sydney: F. Cunninghame and Co., 1902).

37. Colwell, "The Church Sustentation and Extension Society", p. 8.

38. *Australasian Methodist Conference* (1904), p. 28; *Messenger* (21 July 1905); *N.S.W. Baptist Year Book* (1910–11), p. 104.

39. *Methodist* (6 May 1905).

40. See my thesis, pp. 116–17, for a detailed analysis of growth which was calculated from the annual church reports and directories and also Rev W. L. Patison *Congregational Home Missions in N.S.W. October 1903–September 1928. A Superintendent's Review and Impressions* (Sydney, 1929); Prior, *Some Fell on Good Ground,* for list of Baptist churches and their foundations, pp. 260– 312.

3. PASTORAL CARE IN THE SLUMS AND THE BUSH

1. T. A. Coghlan, *The Wealth and Progress of New South Wales, 1900–01* (Sydney: Government Printer, 1902), p. 522.
2. Quoted in C. M. H. Clark, *Select Documents in Australian History 1851–1900* (Sydney: Angus and Robertson, 1955), vol. 2, p. 676.
3. B. K. de Garis, "1890–1900", in *A New History of Australia*, ed. F. K. Crowley (Melbourne: Heinemann, 1974), p. 225.
4. "Prices, Purchasing Power of Money, Wages, Trade Unions, Unemployment, and General Industrial Conditions, 1914–1915", *Labour and Industrial Branch, Report No. 6, Commonwealth Bureau of Census and Statistics* (Melbourne: Government Printer, 1916), pp. 16, 25–27; C. Foster, "Australian Unemployment", *Economic Record* 41, no. 95 (September 1965): 429; P. G. McCarthy, "Wages in Australia 1891 to 1914", *Australian Economic History Review* 10, no. 1 (March 1970): 67, 74–76; *S.M.H.* (25 February and 29 April 1902).
5. *Report on the Working of the Factories and Shops Act, Conciliation and Arbitration Act and Early Closing Act During the Year 1900. N.S.W.P.P.* (1901), vol. 6, pp. 711–46; M. Cannon, *Life in the Cities* (Melbourne: Nelson, 1975), chaps. 16–17.
6. B. Kingston, *My Wife, My Daughter and Poor Mary Anne* (Melbourne: Nelson, 1975), chap. 3.
7. F. Adams, *The Australians: A Social Sketch* (London: T. Fisher Unwin, 1893), p. 31.
8. H. Moran, *Viewless Winds. Being the Recollections and Digressions of an Australian Surgeon* (London: Peter Davis, 1939), p. 18.
9. *N.S.W. Statistical Register* (1902), p. 712; and (1910), p. 938.
10. *Report of the Royal Commission on Alleged Chinese Gambling and Immorality and Charges of Bribery Against Members of the Police Force, N.S.W.P.P.* (1891–92), vol. 8, pp. 467–90.
11. W. M. Hughes, *Crusts and Crusades* (Sydney: Angus and Robertson, 1948), pp. 174–75.
12. Jackson, "Owner Occupation of Houses in Sydney, 1871–1891", *Australian Economic History Review* 10, no. 2 (September 1970): 141.
13. N. Hicks, "Demographic Transition in the Antipodes. Australian Population Structure and Growth, 1891–1911", *Australian Economic History Review* 14, no. 2 (September 1974): 123–42.
14. L. C. Rodd, *A Gentle Shipwreck* (Melbourne: Nelson, 1975), especially pp. 25–26, 50–55.
15. *Report of the Royal Commission of Inquiry into the Question of the Constitution of a Greater Sydney, N.S.W. P.P.* (1913), 2nd session, vol. 2, pp. 411–13.
16. H. Lawson, "Faces in the Street", in *Henry Lawson: Autobiographical and other Writings 1887–1922*, ed. C. Roderick (Sydney: Angus and Robertson, 1972), pp. 69–73, 204–214.
17. *Second Report of the Royal Commission on Public Charities, N.S.W.P.P.* (1898), 2nd session, vol. 3, p. 414.
18. *N.S.W. Statistical Register* (1904), pp. 472–3; Coghlan, *Wealth and Progress of New South Wales, 1900–01*, pp. 525–35.
19. *Report from the Select Committee on Old Age Pensions, N.S.W.P.P.* (1896), vol. 5, p. 68.
20. Moran, *Viewless Winds*, p. 6.
21. Report of the "Centennial Church Extension Fund", *Sydney Synod* (1900), p. 133.

22. Canon F. B. Boyce, *Fourscore Years and Seven: The memoirs of Archdeacon Boyce*, (Sydney: Angus and Robertson, 1934), p. 93.
23. "Report of the Synod Committee on Sydney Church Extension", *Sydney Synod* (1901).
24. *Australian Churchman* (31 May 1902).
25. *Australian Churchman* (25 October 1902).
26. *Australian Churchman* (16 April 1904).
27. *Australian Churchman* (26 May 1906 and 31 July 1909); *Glimpses of the Work of the Mission Zone Fund in the Crowded and Congested Parts of Sydney* (Sydney: Genet Bros., n.d.), p. 1.
28. *Australian Churchman* (14 September 1901).
29. *Church Commonwealth* (26 September 1901); *Sydney Synod* (1903), p. 59.
30. *Home Mission (formerly Church) Society Report* (1913), p. 24.
31. *Glimpses of the Work of the Mission Zone Fund*, p. 3.
32. *Home Mission Society Report* (1913), pp. 26–27.
33. Rodd, *A Gentle Shipwreck*, p. 28.
34. Quoted in B. G. Judd, *He That Doeth. The Life Story of Archdeacon R. B. S. Hammond, O.B.E.* (London: Marshall Morgan and Scott, 1951), p. 57.
35. Ibid., p. 51.
36. *Church Society Report* (1905), p. 19.
37. *Australian Churchman* (28 May 1910).
38. Rev W. G. Taylor, *The Life-story of an Australian Evangelist. With an Account of the Origins and Growth of the Sydney Central Methodist Mission* (London: The Epworth Press, 1920), p. 246.
39. *Methodist* (12 September 1903).
40. *Methodist* (27 May 1905 and 7 July 1906).
41. *Methodist* (5 May 1906).
42. "Methodist Papers", item 34, "Balmain West End Quarterly Meeting Minutes, 1902–1917" (16 October 1912).
43. *Methodist* (23 June 1906).
44. *Methodist* (27 April 1907).
45. *N.S.W. Presbyterian Assembly* (1906), pp. 147–48.
46. *Australian Presbyterian Assembly* (1902), p. 66.
47. *Messenger* (22 May 1903), and Rev J. Walker, *The King's Business: Pastoral Addresses on the Work of the Ministry* (Sydney: Angus and Robertson, 1908), p. 54.
48. *N.S.W. Presbyterian Assembly* (1905), p. 97.
49. *Messenger* (19 May 1905).
50. *Baptist* (1 July 1905).
51. M. Cannon, *Life in the Country* (Melbourne: Nelson, 1973), especially chaps. 5 and 8.
52. W. Evans, ed., *Diary of a Welsh Swagman 1869–1894* (Melbourne: Macmillan, 1975), p. 143.
53. S. Rudd, *On Our Selection* (Sydney: Pacific Books, 1970), p. 43.
54. Evans, ed., *Diary of a Welsh Swagman*, p. 173.
55. *N.S.W. Baptist Year Book* (1909–10), p. 40.
56. "Congregational Papers", Box 10, "Home Mission Board Superintendent's Reports" (March 1904), p. 50.
57. Rev C. H. S. Matthews, *A Parson in the Australian Bush* (London: Edward Arnold, 1908), p. 10.
58. Rev J. Cameron, *Centenary History of the Presbyterian Church in New South Wales* (Sydney: Angus and Robertson, 1905), p. 211.
59. *Methodist* (16 March 1901).

60. *Messenger* (20 October, 10 and 24 November 1905).
61. *Messenger* (30 December 1904).
62. *Messenger* (19 May 1905).
63. *Bush Brother* (July 1908).
64. See *Australian Church Congress* (1902), pp. 39–48, 58; and Matthews, *A Parson in the Australian Bush*, p. 77.
65. *N.S.W. Methodist Conference* (1906), p. 75.
66. *N.S.W. Presbyterian Assembly* (1907), pp. 75–80.
67. *Baptist* (30 June 1904).
68. Rev R. Robertson, *Outwest for Thirty Years. Notes of a Ministry in the Real Australia* (Sydney: W. C. Penfold and Co. Ltd., 1920), pp. 100–04; Rev S. Brown, *A.C.W.* (12 July 1907); Rev T. Morgan, *Messenger* (14 April to 5 May 1905).
69. Bishop Feetham, "Bush Brotherhoods in Australia", *Missions Overseas*, 8 (1915): 33.
70. *New South Wales Bush Missionary Society Messenger* (17 May 1911).
71. "Congregational Papers", Box 10, "Home Mission Board Superintendent's Reports" (May 1904), p. 49.
72. Certainly Russel Ward in his *The Australian Legend* (Melbourne: Oxford University Press, 1966), pp. 89–94 has viewed this as one of the traits of the bushmen.
73. W. F. Wannan, ed., *With Malice Aforethought: Australian Insults, Invective, Ridicule and Abuse* (Melbourne: Lansdowne, 1973), p. 85.
74. Matthews, *A Parson in the Australian Bush*, chap. 18; Robertson, *Outwest for Thirty Years*, p. 60 and p. 177.
75. H. Lawson, "The Shearers" (1901).
76. *Bush Brother* (October 1911).
77. *Church Commonwealth* (6 February 1902).
78. *Messenger*, (3 May 1907).
79. *N.S.W. Statistical Register* (1900), pp. 688–89; see also A. R. Crane and W. C. Walker, *Peter Board: His Contribution to the Development of Education in New South Wales* (Melbourne: Australian Council for Educational Research, 1957), chap. 9.
80. See for instance the nature of the Presbyterian schools outlined in Cameron, *Centenary History*, pp. 161–69.
81. J. Perry's statement is in *S.M.H.* (23 July 1903); see *S.M.H.* (24 and 27 July and 1 August 1903) for the replies.
82. *Messenger* (31 July 1903).
83. *Daily Telegraph* (28 July 1903).
84. *Report of the Minister for Public Instruction* (1904), p. 20; (1912), p. 82.
85. R. Broome, "Protestantism in New South Wales Society 1900–1914" (Ph.D. thesis, University of Sydney, 1974), appendixes 11–13.
86. *Methodist* (22 January 1910).
87. C. C. Jones, *An Australian Sunday School at Work* (Sydney: Epworth, 1915), p. 50.
88. *N.S.W. Presbyterian Assembly* (1907), p. 102.
89. *Australian Churchman* (18 January 1902).
90. *Messenger* (12 November 1909).
91. *A.C.W.* (8 October 1909).
92. Rev W. H. Wheen, ed., *Child Study. The Archibald Red Book: Being Mr G. Hamilton Archibald's Lectures in Australia in 1912 and other Papers* (Sydney: Australian Christian World, 1912).
93. Statistical tables in *N.S.W. Methodist Conference* (1911 and 1914).

94. *Sydney Synod* (1907), pp. 95–96.
95. Statistical reports were published annually in the November issue of the Christian Endeavour journal, the *Roll Call.*
96. *Proceedings of Christian Endeavour Seventh Australasian Biennial Convention* (1903), p. 11.
97. "Methodist Papers", item 38, "Balmain Central Mission Christian Endeavour Mins. 1913–1915" (16 June 1913).
98. *Messenger* (30 October 1902).

4 MISSIONS AND EVANGELISTS

1.   *N.S.W. Methodist Conference* (1905), p. 49.
2.   Quoted in K. J. Cable, "Protestant Problems in New South Wales in the Mid-Nineteenth Century", *Journal of Religious History* 3, no. 2 (December 1964): 120.
3.   Rev J. Watsford, *Glorious Gospel Triumphs as Seen in My Life and Work in Fiji and Australasia* (London: Charles H. Kelly, 1901), p. 123.
4.   Rev J. E. Carruthers, *Memories of an Australian Ministry 1868 to 1921* (London: The Epworth Press, 1922), p. 86.
5.   Ibid., p. 103.
6.   *Census of New South Wales* (1901), p. 253.
7.   For the Evangelical Council's origins and aims see *A.C.W.* (12 May 1899 and 20 July 1900). For its membership see "Evangelical Council of New South Wales Minute Book" 2 Vols. (M.L.).
8.   *Methodist* (21 September 1901); *S.M.H.* (29 October 1901).
9.   *A.C.W.* (29 November 1901).
10. *Daily Telegraph* (2 December 1901); *Census of New South Wales* (1901), p. 242.
11. *S.M.H.* (30 November 1901).
12. *N.S.W.P.D.* (28 November 1901), vol. 4, p. 3772.
13. *Australasian Independent* (16 January 1902).
14. *Australasian Independent* (16 December 1901).
15. *Presbyterian* (5 December 1901).
16. *Methodist* (8 February 1902).
17. *A.C.W.* (6 December 1901).
18. *Methodist* (30 November 1901).
19. *Australian Churchman* (21 September 1901).
20. *Australian Churchman* (6 September 1902).
21. *Presbyterian* (1 May 1902).
22. *A.C.W.* (23 January 1903); Rev W. G. Taylor, *Life story of an Australian Evangelist. With an Account of the Origins and Growth of the Sydney Central Methodist Mission* (London: The Epworth Press, 1920), p. 262; Rev J. Colwell, "The Passing of a Great Philanthropist" (typescript, M.L.), p. 12.
23. See chapter 2.
24. *Report of the Royal Commission together with Minutes of Evidence and Exhibitions on Mount Kembla Colliery Disaster 31 July 1902, N.S.W.P.P. (L.A.)* (1903), vol. 5, pp. 1–1050.
25. *A.C.W.* (30 October 1902).
26. *Methodist* (28 February 1903).
27. Quoted in Rev J. Colwell, *The Illustrated History of Methodism* (Sydney: William Brookes and Co., 1904), p. 625.

28. "Methodist Papers", item 524, "Wagga Circuit Quarterly Mins. 1874–1919" (9 July 1902) and item 465, "Port Macquarie Circuit Quarterly Mins. 1893–1902" (8 October 1902).

29. "Methodist Papers", item 356, "Grafton District Synod Mins. 1885–1912" (31 October 1902), p. 283.

30. "Methodist Papers", items 497, 477, 303 and 319 respectively; refer to Quarterly minutes for 1902 and 1903.

31. "Methodist Papers", item 341, "Glen Innes Circuit Quarterly Mins. 1883–1905" (21 July 1902).

32. Quoted in Colwell, *History of Methodism*, p. 630.

33. *Presbyterian Record* (30 August 1902).

34. Quoted in A. Richardson, ed., *Dictionary of Christian Theology*, 3rd ed. (London: S.C.M. Press, 1974), p. 74.

35. Quoted in R. H. Thouless, *An Introduction to the Psychology of Religion*, 3rd ed. (Cambridge: Cambridge University Press, 1971), chap. 14.

36. *Methodist* (7 March 1903).

37. Quoted in Colwell, *History of Methodism*, pp. 632–33.

38. Ibid., p. 632.

39. *A.C.W.* (3 October 1902).

40. Thouless, *The Psychology of Religion*, pp.104, 113–15.

41. Colwell, *History of Methodism*, p. 630; *A.C.W.* (19 September 1902).

42. *S.M.H.* (20 November 1902).

43. *Royal Commission to Inquire into the Condition of the Crown Tenants, N.S.W.P.P.* (1901) vol. 4, pp. v–xxv; see also *S.M.H.* (20, 22, 24 and 26 November 1902).

44. *Report of the N.S.W. Drought Relief Lord Mayor's Fund, Sydney* (1904), and *S.M.H.* (27 November 1902).

45. *S.M.H.* (26 November 1902).

46. Rev C. H. S. Matthews, *A Parson in the Australian Bush* (London: Edward Arnold, 1908), p. 191.

47. R. D. Barton, *Reminiscences of an Australian Pioneer* (Sydney: Tyrell's Ltd., 1917), p. 267.

48. *Watchman* (28 June 1902).

49. *Baptist* (1 February 1902).

50. *Messenger* of Willoughby-Gordon Methodist Circuit (1 October 1906).

51. *A.C.W.* (13 August 1902). See the special Torrey-Alexander Mission daily issues of the *A.C.W.*

52. *Methodist* (8 May 1909).

53. *Messenger* (7 May 1909).

54. *A.C.W.* (27 May 1909).

55. Ibid.

56. *S.M.H.* (24 June 1909).

57. *S.M.H.* (15 June 1909).

58. W. W. Sweet, *The Story of Religion in America* (New York: Harper and Row, 1950), p. 347.

59. *Alexander's Enlarged Hymn Book* (Melbourne: T. S. Fitchett, 1912), no. 59.

60. *A.C.W.*, special mission daily issue (16 and 17 June 1909).

61. *A.C.W.*, special mission daily issue (9 June 1909).

62. *Baptist* (1 July 1909).

63. *Methodist* (26 June 1909).

64. *Baptist* (1 July 1909).

65. *Daily Telegraph* (28 and 29 June 1909).

66. See statistics in *N.S.W. Methodist Conference* (1908, 1909 and 1910); *Messen-*

ger (24 September 1909); *Congregationalist* (1 September 1909); *N.S.W. Baptist Year Book* (1909–10), p. 79.

67. *Messenger* (18 June 1909), contains reports from other suburban centres in a similar vein.
68. *A.C.W.*, special mission daily issue (1 June 1909).
69. *A.C.W.* (20 August 1909) and *S.M.H.* (29 June 1909).
70. *Methodist* (25 September 1909).
71. *Newcastle Synod* (1907), p. 17.
72. *Messenger* (1 November 1907); also Report on the Conference on Evangelism, *Congregationalist* (1 November 1912).
73. *Church Commonwealth* (30 June 1911).
74. Rev F. E. Harry, "The Problem of the Outsider", *First Australasian Baptist Congress* (1908), pp. 74–78; Rev F. B. Cowling, "Congregational Papers", Box 10, "Ocean St Woollahra Monthly Deacon's Mins." (28 September 1908).
75. Harry, "The Problem of the Outsider", p. 78.
76. "Evangelical Council of New South Wales, Minute Book", vol. 1 (21 December 1909, 15 November 1910).
77. *A.C.W.* (18 November 1910).
78. *A.C.W.* (9, 16 and 23 December 1910).
79. *A.C.W.* (23 December 1910).
80. *A.C.W.* (9 December 1910).
81. *A.C.W.* (23 December 1910).
82. *A.C.W.* (2 July 1912).
83. *A.C.W.* (15 September 1911).
84. *Methodist* (30 July 1912).
85. *A.C.W.* (15 August 1913) letter.

5 UNITY AND SCHISM WITHIN PROTESTANTISM

1. "Methodist Papers", item 55, "Balmain Sunday School Montague St. Admission Book, 1894–1904". This is the only Sunday school admission book for this period which has apparently survived, but scattered literary evidence supports the trends on interdenominationalism it reveals.
2. *Proceedings of Inter-State Congregational Conference, Brisbane-Ipswich* (1903), p. 72.
3. *Methodist* (13 May 1899); see also Rev J. E. Carruthers, *Memories of an Australian Ministry 1868 to 1921* (London: The Epworth Press, 1922), p. 236.
4. *A.C.W.* (12 May 1899).
5. *A.C.W.* (19 May 1899).
6. "Evangelical Council of New South Wales Minute Book", vol. 1, pp. 88–90, 97–98 in conjunction with *Moore's Australian Almanac and Country Directory* (1904).
7. *Australasian Independent* (15 June 1900).
8. *A.C.W.* (15 May 1925). For an assessment of its work see Rev J. E. Carruthers, "A Half Century's Retrospect", VII, newspaper extracts in M.L.; and *Memories of An Australian Ministry*, pp. 236–38.
9. *S.M.H.* (1 November 1902).
10. *Methodist* (1 November 1902).
11. *A.C.W.* (19 June 1903).
12. On Methodist Union see *Methodist Union. A Symposium* (Melbourne: 1887);

Methodist Union in New South Wales. Report of the Federal Council of N.S.W. for 1895 (Sydney: 1896); W. J. Townsend, *The Story of Methodist Union* (London: Milner and Co., n.d.), p. 201.

13. *S.M.H.* (28 July 1903).

14. *S.M.H.* (13 March 1901); see also Clouston's "Is a Larger Church Union Possible?", *Presbyterian* (21 March 1901).

15. *Australian Presbyterian Assembly* (1901), pp. 42, 47–48.

16. *S.M.H.* (15 March 1901). *N.S.W. Congregational Year Book* (1902), p. 39.

17. *Australian Presbyterian Assembly* (1903), pp. 101–102.

18. *Methodist* (19 March 1904).

19. *Australasian Methodist Conference* (1904), p. 61.

20. Rev F. V. Pratt, *Congregationalism and Union* (Sydney: 1907), p. 14.

21. "Church Federation by a Presbyterian", *A.C.W.* (28 August 1896).

22. *Proceedings of the Inter-State Congregational Conference* (1903), especially the papers by Revs M. L. Johnson, Dr Bevan, and G. Campbell.

23. Reports of the conferences found in *A.C.W.* (3 January 1908) and *General Synod* (1910), pp. 86–90.

24. *A.C.W.* (20 November 1908).

25. *Australasian Methodist Conference* (1907), pp. 75–76; see the debate in *Daily Telegraph* (12 June 1907).

26. *Methodist* (3 August and 9 November 1907).

27. *A.C.W.* (6 March, 20 and 27 November 1908).

28. *Messenger* (26 October, 9 and 23 November, 7 December 1906, and 8 November 1907).

29. *Methodist* (28 May 1910).

30. *Australasian Methodist Conference* (1910), p. 101.

31. *S.M.H.* (6 October 1910).

32. *Report of the Committee on Federation of Churches. Proposed Basis of Doctrine and Scheme of Polity* (Sydney: Samuel E. Lees, Printer, 1911), p. 10.

33. *Methodist* (20 May 1911).

34. *A.C.W.* (14 April and 12 May 1911).

35. *Methodist* (February and March 1911); *Congregationalist* (1 April 1911).

36. *Congregationalist* (1 November 1911).

37. "Congregational Papers", Box 12, "Ministerial Sec. of Congregational Union Letter Book 1910–1913" (15 August 1912), pp. 406–408.

38. *N.S.W. Presbyterian Assembly* (1912), pp. 56–58.

39. *Australasian Methodist Conference* (1913), p. 113.

40. *A.C.W.* (8 November 1912).

41. *Congregationalist* (10 March 1913).

42. Articles by Carruthers, *Methodist* (29 October 1910) and *A.C.W.* (8 November 1912). H. E. Wooton letter to *A.C.W.* (7 July 1911).

43. *Congress on Union of Churches Report* (Melbourne: 1914).

44. *Daily Telegraph* (27 July 1912) printed an interview with Dr Gordon, principal of Queen's University, Kingston, Canada.

45. See chapter 7.

46. Rev J. Cameron, *Centenary History of the Presbyterian Church in New South Wales* (Sydney: Angus and Robertson, 1905), p. 246.

47. *Souvenir of the Presidency of Rev J. Penman*, (Sydney: Epworth Press, 1908), p. 4.

48. Rev J. Walker, *The King's Business: Pastoral Addresses on the Work of the Ministry* (Sydney: Angus and Robertson, 1908), p. 244.

49. Rev J. D. McCaughey, "Church Union in Australia", *Ecumenical Review* 17, no. 1 (January 1965): 49.

50. A. M. Ramsey, *From Gore to Temple: The Development of Anglican Theo-*

logy, Between Lux Mundi and the Second World War 1889–1939 (London: Longmans, Green and Co. Ltd., 1961), pp. 3–9.

51.   R. Lloyd, *The Church of England 1900–1965* (London: SCM Press Ltd., 1966), pp. 126–27.

52.   O. Chadwick, *The Victorian Church,* part II, (London: Adam and Charles Black, 1970) p. 355.

53.   *Church Commonwealth* (18 April 1901).

54.   *Australian Churchman* (20 April 1901, 25 February and 14 October 1905).

55.   *Church Commonwealth* (2 January 1902).

56.   *Daily Telegraph* (26 November 1907).

57.   *Church Standard* (30 September 1899).

58.   *Australian Churchman* (5 August 1905).

59.   *Church Commonwealth* (25 July 1910).

60.   *S.M.H.* (29 April 1905).

61.   K. J. Cable, *A Short Story of Historic St. James', Sydney* (Sydney: St. James' Church, 1963), pp. 11–12.

62.   *S.M.H.* (1 December 1903).

63.   R. Teale, "Party or Principle. The Election to the Anglican See of Sydney in 1889–1890", *Journal of Royal Australian Historical Society,* 55, pt. 2 (June 1969), pp. 141–58.

64.   Canon F. B. Boyce, *Fourscore Years and Seven: The Memoirs of Archdeacon Boyce* (Sydney: Angus and Robertson, 1934), p. 79.

65.   *Church of England Outlook* (21 September 1903).

66.   *Sydney Diocesan Magazine* (1 March 1910).

67.   *Australian Churchman* (29 November 1902).

68.   *A.C.W.* (29 March 1907).

69.   *Australian Churchman* (29 November 1902), letter.

70.   Ibid., letter.

71.   *Watchman* (31 May 1902).

72.   *A.C.W.* (19 May 1899).

73.   *S.M.H.* (1 December 1903).

74.   *A.C.W.* (7 October 1898 and 3 February 1899).

75.   *A.C.W.* (19 May 1899).

76.   *A.C.W.* (4 May 1900).

77.   *Australian Churchman* (23 May 1903).

78.   T. B. McCall, *The Life and Letters of John Stephen Hart* (Sydney: Church of England Information Trust, 1963), pp. 21–22.

79.   *Australian Churchman* (9 April 1910).

80.   *Church of England Outlook* (24 October 1903).

81.   *Church Commonwealth* (1 January 1904); *Australian Churchman* (24 April 1904); *Watchman* (12 September 1903).

82.   Presidential addresses to the Sydney Synod, *A.C.W.* (9 October 1896) and *Church Standard* (23 September 1899).

83.   Presidential address to the Provincial Synod, *Australian Churchman* (10 August 1901).

84.   Presidential address to the Sydney Synod, *A.C.W.* (30 September 1898).

85.   *Sydney Synod* (1904), pp. 64, 66 and 188; *Church Commonwealth* (24 February 1905).

86.   *Church Commonwealth* (24 February 1905).

87.   Ibid.

88.   *Sydney Synod* (1904), appendixes 1 and 41; *The Constitution and Ordinances of the Synod of Diocese of Sydney* (Sydney: By Authority, W. M. Madgwick and Sons, Printers, 1908), p. 439.

89. *Church Commonwealth* (27 November 1903).
90. Rev F. J. Albery, *A Brief Statement with Regard to the Use of The Eucharistic Vestments and The Ornaments Rubric Together with a Few Remarks upon the Privy Council's Judgement* (Sydney: D. S. Ford, Printer, 1903); Canon M. Archdall, *The Vestments of the Church of England. Not the Vestments of the Mass. An Historical Enquiry* (Sydney: Protestant Church of England Union, 1903).
91. *Church Commonwealth* (27 November 1903).
92. *Australian Churchman* (2 January 1904).
93. Ibid.
94. *S.M.H.* (9 February 1904) letter.
95. *Australian Churchman* (3 September 1904).
96. *Australian Churchman* (1 October 1904).
97. G. K. A. Bell, *Randall Davidson. Archbishop of Canterbury,* 3rd. ed., (London Oxford University Press, 1952), pp. 469–73.
98. *Month by Month* of St Andrew's Cathedral (1 May 1909).
99. *Australian Churchman* (24 July 1909), reprinted Wright's speech against vestments at the 1909 York Convocation.
1. *Australian Churchman* (11 December 1899).
2. *S.M.H.* (13 May 1910).
3. *Church Commonwealth* (30 July 1910).
4. *Daily Telegraph* (16 and 18 May 1910) for some of the correspondence.
5. *Daily Telegraph* (11 April 1910).
6. *Australian Churchman* (11 June 1910).
7. *S.M.H.* (11 August 1910).
8. *Australian Churchman* (11 June 1910); *Church Commonwealth* (30 June 1910).
9. Canon W. Hey Sharp, *The Crisis at St James'* (Sydney: Angus and Robertson, 1910).
10. *The Monthly Paper, Christ Church St Laurence* (October 1910, April, June, July, August 1911); L. Allen, *A History of Christ Church, St Laurence* (Sydney: Finn Bros., 1939), pp. 99–108.
11. L. C. Rodd, *John Hope of Christ Church St Laurence* (Sydney: Alpha Books, 1972), pp. 38–41.
12. Boyce, *Fourscore Years and Seven,* pp. 142–43.
13. *Month by Month* of St Andrew's Cathedral (1 May 1909).
14. *Australian Churchman* (23 May 1903).
15. *Church Commonwealth* (22 August 1901).
16. Quoted in Canon M. Archdall, *Liturgical Right and National Wrong* (London: Church Association, 1900), p. 305.
17. *Methodist,* 28 July 1900.

6 SECTARIAN UPROAR 1895–1904

1. *S.M.H.* (2 and 14 January 1901; see also P. Ford, *Cardinal Moran and the A.L.P.* (Melbourne: Melbourne University Press, 1966), pp. 242–43 and R. Ely, *Unto God and Caesar* (Melbourne: Melbourne University Press, 1976), pp. 111–17.
2. M. Weber, *The Sociology of Religion* 1922 (London: Methuen, 1965) intro. T. Parsons, see especially chaps. 13 and 15; R. Niebuhr, *The Social Sources of Denominationalism* 1929 (New York: Meridian Books, 1965), comments on

p. 6 that "the division of the churches closely follows the division of men into the castes of national, racial and economic groups". See also G. Lenski, *The Religious Factor,* revised ed. (New York: Anchor Books, 1963).

3. See the discussion in the introduction.

4. S. G. Firth, "Social Values in the New South Wales Primary School 1880–1914: An Analysis of School Texts", in *Melbourne Studies in Education,* ed. J. W. Selleck (Melbourne: Melbourne University Press, 1970), p. 158.

5. Related by Ms Ged Thompson whose grandmother heard it as a child in Griffith in the early twentieth century. See also I. Turner, *Cinderella Dressed in Yella* (Melbourne: Heinemann Educational Australia, 1969).

6. *S.M.H.* (18 June 1895).

7. *S.M.H.* (24 and 25 June 1895).

8. *S.M.H.* (3 July 1895).

9. *A.C.W.* (4 October 1895).

10. *S.M.H.* (26 June 1899).

11. *Daily Telegraph* (28 June 1899).

12. *Daily Telegraph* (12 July 1899).

13. *Methodist* (29 July 1899).

14. Ibid.

15. Rev E. T. Dunstan, *Protestant Missions in the Pacific: A Reply to Cardinal Moran* (Sydney: Christian World Publishing House, 1899), p. 10.

16. *S.M.H.* (26 July 1899).

17. *Daily Telegraph* (27 July 1899).

18. *Daily Telegraph* (4 September and 7 August 1899 respectively).

19. *S.M.H.* (28 January 1903).

20. *S.M.H.* (10 September 1900).

21. *S.M.H.* (18 September 1900) letter.

22. *S.M.H.* (24 September 1900).

23. *Daily Telegraph* (25 September 1900).

24. *Methodist* (29 September 1900).

25. *S.M.H.* (29 March 1901). For the whole controversy see *S.M.H.* (4 to 15 December 1900 and 12 March to 3 April 1901). Also, C. Pearl, *Wild Men of Sydney* (London: Universal Books 1958), pp. 135–58.

26. *S.M.H.* (19 April 1901) letter.

27. *Methodist* (4 May 1901).

28. *S.M.H.* (23 May 1901).

29. P. J. O'Farrell, *The Catholic Church in Australia. A Short History, 1788–1967,* (Sydney: Nelson, 1968), p. 177; Ford, *Cardinal Moran and the A.L.P.,* pp. 208–218; J. D. Bollen, *Protestantism and Social Reform in New South Wales 1890–1910* (Melbourne: Melbourne University Press, 1972), p. 145.

30. P. J. O'Farrell, *The Catholic Church in Australia,* chap. 4.

31. See O'Farrell's interpretation of Moran's 1897 candidature for the federal convention, ibid., p. 173.

32. Fr E. O'Brien, "Cardinal Moran's Part in Public Affairs", *Journal of Royal Australian Historical Society,* 28, pt. 1 (1942): 27.

33. Fr J. M. Mahon "Cardinal Moran's Candidature", *Manna* 6 (1963); 64.

34. *S.M.H.* (15 January 1901) letter.

35. *S.M.H.* (21 May 1901).

36. *A.C.W.* (24 May 1901).

37. *S.M.H.* (27 July 1901).

38. J. Waldersee, *Catholic Society in New South Wales 1788–1860,* (Sydney: Sydney University Press, 1974), chap. 1.

39. Cardinal P. F. Moran, *History of the Catholic Church in Australia,* 2 vols., (Sydney: Oceanic Publishing Co., 1895), especially pp. 24–25.

40. Fr P. Dowling, "Some Dangers and Difficulties of Australian Catholics", *Proceedings of the Third Australasian Catholic Congress* (1909), p. 112. See also Dean Hegarty, "A Plea for a Catholic Truth Society in Australia", *Proceedings of the Third Australasian Catholic Congress* (1905), pp. 592–98.
41. "James the less", *A.C.W.* (17 September 1909).
42. *S.M.H.* (1 March 1902).
43. Fr Francis quoted in R. J. C. Ferguson, *Cardinal Moran's Church in New South Wales* (Sydney: The Watchman Newspaper Ltd., 1909), p. 157.
44. Bishop P. Delaney, "The Relation of the Church to the Non-Catholic World in Australia", *Proceedings of the First Australasian Catholic Congress* (1900), p. 142.
45. *A.C.W.* (14 October 1904).
46. *Watchman* (1 February 1902).
47. *Watchman* (20 September 1902).
48. "A.O.P." in *Church Commonwealth* (27 March 1902).
49. *Daily Telegraph* (1 June 1904).
50. Computated from the *New South Wales Public Service List* (1903–1905).
51. *Church Commonwealth* (28 November 1901).
52. *S.M.H.* (15 August 1902).
53. *Watchman* (4 October 1902).
54. *S.M.H.* (27 November 1902) letter.
55. "James the less", *A.C.W.* (22 November 1912).
56. "Methodist Papers", item 497, "Manning River Quarterly Meeting Mins. 1901–1924" (6 July 1901), p. 10.
57. *N.S.W.P.P. (L.A.)* (1902), vol. 2, pp. 415–16.
58. *S.M.H.* (28 September 1905).
59. See reports, *S M.H.* (15 September to 28 September 1905), and *Report from the Select Committee on an Allegation by the Rev W. Woolls Rutledge Respecting an Appointment to the Public Service*, *N.S.W.P.P. (L.A.)* (1905), vol. 2, pp. 195–243.
60. *Methodist* (9 December 1905); Rev F. H. McGowan, "The Rev W. Woolls Rutledge", *Australasian Methodist History Society Journal* 6, p. 3 (April 1938): 292.
61. Rev J. E. Carruthers, *Memories of an Australian Ministry 1868 to 1921* (London: The Epworth Press, 1922), p. 140.
62. A. L. Kenny, "On Catholic Registration", *Proceedings of the First Australasian Catholic Congress* (1900), p. 200.
63. O'Farrell, *The Catholic Church in Australia*, p. 192.
64. J. C. Watson in *Commonwealth Parliamentary Debates* (4 March 1904), vol. 18, p. 144; and Sir William Lyne in *Watchman* (26 December 1903).
65. *Watchman* (31 October 1903). The report at least third hand via Ireland was probably at error, rather than Moran himself.
66. V. Jansen, "The Social Background of the Members of the New South Wales Legislative Assembly 1901–1959", 3 vols., (M.Ec. thesis, University of Sydney, 1962), pp. 127–28.
67. See letters to *Daily Telegraph* (10 and 12 March 1903).
68. *S.M.H.* (3 March 1903).
69. *Daily Telegraph* (9 March 1903).
70. Jansen, "The Social Background of the Members of the New South Wales Legislative Assembly 1901–1959", pp. 127–28.
71. O'Farrell, *The Catholic Church in Australia*, p. 192.
72. *Methodist* (29 April and 29 July 1905); *Messenger* (24 February and 23 June 1905); *Australian Churchman* (25 March and 8 April 1905); and letters in *S.M.H.* (15, 17, 20, 21 and 25 March 1905).

73. *S.M.H.* (26 July 1905).
74. See A. E. Cahill, "Catholics and Socialism – The 1905 Controversy in Australia", *Journal of Religious History*, 1, no. 2 (December 1960): 88–101.
75. *Methodist* (25 May 1901); and *Daily Telegraph* (25 September 1900).
76. Sermons by Rev A. White and Rev W. Allen in *A.C.W.* (14 August 1903 and 14 November 1902 respectively).
77. *S.M.H.* (14 July 1902).
78. *Watchman* (29 August 1903 and 9 January 1904).
79. J. Britten, *The Slatterys* (Melbourne: "The Advocate" office, 1899), p. 13.
80. *Watchman* (21 June and 12 July 1902).
81. Cardinal P. F. Moran, *Address to the Admiral, Officers and Men of the American Fleet* (Sydney: Catholic Book Depot, 1908): see *A.C.W.* (11 and 18 September 1908) for the Protestant shocked reaction to this.
82. Canon F. B. Boyce, *Empire Day* (Sydney: The British Empire League in Australia, 1921).
83. The allegations printed in the *Watchman* (20 June to 11 July 1903) were reprinted in a pamphlet entitled *Convent Horrors*. See the *Report Respecting the Management of the Roman Catholic Orphanage, Manly* in *N.S.W.P.P. (L.A.)* (1904), 2nd session, vol. 2, pp. 901–910.
84. *Watchman* (22 and 29 August 1903).
85. Convent launderies being on church property were exempt from such overheads as land and water rates. See the pamphlet of the Australian Protestant Defence Association, *Respecting Charitable Launderies and Institutions* (Sydney: A.P.D.A., 1906).
86. *A.C.W.* (15 February 1901).
87. C. Fetherstonhaugh, "My Religious Experiences" (typescript, M.L.).
88. Quoted in *Life Story of W. M. Dill Macky D.D.* (Sydney: 1904) held in Susannah Dill Stevenson family papers (M.L.).
89. *A.C.W.* (15 January 1909).
90. See reports and reprints of his sermons in *A.C.W.* (15 January 1909 and 9 September 1910); *Messenger* (16 August 1907).
91. *A.C.W.* (7 June 1907); see also *S.M.H.* (9, 10, 11, 16 and 30 May and 12 June 1907).
92. "E.H.", *A.C.W.* (9 September 1910).
93. For biographical information see Susannah Dill Stevenson family papers (M.L.) and my forthcoming article in *Australian Dictionary of Biography*, 1891–1939.
94. *S.M.H.* (13 January 1903).
95. Susannah Dill Stevenson (Dill Macky's oldest daughter) in her manuscript reminiscences written in 1952, p. 23, Susannah Dill Stevenson family papers, (M.L.).
96. *S.M.H.* (12 October and 14 December 1904). The Presbytery amended the motion to read that as Ferguson was holidaying at the time it was an acceptable unofficial visit.
97. *A.C.W.* (15 January 1909).
98. Delaney, "The Relation of the Church to the Non-Catholic World in Australia", p. 142.
99. *S.M.H.* (22 June 1901).
1.   The *Watchman*'s directors were A.J.C. Wood, funeral director, office holder in the Druids, the Oddfellows and the Masons, and a Balmain resident, *The Cyclopedia of N.S.W.* (McCarron, Stewart and Co., 1907), p. 666; J. Wheeler, J.P., former Mayor of Petersham, and former M.L.A. for Canterbury R.G.W.M. of L.O.L. of N.S.W. 1894–1899, general manager of Newcastle-Wallsend Coal

Co., *The Cyclopedia of N.S.W.*, p. 491; J. P. Josephson, former engineer in Department of Public Works, consultant after 1896, obituary, *Journal of Royal Society of New South Wales* 46 (1912): 12–13; and T. B. Watt, a member of Scot's church.

2. *Watchman* (24 January 1903).
3. *S.M.H.* (13 October 1902).
4. *S.M.H.* (14 October 1902).
5. *Watchman* (31 January 1903).
6. See the reports of branch formations, *Watchman* (October 1902 to May 1903).
7. *S.M.H.* (16 October 1903).
8. *Watchman* (28 February and 7 March 1903).
9. *Watchman* (7 March 1903).
10. Both *Daily Telegraph* and *S.M.H.* (28 March 1903); see Dill Macky's account in *Watchman* (4 April 1903).
11. Both *Daily Telegraph* and *S M.H.* (30 March 1903); *Watchman* (14 April 1903).
12. *Watchman* (4 and 25 April 1903).
13. Calculated from *New South Wales Census* (1901), pp. 251–52.
14. *S.M.H.* (2 April 1903) letter F. Neeld.
15. *S.M.H.* (30 March 1903).
16. *Watchman* (21 and 28 November 1903).
17. *Watchman* (6 December 1902).
18. *Watchman* (21 February 1903).
19. These are the findings of an extensive search of Protestant journals which form part of work in progress on the A.P.D.A. Unfortunately the offices of the *Watchman* were burnt around 1910 and all the branch records were destroyed.
20. *Watchman* (28 November 1903).
21. *S.M.H.* (12 June 1907) letter Dill Macky; *Methodist* (19 March 1904).
22. M. Lyons, "Aspects of Sectarianism in New South Wales Circa 1865 to 1880" (Ph.D. thesis, A.N.U., 1972), pp. 285–89.
23. *Watchman* (2 January 1904).
24. *Watchman* (16 January 1904).
25. *S.M.H.* (27 April 1903) for a copy of the L.R.A. Party manifesto.
26. *Watchman* (16 July 1904).
27. *S.M.H.* (23 April and 4 July 1904).
28. *S.M.H.* (16 July 1904).
29. *Watchman* (13 August 1904).
30. For the machinations behind this alliance see J. D. Bollen, "The Temperance Movement and the Liberal Party in New South Wales Politics, 1900–1904", *Journal of Religious History* 1, no. 3 (June 1961): 160–82.
31. *S.M.H.* (23 May 1904).
32. W. Affleck, *Reminiscences from Infancy to Present Day* (Sydney: R. Dey, Son and Co., 1916), p. 71.
33. *S.M.H.* (1 December 1904).
34. Though now missing, this minute book was used by M. B. Marshall in her "Some Aspects of the Australian Protestant Defence Association 1901–1904" (Government III hons. thesis, University of Sydney, 1961).
35. *S.M.H.* (18 October 1913).
36. *S.M.H.* (17 June 1902).

7 WOWSERISM TRIUMPHANT 1904–1910

1. J. D. Bollen, *Protestantism and Social Reform in New South Wales 1890–1910* (Melbourne: Melbourne University Press, 1972), especially p. 135; see also my comments on Bollen's views in chapter one above.
2. *Methodist* (1 June 1901).
3. J. D. Bollen, "The Temperance Movement and the Liberal Party in New South Wales Politics, 1900–1914, *Journal of Religious History* 1, no. 3 (June 1961).
4. A. Summers, *Damned Whores and God's Police* (Ringwood, Victoria: Penguin, 1975), especially pp. 358–70.
5. *Australian Churchman* (20 October 1906).
6. For a good general account of the 1890s see B. de Garis, "1890–1900", in *A New History of Australia,* ed. F. K. Crowley (Melbourne: Heinemann, 1974), pp. 216–59.
7. See my earlier discussion of this in chapter 3 above.
8. B. Shaw, preface to *Saint Joan* (Harmondsworth, Middlesex: Penguin, 1964), p. 36.
9. *Methodist* (6 July 1907).
10. *St Paul's Parish Paper* Burwood (October 1905).
11. *S.M.H.* (23 October 1902).
12. *Methodist* (6 July 1907).
13. Rev J. A. Soper, *Straight Talks, A Bundle of Arrows Meant to Hit* (Sydney: Christian World Publishing House, 1899), p. 93.
14. *Messenger* (24 July 1908).
15. *Baptist* (1 March 1911).
16. Rev W. Allen, *At Starting: Plain and Friendly Words for Beginners in the Christian Life* (Sydney: Christian World Publishing House, 1900), pp. 11–12.
17. *S.M.H.* (8 November 1910).
18. *A.C.W.* (26 October 1906).
19. See J. D. Bollen's useful discussion of this question in *Religion in Australian Society. An Historian's View*, Leigh College open lectures, Winter Series (Sydney: Leigh College, 1973), lectures 3 and 4.
20. *Methodist* (10 November 1900).
21. S. Rudd, *On Our Selection* (Sydney: Pacific Books, 1970), p. 43.
22. *Messenger* (5 May 1905).
23. *A.C.W.* (30 November 1900).
24. *A.C.W.* (20 January 1905).
25. United declaration of the Protestant churches on Sunday observance, in *Australian Churchman* (23 November 1907).
26. Memo to Inspector-General of Police (5 July 1900), C.S. 00/7142, Box 5269.
27. *S.M.H.* (31 May 1900).
28. *S.M.H.* (29 November 1900); *Daily Telegraph* (28 November 1900).
29. Memo to Inspector-General of Police (6 February 1902), C.S. (no file number) Box 5269.
30. *S.M.H.* (4, 8 and 9 November 1910); see also fruitless deputation of clergy to Labour Chief Secretary, D. MacDonnell, *Daily Telegraph* (7 December 1910).
31. *S.M.H.* (3 November 1910). The Inspector-General of Police, J. Gavin actually released a very liberal interpretation of MacDonnel's original minute to the press. See R. Broome, "Protestantism in New South Wales Society 1900–1914" (Ph.D. thesis, University of Sydney, 1974), pp. 470–73.
32. Chief Secretary's minute 24 March 1915, C.S. (no file number), Box 5403.
33. Ibid., minute no. 425 (1 September 1916), which modified the Sunday Trading (Refreshment Rooms) Act 1916.

34.   Quoted in C. Pearl, *Wild Men of Sydney* (London: Universal Books, 1970), pp. 113–14. For an interpretation of the word's origins and its meanings see K. Dunstan, *Wowsers* (Sydney: Angus and Robertson, 1974), chap. 1.

35.   H. Moran, *Viewless Winds. Being the Recollections and Digressions of an Australian Surgeon* (London: Peter Davis, 1939), p. 15.

36.   Report on Lane by Sub-Inspector of No. 2 Police Station, Sydney (18 February 1904), C.S. 04/1104, Box 5269.

37.   Lane wrote seven letters to the Chief Secretary between November 1902 and August 1903; see C.S. Box 5269.

38.   Ibid., letters 1 June 1903 and 25 January 1904.

39.   Ibid., letters C.S. 05/6838 and 05/4504.

40.   Ibid., C.S. 01/908 revealed that of the 808 Sydney shopkeepers observed trading illicitly (but not charged) on the Sunday prior to 20 September 1901, 586 were British, 106 were other foreign born and 116 were Italian. However, C.S. 05/7917, listing convictions (and prior offences of those convicted) between 1 January and 7 May 1905, reveals that 8 shopkeepers with "British" names had been convicted a total of twenty-one times, an average of two and a half convictions each, and at an average of 4/- for their last fine; whereas 20 shopkeepers with southern European names had been convicted a total of 104 times, an average of over five times each, and at an average of £1 for their last fine.

41.   *N.S.W.P.D.,* (4 July 1905) vol. 18, p. 523.

42.   Memo to Superintendent of Police, West Maitland (31 August 1909), C.S. 10/941, Box 5269.

43.   *Methodist* (10 November 1900).

44.   Rev G. Campbell Morgan, *Baptist* (15 September 1903).

45.   *N.S.W. Methodist Conference* (1906), p. 50.

46.   *A.C.W.* (8 July 1910).

47.   *A.C.W.* (21 April 1911).

48.   *Australian Churchman* (29 June 1907).

49.   T. A. Coghlan, *The Wealth and Progress of New South Wales, 1900–1901* (Sydney: Government Printer, 1902), pp. 972, 977.

50.   *A.C.W.* (22 July 1904).

51.   "Congregational Papers", Box 12, "Ministerial Secretary of the N.S.W. Congregational Union Letter Book 1908–1910", pp. 402–12, 427–28, 436; and "Letter Book 1910–1913", pp. 30–31, 168–70, 211–12.

52.   Coghlan, *Wealth and Progress of New South Wales,* pp. 989, 991.

53.   Petition from Women's Political Educational League, *N.S.W.P.P. (L.A.) (1905), vol. 2, p. 113.*

54.   *See N.S.W. State Archives A.G.J. Box 7747.*

55.   *Methodist* (4 November 1899); *Australian Churchman* (11 January 1902); Congregationalist (11 September 1913).

56.   Reported in *Roll Call* (1 July 1899).

57.   See minutes of Evangelical Council deputation of 28 February 1906, C.S. 06/4555 and correspondence from Public Morals Association, C.S. 07/23877 and Treasury file no. C926, in C.S. Box 4/966.

58.   "V.S.", *Australian Churchman* (2 January 1909).

59.   Letters to Carruthers (18 August and 9 September 1906), "Carruthers Papers" Box 11(28).

60.   A. C. Wilson, *Letter to a Girl* (Sydney: White Cross League, n.d.).

61.   Ibid. See also anonymous, *Chastity and Health*, (Sydney: White Cross League n.d.); and Dr R. Arthur, *The Choice between Purity and Impurity: An Appeal to Young Men* (Sydney: White Cross League, n.d.), both in M.L. pam. file 196/A.

62. V. Cooper Mathieson, *The Woman's White Cross Moral Reform Crusade* (Sydney: White Cross League, n.d.), pp. 17, 7.

63. T. A. Coghlan, *The Decline in the Birth-Rate of New South Wales and other Phenomena of Child Birth: An Essay in Statistics* (Sydney: Government Printer, 1903).

64. For an admirable interpretation of this royal commission see, N. Hicks, *"This Sin and Scandal": Australia's Population Debate 1891–1911* (Canberra: Australian National University Press, 1978).

65. *Royal Commission on the Recent Decline in the Birth-Rate, N.S.W.P.P. (L.A.)* (1904), 2nd session, joint vol. 4, pp. 791–956, especially p. 17 of the report.

66. Reprinted in *Church Commonwealth* (30 November 1905).

67. Rev E. Owen in *S.M.H.* (7 December 1903); see also Archbishop Smith in *Australian Churchman* (1 October 1904).

68. *A.C.W.* (8 April 1904).

69. *S.M.H.* (27 May 1909).

70. *Australian Presbyterian Assembly* (1909), p. lxxiv.

71. *S.M.H.* (20 August 1909).

72. Computated from statistics supplied by government minister without port folio, J. N. Brunker, *N.S.W.P.P. (L.C.)* (1905), vol. 68, p. 114.

73. *N.S.W. Police Department Report* (1900), appendix A, p. 3 in *N.S.W.P.P. (L.A.)*, (1901), vol. 2.

74. Statistics supplied by Canon F. B. Boyce in *Church Standard* (17 June 1899).

75. *N.S.W. Police Department Report* (1904), p. 233 in *N.S.W.P.P. (L.A.)*, (1905), vol. 3, pt. 1.

76. Coghlan, *Wealth and Progress of New South Wales*, p. 260.

77. Compiled from the hotels listed in *Sand's Sydney and Suburban Directory for 1900* (Sydney: John Sands, 1900).

78. *Watchman* (5 July 1902).

79. Rev G. Campbell, *The Drink Traffic: A Social and Political Menace* (Sydney: W. G. Penfold and Co., 1903), p. 8.

80. Ibid., p. 9.

81. Canon F. B. Boyce, *Fourscore Years and Seven: The Memoirs of Archdeacon Boyce* (Sydney: Angus and Robertson, 1934), p. 97.

82. Rev R. B. S. Hammond, *The Curse of Drink in New South Wales* (Sydney: H. Bethel and Co., 1903).

83. *Report from the Select Committee on Tied Houses, N.S.W.P.P. (L.A.)* (1901), vol. 6, p. 4 of report.

84. Rev J. Fordyce, *Aspects of the Temperance Problem* (Sydney: Christian World Publishing House, 1905), p. 11.

85. *N.S.W. Methodist Conference* (1903), p. 50.

86. G. D. Clark, *The Good Templar Movement: Its History and Work* (Sydney: by authority, 1928), p. 49.

87. *S.M.H.* (6 July 1901 and 3 May 1905).

88. Reprinted in *N.S.W. Methodist Conference* (1904), pp. 180–81.

89. *Methodist* (4 March 1905).

90. *Church Commonwealth* (1 April 1901).

91. Moran, *Viewless Winds*, p. 15.

92. *A.C.W.* (5 June and 4 December 1914); Rev J. E. Carruthers, *Memories of an Australian Ministry 1868 to 1921* (London: The Epworth Press, 1922), pp. 237 –38.

93. *Methodist* (21 September 1901).

94. In 1882 twenty-eight per cent voted and in 1900 it had dropped to twenty per cent. *N.S.W. Police Department Report* (1901), *N.S.W.P.P. (L.A.)* (1902), vol.

2, p. 2 of report. For criticisms of the act see *Messenger* (6 February 1903) letter from Canon Boyce; *Methodist* (25 May 1903).

95.   W. Lawson Dash, hon. sec. of N.S.W. Alliance, in *A.C.W.* (2 June 1899). See also Bollen, "The Temperance Movement and the Liberal Party", pp. 166–70.

96.   *S.M.H.* (22 June 1904).

97.   Bollen, "The Temperance Movement and the Liberal Party", p. 170.

98.   Forty-nine per cent were Anglicans, slightly above their state average, and the rest were assorted Protestants and others. V. Jansen, "The Social Background of the members of the New South Wales Legislative Assembly 1901–1959", 3 vols. (M.Ec. thesis, University of Sydney, 1962), p. 421.

99.   *S.M.H.* (17 April 1905).

1.   Quoted in D. Walker, *Dream and Disillusion: A Search for Australian Cultural Identity* (Canberra: Australian National University Press, 1976), p. 19.

2.   *Daily Telegraph* (20 April 1905).

3.   Wade borrowed these books on 6 May 1905 from the parliamentary library and held them on loan till 8 November 1905. Information kindly supplied by researcher Ms Jane Carmichael.

4.   *N.S.W.P.D.,* (10 August 1905) vol. 19, pp. 1394–1410; and (30 October 1905) vol. 20, pp. 2520–34.

5.   *S.M.H.* (4, 15, 19, 20 and 27 October 1905); *Daily Telegraph* (4, 20, 25–27 October 1905).

6.   *N.S.W.P.P. (L.A.)* (1905), vol. 2, pp. 347–65.

7.   Ibid., p. 367.

8.   *N.S.W.P.D.,* (30 October 1905) vol. 20, p. 2591.

9.   *Methodist* (4 November 1905).

10.   *Messenger* (13 April 1906).

11.   Reprinted in *Church Commonwealth* (30 November 1905).

12.   Rev P. J. Stephen, *The Microbe of Gambling: Or What Makes It Wrong?* (Sydney: Watchman Print, n.d.); see also his *The Totalizator: Shall We Legalize it?* (Sydney: New South Wales Christian Endeavour Union, 1900).

13.   *N.S.W. Methodist Conference* (1902), p. 173.

14.   L. Stone, *Jonah* (Sydney: Angus and Robertson, 1972), p. 159.

15.   Quoted in *A.C.W.* (30 October 1903).

16.   *S.M.H.* (4 April 1905).

17.   *S.M.H.* (10 April 1905) letter.

18.   *S.M.H.* (14 April 1905).

19.   *S.M.H.* (24 May 1905).

20.   Stone, *Jonah*, p. 163.

21.   *S.M.H.* (16 and 24 April 1906).

22.   A. J. Kelly in *N.S.W.P.D.,* (7 December 1905) vol. 21, p. 4781. For the short but not sweet debate see pp. 4780–83.

23.   For a report of the incident see *S.M.H.* (16 July 1906); For church opinions see *Australian Churchman* (21 July and 4 August 1906); *Church Commonwealth* (31 July 1906).

24.   *S.M.H.* (25 July 1906).

25.   *N.S.W.P.D.,* (23 August 1906) vol. 23, pp. 1377–80.

26.   Ibid., p. 1434.

27.   This was actually stated during the first reading, *N.S.W.P.D.,* (1 August 1906) vol. 22, p. 828.

28.   *S.M.H.* (2 August 1906 and 31 August 1906).

29.   *Daily Telegraph* (30 August 1906).

30.   *N.S.W.P.D.,* (14 December 1906) vol. 25, pp. 4946–47.

31.   *N.S.W.P.P. (L.A.)* (1906), vol. 2, p. 1350, presented on 4 October 1906.

32.   *Daily Telegraph* (24 November 1906).

33.   C.S. 07/14067, Box 7747. C. G. Wade referred to this in parliament, *N.S.W. P.D.* (29 September 1908), vol. 31, p. 1267.

34.   *Australian Churchman* (27 July and 7, 14 and 21 September 1907). For the manifesto see *S.M.H.* (9 September 1907).

35.   *S.M.H.* (8 December 1905, 10 and 14 August 1906); *Daily Telegraph* (15 December 1905 and 11 July 1907). For the land scandals see H. V. Evatt, *Australian Labour Leader. The Story of W. A. Holman and the Labour Movement*, 2nd ed., (Sydney: Angus and Robertson, 1954), chaps. 21–22.

36.   *S.M.H.* (10 August 1906).

37.   *S.M.H.* (12 March 1907).

38.   *S.M.H.* (18 July 1907).

39.   *S.M.H.* (5 September 1907).

40.   Quoted in Evatt, *Australian Labour Leader*, p. 147.

41.   *Methodist* (21 September 1907).

42.   *S.M.H.* (21 September 1907).

43.   Letter to Premier Carruthers (1 October 1907), "Carruthers Papers", Box 8(28).

44.   Computated from statistics tabulated in *S.M.H.* (14 September 1907) and the local option returns in *N.S.W.P.P. (L.A.)* (1908), 2nd session, vol. 2, pp. 19–58.

45.   Ibid. The figure for "reduction" was 59.6 per cent, just short of the 60 per cent needed for prohibition in that area.

46.   *Daily Telegraph* (17 September 1907).

47.   *N.S.W.P.P. (L.A.)* (1908), 2nd session, vol. 2, pp. 19–53.

48.   *N.S.W. Police Department Report* (1907), in *N.S.W.P.P. (L.A.)* (1908), vol. 1, p. 310.

49.   J. Rowntree and A. Sherwell, *The Temperance Problem and Social Reform* (London: Hodder and Stoughton, 1900), especially pp. ix–x, 367.

50.   *S.M.H.* (6, 7, 8 and 12 June 1907).

51.   See R. Broome, "The Australian Reaction to Jack Johnson, Black Pugilist, 1907–9", in *Sport in History. The Making of Modern Sporting History*, ed. R. Cashman and Michael McKernan (St Lucia, Queensland: University of Queensland Press, 1979).

52.   *S.M.H.* (31 December 1908).

53.   Ibid.

54.   Liquor Trades Defence Union of New South Wales, *The Truth About No-License in New Zealand* (Sydney: by authority 1910) and also, *Prohibition Abroad* (Sydney: by authority 1910).

55.   *Methodist* (16 July 1910); see also Canon F. B. Boyce, *The Case for No-License*, 2nd ed., (Sydney: New South Wales Alliance, 1912); and Presbyterian Temperance Committee, *Is No-License a Failure in New Zealand?* (Sydney: by authority, 1910).

56.   Compiled to the nearest per cent from *S.M.H.* (15 December 1915) and G. D. Clark, *The Good Templar Movement*, p. 199.

57.   Compiled from electoral returns in *N.S.W.P.P.* (1908), 2nd session, vol. 2, pp. 19–58; *N.S.W.P.P.* (1911–1912), joint vol. 3, pp. 41–76; *N.S.W.P.P.* (1915–1916), joint vol. 4, pp. 105–141.

58.   *N.S.W.P.D.* (19 September 1906), vol. 23, p. 2205.

59.   *N.S.W.P.P. (L.A.)* (1908), 2nd session, vol. 2, pp. 19–53; *N.S.W.P.P. (L.A.)* (1911–1912), vol. 3, p. 41; *N.S.W. Statistical Register* (1910), p. 769.

60.   Summers, *Damned Whores and God's Police*, p. 339.

61.   Unlike the earlier flood of protests (eighty-four in 1899 alone) against private member's Totalizator Bills, only two church petitions were sent in 1916, see *N.S.W.P.P. (L.A.)*, (1916), vol. 6, pp. 1117, 1119.

62. Boyce, *Fourscore Years and Seven,* p. 163.
63. *Methodist* (22 October 1910).
64. *Roll Call* (November 1913).

8. CONCLUSION

1. Quoted in R. Bainton, *Here I Stand* (New York: Mentor, 1950), pp. 184–85.
2. See the figures and discussion in R. Broome, "Protestantism and New South Wales Society 1900–1914" (Ph.D. thesis, Sydney University, 1974), pp. 565–. 71.
3. St Clair Donaldson, "Australia", in *Church and Empire*, ed. Rev J. Ellison and Rev G. H. S. Walpole (London: Longmans, Green and Co., 1907) pp. 157–58.

SELECT BIBLIOGRAPHY

GOVERNMENT SOURCES

Printed

Commonwealth of Australia

Census of Commonwealth of Australia for the years 1911 and 1921.
"Prices, Purchasing Power of Money, Wages, Trade Unions, Unemployment, and General Industrial Conditions, 1914–1915". *Labour and Industrial Branch, Report no. 6*. Melbourne: Bureau of Census and Statistics, 1916.

New South Wales

Census of New South Wales for the years 1881, 1891, and 1901.
Legislation Reforms During the Tenure of Office of the Carruthers' Government, 1907.
New South Wales Parliamentary Debates, 1900–1914.
New South Wales Parliamentary Papers, 1900–1914.
New South Wales Public Service List, 1898–1914.
New South Wales Statistical Register, 1897–1916.
Number of Persons Employed of Each of Principal Religious Denominations, 1902.
Report of the Royal Commission on Alleged Chinese Gambling and Immorality and Charges of Bribery Against Members of the Police Force, 1891.
Report from the Select Committee on Old Age Pensions, 1896.
Second Report of the Royal Commission on Public Charities: "Benevolent Society of New South Wales", 1898.
Report on the Working of the Factories and Shops Act, Conciliation and Arbitration Act and Early Closing Act during the year 1900, 1901.
Report of the Royal Commission to Inquire into the Condition of the Crown Tenants, 1901.
Report from the Select Committee on Tied Houses, 1901.
Report of the Royal Commission Together with Minutes of Evidence and Exhibitions on Mount Kembla Colliery Disaster 31 July 1902, 1903.
Report of Assembly Select Committee into Allegations by Rev W. W. Rutledge that Mr Hall, Acting Government Statistician, Unable to Obtain Re-employment Until Joined Roman Catholic Church, 1905.
Report of the Royal Commission for the Improvement of the City of Sydney and Its Suburbs Together with Copy of Commission, Evidence, Appendices and Plans, 1909.
Report of the Royal Commission of Inquiry Respecting the Question of Legalising and Regulating the Use of the Totalizator in N.S.W., Together with Evidence and Appendices, 1912.
Report of the Royal Commission of Inquiry into the Question of the Constitution of a Greater Sydney, 1913.
The Statutes of New South Wales, 1900–1914.

Departmental Records (N.S.W. State Archives)

Attorney General and Justice Special Bundles

"1900, 1905–9. Working of and Amendments to Inebriates Act", nos. 7754–55.
"1904–8. Proposed Amendments to Police Offences Act", no. 7747.
"1905–1912. Neglected Children and Juvenile Offenders Act – Working and Proposed Amendments", no. 7779.

Colonial Secretary Special Bundles

"1904–1908. Public Entertainments Act Amendment – Letters Received", nos. 4/965.2 and 4/966.
"1907–14. Papers re Suggested Legalization of the Totalizator – Letters Received", no. 5281.
"1911–1913. Sunday Trading Papers – Letters Received", nos. 5268–69.
"1914–1915. Sunday Trading – Letters Received", no. 5291.1.
"1914–32. Sunday Trading – Letters Received", no. 5403.
"1910–31. Sunday Sport – Letters Received", no. 5430.

REFERENCE SOURCES

Australian Dictionary of Biography. 3–7. Melbourne: Melbourne University Press, 1966–.
The Cyclopedia of New South Wales: An Historical and Commercial View. Sydney: McCanon, Stewart and Co., Printers, 1907.
Hughes, C. A. and Graham, B. D. *A Handbook of Australian Government and Politics 1890–1964.* Canberra: Australian National University Press, 1968.
New South Wales Legislative Council Consolidated Index. 3–4. Sydney: Legislative Council, 1959 and 1960.
Martin, A. W. and Wardle, P. *Members of the Legislative Assembly of New South Wales 1851–1901.* Canberra: Australian National University Press, 1959.
Moore's Australian Almanac and New South Wales Country Directory and Tourist Guide. 1900–1914.
Sands Sydney Directory. 1900–1914.
Wilson's Authentic Director: Sydney and Suburbs 1906–07.
Serle, P. *Dictionary of Australian Biography.* 1–2. Sydney: Angus and Robertson, 1949.

CHURCH SOURCES

Printed

Baptist

Baptist Union of New South Wales Year Book. 1901–02 to 1914–15.
Australasian Baptist Congress Proceedings. 1908 and 1911.

Church of England

The Brotherhood of the Good Shepherd. Sydney: by authority, 1908.
The Church of England Outlook and Ecclesiastical Gazette for the Diocese of Sydney Nos. 1–14. 1902–1903.
The Church Review for the Diocese of Sydney. A Monthly Record of News, Work and Thought. 1907.
The Church Society for the Diocese of Sydney. The Home Mission: Advent Season Appeal. Sydney: by authority, 1910.
Church Society of the Sydney Diocese, Papers Read at the Conference on Church Finance, Sydney 23 April 1912. Sydney: by authority, 1912.
The Constitutions and Ordinances of the Synod of the Diocese of Sydney. Sydney: by authority, 1908.
The Diocesan News (of the Diocese of Grafton and Armidale). 1900–1908.
Glimpses of the Work of the Mission Zone Fund in the Crowded and Congested Parts of Sydney. Sydney: by authority, n.d.
Official Report of the Proceedings of the Australian Church Congress. 1898, 1902, 1906 and 1909.
Proceedings of the General Synod of the Dioceses in Australia and Tasmania. 1900–1916.
Proceedings of the Provincial Synod of New South Wales. 1900–1914.
Proceedings of the Synod of the Diocese of Newcastle. 1900–1914.
Proceedings of the Synod of the Diocese of Sydney. 1900–1914.
Progress Report of the Executive Committee of the Century Church Thanksgiving Fund. Diocese of Sydney September 1901. Sydney: by authority, 1901.
Report of the Church Society for the Diocese of Sydney. 1900–1914.
Sydney Diocesan Directory. 1900–1914, 1920 and 1930.
Sydney Diocesan Magazine. 1910–1914.
Year Book of the Diocese of Grafton–Armidale. 1900–1914.
Year Book of the Church of England in the Diocese of Goulburn. 1900–1914.

Congregational

Congregational Union of New South Wales Home Mission Board. Annual Reports and Balance Sheets. 1904–1914.
Jubilee of Queensland Congregationalism and Australasian Inter-State Conference, Brisbane-Ipswich, 1903. Brisbane: by authority, 1903.
New South Wales Congregational Year Book. 1900–1914.
Proceedings of the Australasian Congregational Union. 1904–1914.

Methodist

Australian Methodist Centenary Commemoration Committee: Statement and Appeal 1915. Sydney: 1915.
The Laws and Regulations of the Australasian Wesleyan Methodist Church. Revised ed. 1895 with 1897 supplement. Melbourne: 1895.
Minutes of the Conference of the Australasian Wesleyan Methodist Church in New South Wales. 1900–1902.
Minutes of the Conference of the Methodist Church of Australasia. 1904–1914.
Minutes of the Conference of the Methodist Church in Australasia in New South Wales. 1902–1914.
The Methodist Hymn Book. Australasian ed. 1904.

Methodist Ministerial Index for Australia. 1889–1936.

The Methodist School Hymnal. Australasian ed. 1911c.

Methodist Union: A Symposium. Melbourne: 1887.

*Methodist Union in New South Wales: Report of the Federal Council for 1895.
Draft Scheme and Suggested Plan of Readjustment of Circuit Boundaries.*
Sydney: 1896.

*Methodist Union. Report Containing Recommendations and Proposed Basis of
Union of the Various Branches of the Methodist Church of Australasia as
finally adopted by the New South Wales Joint Committee on Methodist
Union.* Sydney: 1892.

*Report of the Sustentation and Home Mission Society of the Methodist Church of
Australasia in New South Wales.* 1902–1914.

Presbyterian

Are We Up to Date? If Not, Why? Facts and Aspirations. Sydney: n.d.

*The Church and Industrial Unrest also The Drift from the Churches. Being a Collec-
tion of Opinion and Suggestions Gathered in New South Wales.* Sydney: 1913.

Committee on Religious Instruction in Public Schools. Sydney: n.d.

Is No-License a Failure in New Zealand? By authority of the Presbyterian Church
Temperance Committee. 1910.

*Minutes of the Proceedings of the General Assembly of the Presbyterian Church of
Australia.* 1901–1914.

*Minutes of the Proceedings of the General Assembly of the Presbyterian Church of
Australia in New South Wales.* 1900–1914.

Presbyterian Centenary Thanksgiving Fund 1899–1902. n.d.

*Report of the Committee of the Federation of the Churches. Proposed Basis of Doc-
trine and Scheme of Polity.* Sydney: 1911.

The Year Book of the Presbyterian Church of Australia, 1903–1911.

Catholic

Proceedings of the First Australasian Catholic Congress 1900. Sydney: 1900.

Proceedings of the Second Australasian Catholic Congress 1904. Melbourne: 1905.

Proceedings of the Third Australasian Catholic Congress 1909. Sydney: 1910.

Manuscript

Papers of the Methodist Church of Australia. M.L.

Papers of the New South Wales Congregational Union. M.L.

Clerical Writings

Albery, F. J. *A Brief Statement With Regard to the Use of The Eucharistic Vestments and The Ornaments Rubric Together with a Few Remarks upon the
Privy Council's Judgement.* Sydney: D. S. Ford, Printer, 1903.

Allen, W. *At Starting: Plain and Friendly Words for Beginners in the Christian Life.*
3rd ed. Sydney: Christian World Publishing House, 1903.

Archdall, H. K. *Mervyn Archdall: A Memorial of the Late Reverend Canon Mervyn
Archdall, M.A.* Sydney: Angus and Robertson, 1922.

Archdall, M. *Liturgical Right and National Wrong.* London: Church Association, 1900.
    . *The Vestments of the Church of England. Not the Vestments of the Mass. An Historical Enquiry.* Sydney: Protestant Church of England Union, 1903.
    . *Analytical Higher Criticism of the Old Testament.* Sydney: W. M. Madgwick and Sons, Printers, 1903.
    . *Murder and the Birth-Rate: or, how to lose life by saving it; and how to save life by losing it: a sermon.* Sydney: Protestant Church of England, 1904.
    . *The Analytical Higher Criticism, Darwinism and the Virgin Birth.* 2nd ed. Sydney: W. M. Madgwick and Sons, Printers, 1905.
    . *Darwinism: The Latest German Criticism of an Exploded Theory.* Sydney: W. M. Madgwick and Sons, Printers, 1906.
    . *The Church and the Churches, or, Church and Churchdom.* Sydney: G. B. Philip and Son, 1912.
    . *The Prayer Book Under Fire: A Word on Romanism and Rationalism.* Sydney: Lancett and Jackson, 1914.
    . *The Gospel in Relation to the Symbolical and the Artistic in Our Worship* Sydney: Lancett and Jackson, n.d.
Ash, W. H. *A Presbyterian Handbook.* Sydney: Angus and Robertson, n.d.
Bavin, R. *Official Address and Ordination.* Sydney: Epworth Press, n.d.
Beale, W. H. *Souvenir of the Official Year of the Rev W. H. Beale; President of the New South Wales Conference 1900–1901.* Sydney: Epworth Press, 1901.
    . *The Bible and the Land; with an Appreciation of Henry George.* Sydney: Samuel E. Lees, Printer, 1904.
Socialist or – What? Sydney: Christian World Publishing House, 1908.
Binns, F. *Annual Report of the Evangelical Council, 1910 and Presidential Address.* Sydney: Evangelical Council, 1910.
Boyce, F. B. *The Drink Problem in Australia: or the Plagues of Alcohol and the Remedies.* London: National Temperance League Publication Depot, 1893.
    . *The Drink Bills of New South Wales.* Sydney: Christian World Publishing House, 1898.
    . *"Shall I Vote for No-License?"* 3rd. ed. Sydney: New South Wales Alliance, 1913.
    . *A Campaign for the Abolition of the Slums in Sydney.* Sydney: Andrews Printing Co., 1913.
    . *Empire Day.* Sydney: Christian World Publishing House, 1921.
    . *Fourscore Years and Seven: the Memoirs of Archdeacon Boyce.* Sydney: Angus and Robertson, 1934.
    . *The New Testament and Intoxicants.* Sydney: W. Andrew Printing Co., n.d.
    . *How the Old Age Pensions Came to New South Wales.* Sydney: William Blanchard Printer, n.d.
Boyer, F. C. *The Romanising of the Church of England.* Sydney: Epworth Press, 1899.
Cameron, J. *Centenary History of the Presbyterian Church in New South Wales.* Sydney: Angus and Robertson, 1905.
Campbell, A. P. *Where's the Harm in Games on Sunday?* Sydney: New South Wales Congregational Union, n.d.
Campbell, C. *"That They All May Be One": A Plea for "Reunion".* Melbourne: George Robertson and Co., 1893.
Campbell, G. *The Drink Traffic: a Social and Political Menace.* Sydney: W. G. Penfold and Co., 1903.
    . *Catechism of Christian Truth for the Use of Congregational Sunday Schools and Families.* Sydney: Angus and Robertson, 1907.

Carruthers, J. E. *Suburban Methodism: A Paper Read at the Sydney Ministers' Meeting.* Sydney: Epworth Press, 1901.

——. *Memories of an Australian Ministry 1868 to 1921.* London: J. A. Sharp, 1922.

Carey, S. P. *Protestants and National Life.* Sydney: Watchman Newspaper Ltd., n.d.

Chapman, J. W. *Revival Addresses.* Melbourne: T. Shaw Fitchett, 1909.

——. *How to Fill an Empty Church. A Statement: A Controversy: and a Reply.* Melbourne: T. Shaw Fitchett, 1912.

Colwell, J. *The Illustrated History of Methodism.* Sydney: William Brookes and Co., 1904.

Cooper, W. M. *The Autobiography and Reminiscences of William Macquarie Cowper. Dean of Sydney.* Sydney: Angus and Robertson, 1902.

Dale, R. W. *Impressions of Australia.* London: Hodder and Stoughton, 1889.

Delany, Bishop. "The Relation of the Church to the Non-Catholic World in Australia". *Proceedings of First Australasian Catholic Congress* (1900) pp. 141–46.

Dowling, P. "Some Dangers and Difficulties of Australian Catholics". *Proceedings of Third Australasian Catholic Congress* (1910) pp. 112–19.

Dunstan, E. T. *The Facts and Fancies of Prior Vaughan and Cardinal Moran.* Sydney: S.D. Townsend and Co., 1895.

Protestant Missions in the Pacific (reply to Cardinal Moran) — Sermon Preached in Pitt St Congregational Church Sydney, 22 July 1899. Sydney: Christian World Publishing House, 1899.

Ellison, J. and Walpole, G. H. S. *Church and Empire.* London: Longmans, Green & Co., 1907.

Feetham, J. O. "Bush Brotherhoods in Australia". *Missions Overseas.* (1915) pp. 27–33.

Ferguson, J. *The Economic Value of the Gospel.* Sydney: Worker Print, 1909.

Fordyce, J. *Some Spiritual Ideals and Aspirations of the New Century.* Sydney: Christian World Publishing House, 1900.

——. *The Religious Outlook and the Duty of the Hour.* Brisbane: Christian World Publishing House, 1903.

——. *Christian Unity.* Melbourne: Walker May and Co., 1904.

——. *Aspects of the Temperance Problem.* Sydney: Christian World Publishing House, 1905.

Forsyth, Rev *The New Congregationalism and the New Testament Congregationalism.* Sydney: William Brookes and Co., 1903.

Fraser, A. *Presbyterianism, Its Historic Place.* Newcastle: T. McLuckie, Printer, 1910.

Gainford, H. *Shadows of the Red Hat: The Papacy in the Old and New Worlds.* Sydney: The Watchman, 1907.

——. *The Sting of the Wafer God; or Papal Porcupine Points.* Melbourne: Fraser and Jenkinson, 1914.

——. *Jesuit Papal Octopus: Jesuit Secrets of How to Get Money and Property.* Sydney: W. H. Beade, n.d.

Gawthrop, B. *New Testament Ideals.* Sydney: Australian Baptist Publishing House, 1914.

Glasson, G. *Pulpit and Politics.* Sydney: Epworth Press, 1912.

Glasson, W. *Socialism and Christianity Opposed.* Sydney: F. E. Moore and Co., n.d.

Gosman, A. *The Federation of Free Protestant Churches.* Sydney: Christian World Publishing House, 1901.

——. *A Catechism on Congregational Church Polity.* Melbourne: Stillwell and Co., Printers, 1906.

Hammond, R. B. S. *The Curse of Drink in New South Wales.* 5th ed. Sydney: H. Bethel and Co., 1903.

Harper, A. *Australian Without God: An Appeal to the Churches of Australia to Secure an Acknowledgement of God in the Australian Constitution.* Melbourne: M. L. Hutchinson, 1897.
———. *In Memoriam: Her Gracious Majesty Queen Victoria.* Sydney: Angus and Robertson, 1901.
———. *Christian Essentials.* Melbourne: Student Movement Press, n.d.
Hegarthy, Dean. "A Plea for a Catholic Truth Society in Australia". *Proceedings of the Third Australasian Catholic Congress* (1905) pp. 592–98.
Henry, J. Q. A. *The Slaughter of Young Men.* Melbourne: T. Shaw Fitchett, 1910.
Holdsworth, W. H. ed. *Baptists and Baptism.* Melbourne: Baptist Union of Victoria, n.d.
Howard, H. *Rally! A Message to Christian Endeavourers.* Adelaide: Hussey and Gillingham, 1905.
Hulme, J. and Stephen, P. J. *The Morals and Manners of Cardinal Moran: The Examination of a Recent Controversy.* Sydney: Christian World Publishing House, 1904.
James, A. S. C. *Young Men to the Front.* Bendigo: Bolton Bros., 1896.
Long, G. M. *Papal Pretentions: A Reply to Roman Catholic Assertions.* Sydney: Church Book Store, 1913.
Macauley, J. *Modern Religious Life.* Sydney: H. J. Dunn and Co., 1908.
McGowan, F. H. "The Rev. W. Woolls Rutledge". *Australasian Methodist Historical Society Journal* 6, no. 17 (April 1938) pp. 287–97.
Macintyre, R. G. *Training of the Ministry: An Address delivered at Ordination Service in St Stephen's Church Sydney 25 October 1904.* Kogarah: D. Christian and Co., 1904.
Macqueen, W. S. *Sell your Coat and Buy a Sword.* Paddington: A. K. Murray, 1911.
Mathison, W. *"Lest We Forget". The Old and the New Century and the Australian Commonwealth.* Sydney: Christian World Publishing House, 1901.
———. *The Cross of Christ and Its Bearing Upon the Life of Christian Men.* Sydney: Christian World Publishing House, 1903.
Matthews, C. H. S. *A Parson in the Australian Bush.* London: Edward Arnold, 1908.
Mercer, J. E. *Social Equality.* Sydney: Angus and Robertson, 1905.
Moran, P. F. *History of the Catholic Church in Australia.* 2 vols. Sydney: Oceanic Publishing Co., 1895.
———. *The Reunion of Christendom.* Sydney: F. Cunninghame and Co., 1895.
———. *Address of the Cardinal Archbishop of Sydney to the Catholic Soldiers of the South African Contingent, at St Mary's Cathedral, 14 January, 1900.* Sydney: F. Cunninghame and Co., 1900.
———. *Address to the Admiral, Officers and Men of the American Fleet. 23 August 1908.* Sydney: Catholic Book Depot, 1908.
———. *The Priests and People of Ireland in the Nineteenth Century. A Vindication.* Melbourne: Australian Catholic Truth Society, n.d.
Osborn, A. R. *Method in Teaching. A Text Book for Sunday School Teachers.* Melbourne: Oxford University Press, 1913.
Patison, W. L. *Congregational Home Missions in New South Wales Oct. 1903–Sept. 1928. A Superintendent's Review and Impressions.* Sydney: by authority, 1929.
Penman, J. *Souvenir of the Presidency of the Rev J. Penman. Methodist Church of Australasia New South Wales Conference 1907–8.* Sydney: Epworth Press, 1908.
Pratt, F. V. *Congregationalism and Union.* Sydney: New South Wales Congregational Union, 1907.
Prescott, C. J. *Pastoral Letters.* Sydney: Epworth Press, 1911.

Pritchard, E. Cook-. *Under the Southern Cross: Incidents and Adventures of Missionary Life in Australia*. London: W. A. Hammond, 1914.

Robertson, W. *Sunshine and Shadow. Sketches of a Western Parish*. Sydney: Penfolds and Co., 1918.
. *Out West for Thirty Years. Notes of a Ministry in the Real Australia*. Sydney: Penfolds and Co., 1920.

Rogers, W. H. *A Memento, Being Official Address, Ordination Charge, and Letter to the Young People, by the President of the New South Wales Conference of the Methodist Church of Australasia, 1904*. Sydney: Epworth Press, 1905.

Roseby, T. B. *Social Unrest: Labour*. Melbourne: Walker, May and Co., 1904.

Rutledge, W. W. *Official Address and Ordination Charge, 1902–3*. Sydney: Epworth Press, 1903.
. *Public Control of the Public House*. Sydney: Epworth Press, n.d.

Sharp, W. H. *The Old Testament and Modern Critics*. Sydney: n.p. 1898.
. *The Crisis at St. James'*. Sydney: Angus and Robertson, 1910.

Slattery, P. "Papal Encyclicals of the Nineteenth Century". *Proceedings of First Australasian Catholic Congress* (1900) pp. 113–40.

Soper, J. A. *Straight Talks: A Bundle of Arrows Meant to Hit*. Sydney: Christian World Publishing House, 1899.

Spence, J. *The Re-union of Christendom, or, Fancies and Fallacies of Cardinal Moran* Sydney: Epworth Press, 1895.

Stephen, P. J. *The Totalizator: Shall We Legalise It?* Sydney: New South Wales Christian Endeavour, n.d.
. *The Microbe of Gambling, or, What Makes It Wrong?* Sydney: Watchman Print, n.d.

Taylor, J. G., Morris-. *The Centenary of Methodism in Australia*. Sydney: Epworth Press, 1910.

Taylor, W. G. *Notes of an Address on the National Recognition of God, Being a Comment Upon a Vote Taken in the Recent Federal Convention in Adelaide*. Bathurst: C. and G. S. White, 1897.
. *Official Address and Ordination Charge*. Sydney: Epworth Press, 1897.
. *Restore the Fellowship of the Church*. Sydney: Epworth Press, 1912.
. *Life-Story of an Australian Evangelist, with an Account of the Origin and Growth of the Sydney Central Methodist Mission*. London: Epworth Press, 1920.

Townsend, W. J. *The Story of Methodist Union*. London: Milner and Co., n.d.

Vaughan, J. *The Commonwealth Blessing*. Ashfield: G. Watson, 1901.

Walker, J. *Some Urgent Church Problems. Address at the Opening of the General Assembly of the Presbyterian Church of Australia, in State of New South Wales*. Sydney: Angus and Robertson, 1902.
. *The King's Business. Practical Addresses on the Work of the Ministry*. Sydney: Angus and Robertson, 1908.

Watsford, J. *Glorious Gospel Triumphs as Seen in My Life and Work in Fiji and Australasia*. London: Charles H. Kelly, 1901.

Wheen, H. ed. *Child Study. The Archibald Red Book: Being Mr G. Hamilton Archibald's Lectures in Australia in 1912 and other Papers*. Sydney: Christian World Publishing House, 1912.

Wilson, R. *System in the Sunday School*. Melbourne: Church of England Messenger, 1916.

Wise, P. W. *Obstacles to Religion in Australian Towns Arising from the Conditions of Australian Life*. Goodwood: S. A. Vestry of the Church of St George, 1907.

Wright, J. C. *Thoughts on Modern Church Life and Work*. London: Longmans, Green and Co., 1909.

Yarrington, W. H. H. *Sermon on the "Royal Priesthood"*. Sydney: n.p. 1904.

"Once for All": The Annual Sermon of the Protestant Church of England Union, Preached 12 May 1908, St Barnabas', Sydney. Sydney: Protestant Church of England Union, 1908.

Sonnets on Ritualism and Other Verses. Sydney: Websdale, Shoosmith and Co., n.d.

NEWSPAPERS

Held in the Mitchell Library and Library of New South Wales.

All Soul's (Leichhardt) Parish Paper 1900–1904.
Australasian Independent 1897–1907 (superseded by *Congregationalist*).
Australian Baptist 1913–1914.
Australian Christian World 1890–1925.
Australian Churchman 1901–1914.
Baptist, 1900–1912 (superseded by *Australian Baptist*).
Bush Brother 1904–1914 (Brotherhood of St Laurence).
Chimes 1902–1905 (Congregational paper Newcastle District).
Church Commonwealth 1900–1912 (superseded by *Church Standard*).
Church Standard 1899–1901 (superseded by the *Australian Churchman*).
Church Standard 1912–1914.
Congregationalist 1908–1914.
Daily Telegraph 1900–1914.
Fairplay 1908–1909 (Liquor Trades Defence Union of New South Wales).
Messenger 1902–1914.
Messenger 1905–1907 (Willoughby and Gordon Methodist Circuit).
Messenger 1910–1912 (Petersham Congregational Church).
Methodist 1899–1914.
Monthly Paper 1898–1915 (Christ Church, St Laurence).
New South Wales Bush Missionary Society Messenger 1907–1914.
Parish Paper 1905–1908 (St Paul's Burwood).
Presbyterian 1899–1902 (superseded by the *Messenger*).
Presbyterian Record 1900–1914 (Upper Manning Presbyterian Church).
Protestant Church of England Intelligencer 1899–1900 (Protestant Church of England Union).
Roll Call, 1900–1914 (Christian Endeavour Society).
St Philip's Messenger 1901–1905 (Church Hill, Sydney).
Sydney Morning Herald 1900–1914.
Watchman 1900–1910 (Australian Protestant Defence Association).
Whitefield Press 1903–1904 (Whitefield Congregational Church).
Worker 1905–1906.

TYPESCRIPTS AND MANUSCRIPTS

Bollen, J. D. "The Protestant Churches and the Social Reform Movement in New South Wales 1890–1910". Ph.D., University of Sydney, 1965.
Broome, R. L. "Protestantism in New South Wales Society 1900–1914". Ph.D., University of Sydney, 1974.

Carruthers, J. E. "A Half Century's Retrospect". Newspaper cuttings. M.L.
Carruthers, Sir J. H. Personal Papers. M.L.
Civic League. Minute Book 1907–1910. M.L.
Colwell, J. "The Church Sustentation and Extension Society". Typescript. M.L.
Colwell, J. "The Passing of a Great Philanthropist: Ebenezer Vickery M.L.C." M.L.
Evangelical Council of New South Wales, "Minute Books 1904–1925". 2 vols. M.L.
Fetherstonhaugh, C. "My Religious Experience". Typescript. M.L.
French, M. "Churches and Society in South Australia 1890–1900: An Exercise in Reassurance". M.A., Flinders University, 1969.
Hamilton, C. "Irish-Australian Catholics and the Labour Party: A Historical Survey of Developing Alignment in New South Wales, Victoria and Queensland. 1890–1921." M.A., Melbourne University, 1957.
Hogg, S. N. "Balmain, Past and Present". Typescript, 1924. M.L.
Jansen, V. M. "The Social Background of the Members of the New South Wales Legislative Assembly 1901–1959". 3 vols. M.Ec., University of Sydney, 1963.
Lane, G. "Press Cuttings". M.L.
Marshall, M. B. "Some Aspects of the Australian Protestant Defence Association. 1901–1904." Govt. III Hons., University of Sydney, 1961.
Nicholas, G. R. Collection of notes, letters and newspaper cuttings on the various churches. M.L.
Phillips, W. W. "Christianity and its Defence in New South Wales 1880 to 1890." Ph.D., Australian National University, 1969.
Stevenson, S. D. "Family Papers 1862–1952". M.L.
Teale, R. "By Hook and By Crook: The Anglican Diocese of Bathurst, 1870–1911". M.A., University of Sydney, 1967.
Watson, J. H. "Church Newspaper Cuttings, 1906–1928". 2 vols. M.L.

OTHER SOURCES

Contemporary

Anonymous. *The Forerunner: Report of Congress on Union of Churches*. Melbourne: Brown, Prior and Co., 1913.
Adams, F. *The Australians: A Social Sketch*. London: T. Fisher Unwin, 1893.
"Anglicanus". *The Anglican Church in New South Wales: Its Position and Prospects*. Sydney: William Brooks and Co., 1900.
Affleck, W. *Reminiscences from Infancy to Present Day*. Sydney: R. Dey, Son and Co., 1916.
Alexander, C. *Alexander's Enlarged Hymn Book*. Melbourne: T. S. Fitchett, 1912.
Arthur, R. *Choice Between Purity and Impurity: An Appeal to Young Men*. Sydney: White Cross League, n.d.
Australasian White Cross League. *Purity Series* no. 1–14. Sydney: by authority, n.d.
    A Talk with a Boy; by a Doctor. Sydney: White Cross League, 1917.
Australian Christian World. *Chapman-Alexander Mission Book of Remembrance, 1909*. Sydney: Christian World Publishing House, 1909.
    Chapman-Alexander Mission Souvenir No. 2 Seasons of Revival. Sydney: Christian World Publishing House, 1912.
Australian Protestant Defence Association. *Official Programme and Souvenir: Anniversary Tea and Demonstration, November, 1904*. Sydney: Watchman Print, 1904.
    Constitution and By-Laws for the Use of Branches issued by Authority

of the Council 25 November 1905. 3rd ed. Sydney: Watchman Print, 1905.
   Respecting Charitable Launderies and Institutions. Sydney: Watchman Print, 1906.

Beale, O. C. *Racial Decay: A Compilation of Evidence from World Sources.* Sydney: Angus and Robertson, 1910.

Britten, J. *The Slatterys.* Melbourne: The Advocate Office, 1899.

Buckingham, W. *Ethics in Business.* Sydney: Samuel Jones, 1905.

Christian Endeavour Society. *Souvenir, Sydney, 1903: Being the Official Report of the Seventh Biennial Australasian Christian Endeavour Convention.* Sydney, by authority, 1903.
   . *Prayer Meeting Topics and Daily Readings.* Sydney: by authority, 1907.

Church Union League. *"Union of Churches": Statement of Creed and Polity Drawn up at Mount Martha Conference November 1904.* Melbourne: Brown, Prior and Co. n.d.

Clark, G. D. *The Good Templar Movement: Its history and Work.* Sydney: by authority, 1928.

Coghlan, Sir T. A. *The Wealth and Progress of New South Wales 1900–01.* Sydney: Government Printer, 1902.
   . *The Decline in the Birth-Rate of New South Wales and other Phenomena of Child Birth: An Essay in Statistics.* Sydney: Government Printer, 1903.

Criss, J. *A Friendly Talk with a Catholic Priest.* Coraki: Richmond River Herald, printer, 1909.
   . *Papal Infallibility Defined; by Rev Father Callanan.* Sydney: Deaton and Spencer, 1909.

Ferguson, R. J. C. *Cardinal Moran's Church in New South Wales.* Sydney: Watchman Print, 1909.

Hoare, B. *Catholics and Crime.* Melbourne: Australian Catholic Truth Society, 1905.
   . "Why Catholics Insist on Catholic Schools". *A Treasury of Catholic Doctrine.* Sydney: Treasury Publishing Co., n.d., pp. 622–36.
   . "Catholicity. The Safety of Our Commonwealth. Some Alleged Dangers Considered". *Treasury of Catholic Doctrine.* Sydney: Treasury Publishing Co., n.d., pp. 603–21.

Hughes, W. M. *Crusts and Crusades: Tales of Bygone Days.* Sydney: Angus and Robertson, 1947.

Jones, C. C. *An Australian Sunday School at Work.* Sydney: Epworth Press, 1915.

Kellog, J. H. and Kellog, E. E. *Social Purity: The Purity Pledge. A Talk to Girls.* Melbourne: International Tract Society, n.d.

Liquor Trades Defence Union of New South Wales. *"Prohibition Abroad".* Sydney: Marchant and Co. Ltd., Printer, 1910.
   . *The Truth about No-License in New Zealand 1910.* Sydney: Marchant and Co., Ltd., Printer, 1910.

MacNeil, H. *John MacNeil: A Memoir by His Wife.* London: Marshall Brothers, 1897.

Mathieson, V. Cooper-. *The Woman's White Cross Moral Reform Crusade.* Sydney: White Cross League, 1904.

Moran, H. *Viewless Winds: Being the Recollections and Digressions of an Australian Surgeon.* London: Peter Davis, 1939.

New South Wales Bush Missionary Society. *Annual Reports, 1900–1914.*

Northcott, C. H. *Religion and Politics.* Sydney: Epworth Press, 1907.

Paul, A. *Professor Andrew Harper's "Recent Criticism" Examined.* Melbourne: Mason, Firth and McCutcheon, 1907.

Rowntree, J. and Sherwell, A. *The Temperance Problem and Social Reform.* 8th ed. London: Hodder and Stoughton, 1900.

Shum, W. A. S. ed. *The Official Souvenir of the Chapman-Alexander Campaigns 1909–1913*. Melbourne: T. S. Fitchett, 1912(?)

Sinclair, S. *Thoughts About Sabbath Schools*. Sydney: Presbyterian Church of New South Wales, 1915.

Smith, F. B. *Sins That Kill*. Sydney: Watchman Print, 1906.

Smith, R. Mudie- ed. *The Religious Life of London*. London: Hodder and Stoughton, 1904.

Stewart, W. A. *Early History of the Loyal Orange Institution. New South Wales.* Sydney: Grand Lodge of New South Wales, 1926.

Temple, W. *Principles of Social Progress*. Melbourne: Australasian Student Christian Union, 1910.

Trollope, A. *Australia and New Zealand*. 2 vols. London: Dawsons of Pall Mall reprint, 1968.

Later

Allen, L. M. *A History of Christ Church St Laurence, Sydney*. Sydney: Finn Bros. Ltd., 1939.

Barrett, J. *That Better Country. The Religious Aspect of Life in Eastern Australia 1835–1850*. Melbourne: Melbourne University Press, 1966.

Batley, A. W. *Soldiers of the Cross: The Story of the Church Army in Australia.* 2nd ed. Newcastle: by authority, 1959.

Bell, G. K. A. *Randall Davidson. Archbishop of Canterbury*. 3rd ed. London: Oxford University Press, 1952.

Bennie, P. "Anglicanism in Australia". *Quadrant* (May 1972) pp. 34–44.

Bollen, J. D. "The Temperance Movement and the Liberal Party in New South Wales Politics, 1900–1914". *Journal of Religious History* (June 1961) pp. 160–82.
. *Protestantism and Social Reform in New South Wales 1890–1910*. Melbourne: Melbourne University Press, 1972.
. *Religion in Australian Society. An Historian's View*. Sydney: Leigh College, 1973.

Cable, K. J. *A Short Story of Historic St James', Sydney*. Sydney: St James', 1963.
. "Protestant Problems in New South Wales in the Mid-Nineteenth Century". *Journal of Religious History* (December 1964) pp. 119–36.

Cahill, A. E. "Catholics and Socialism – The 1905 Controversy in Australia". *Journal of Religious History*. (December 1960) pp. 88–101.
. "Catholics and Politics in New South Wales". *Journal of Religious History* (June 1966) pp. 63–70.

Cannon, M. *Life in the Country: Australia in the Victorian Age: 2*. Melbourne: Nelson, 1973.
. *Life in the Cities: Australia in the Victorian Age: 3*. Melbourne: Nelson, 1975.

Chadwick, O. *The Victorian Church*. 2 vols. London: Adam and Charles Black, 1966 and 1970.

Crowley, F. K. ed. *A New History of Australia*. Melbourne: Heinemann, 1974.

Dale, P. *Salvation Chariot. A Review of the First Seventy One Years of the Salvation Army in Australia 1880–1951*. Melbourne: Salvation Army Press, 1952.

Dunstan, K. *Wowsers*. Sydney: Angus and Robertson, 1974.

Elkin, A. P. *The Diocese of Newcastle. A History of the Diocese of Newcastle, N.S.W. Australia*. Sydney: Australian Medical Publishing Co., 1955.

Evans, W. ed. *Diary of a Welsh Swagman 1869–1894*. Melbourne: Macmillan, 1975.

Evatt, H. V. *Australian Labour Leader. W. A. Holman and the Labour Movement.* Abridged ed. Sydney: Angus and Robertson, 1954.

Firth, S. G. "Social Values in the New South Wales Primary School 1880–1914: An Analysis of School Texts". *Melbourne Studies in Education* (1970) pp. 123–59.

Ford, P. *Cardinal Moran and the A.L.P.: A Study of the Encounter Between Moran and Socialism 1890–1907, Its Effects Upon the Australian Labour Party, the Foundation of Catholic Social Thought and Action in Modern Australia.* Melbourne: Melbourne University Press, 1966.

Forster, C. "Australian Unemployment". *Economic Record* (September 1965) pp. 426–50.

Garrett, J. and Farr, L. W. *Camden College. A Centenary History.* Sydney: Camden College, 1964.

Gregory, J. S. *Church and State: Changing Government Policies Towards Religion in Australia; with Particular Reference to Victoria since Separation.* Melbourne: Cassell, 1973.

Gusfield, J. R. *Symbolic Crusade: Status Politics and the American Temperance Movement.* Urbana: University of Illinois Press, 1963.

Hamilton, C. "Irish-Catholics of New South Wales and the Labor Party 1890–1910". *Historical Studies* (November 1958) pp. 254–67.

 "Catholic Interests and the Labor Party: Organized Catholic Action in Victoria and New South Wales, 1910–1916". *Historical Studies* (November 1959) pp. 59–73.

Hicks, N. "Demographic Transition in the Antipodes. Australian Population Structure and Growth, 1891–1911". *Australian Economic History Review* (September 1974) pp. 123–42.

 "This Sin and Scandal". Australia's Population Debate 1891–1911. Canberra: Australian National University Press, 1978.

Howe, R. "Social Composition of the Wesleyan Church in Victoria During the Nineteenth Century". *Journal of Religious History* (June 1967) pp. 206–217.

Inglis, K. *Churches and the Working Classes in Victorian England.* London: Routledge and Kegan Paul, 1963.

Jackson, R. V. "Owner Occupation of Houses in Sydney 1871 to 1891". *Australian Economic History Review* (September 1970) pp. 138–54.

Judd, B. C. *He That Doeth: The Life Story of Archdeacon R. B. S. Hammond O.B.E.* London: Marshall Morgan and Scott, 1951.

Kane, J. J. *Catholic-Protestant Conflicts in America.* Chicago: Regnerz, 1955.

Kingston, B. *My Wife, My Daughter and Poor Mary Ann.* Melbourne: Nelson, 1975.

Lenski, G. E. *The Religious Factor.* 2nd ed. New York: Anchor Books, 1963.

Lloyd, R. *The Church of England, 1900–1965.* London: S.C.M. Press Ltd., 1966.

Loane, M.L. *A Centenary History of Moore Theological College.* Sydney: Angus and Robertson, 1955.

McCall, T. B. *The Life and Letters of John Stephen Hart.* Sydney: Church of England Information Trust, 1963.

McCarthy, P. G. "Wages in Australia 1891 to 1914". *Australian Economic History Review.* (March 1970) pp. 56–76.

McCaughey, J. D. "Church Union in Australia". *Ecumenical Review* (January 1965) pp. 38–53.

McNeil, J. T. *Unitive Protestantism: The Ecumenical Spirit and its Persistent Expression.* London: Epworth Press, 1964.

Mahon, J. M. "Cardinal Moran's Candidature". *Manna* (1963) pp. 63–71.

Martin, D. A. "The Denomination". *British Journal of Sociology* (1962) pp. 1–14.

Mol, H. *Religion in Australia. A Sociological Investigation.* Melbourne: Nelson, 1971.

Neibuhr, R. *The Social Sources of Denominationalism.* New York: World Publishing Co. 1965.

O'Brien, E. "Cardinal Moran's Part in Public Affairs". *Journal of Royal Australian Historical Society* (1942) pp. 1–28.

O'Farrell, P. J. "Irish Catholicism" *Manna* (1966) pp. 55–65.

. *The Catholic Church in Australia. A Short History, 1788–1967.* Sydney: Nelson, 1968.

. ed. *Documents in Australian Catholic History.* 2 vols. London: Geoffrey Chapman, 1969.

Pearl, C. *Wild Men of Sydney.* London: Universal Books, 1970.

Phillips, W. W. "Religious Profession and Practice in New South Wales 1850–1901: The Statistical Evidence". *Historical Studies* (October 1972) pp. 378–400.

Prior, A. C. *Some Fell on Good Ground: A History of the Beginnings and Development of the Baptist Church in N.S.W. Australia 1831–1965.* Sydney: Baptist Union of N.S.W., 1966.

Ramsey, A. M. *From Gore to Temple. The Development of Anglican Theology between Lux Mundi and the Second World War 1889–1939.* London: Longmans, Green and Co., 1961.

Robin, A. de Q. "Theology and Theological Training in Australia: An Outline Historical Survey". *Journal of the Royal Australian Historical Society* (December 1968) pp. 356–67.

Rodd, L. C. *John Hope of Christ Church. A Sydney Church Era.* Sydney: Alpha Books, 1972.

. *A Gentle Shipwreck.* Melbourne: Nelson, 1975.

Roe, J. "Challenge and Response: Religious Life in Melbourne 1876–86". *Journal of Religious History* (December 1968) pp. 149–66.

Rouse, R. and Neill, S. C. ed. *A History of the Ecumenical Movement 1517–1948.* London: S.P.C.K., 1967.

Rydon, J. and Spann, R. W. *New South Wales Politics 1901–1910.* Melbourne: F. W. Cheshire, 1961.

Summers, A. *Damned Whores and God's Police.* Ringwood: Penguin, 1975.

Swynny, F. R. "Woolloomooloo Methodism". *The Australian Methodist Historical Society Journal* (August 1933) pp. 43–54.

Sydney City Mission, *Presenting Ten Decades: The History of the Sydney City Mission 1862–1962.* Sydney: by authority, 1962.

. *The Tragedy of Human Failure: The Story of the Sydney Night Refuge and Soup Kitchen. What it is, it does, the men it serves.* Sydney: by authority, 1963.

Teale, R. "Party or Principle. The Election to the Anglican See of Sydney in 1889–90". *Journal of the Royal Australian Historical Society* (June 1969) pp. 141–58.

Thouless, R. H. *An Introduction to the Psychology of Religion.* 3rd ed. Cambridge: Cambridge University Press, 1971.

Waldersee, J. *Catholic Society in New South Wales, 1788–1860.* Sydney: Sydney University Press, 1974.

Walker, R.B. "Presbyterian Church and People in the Colony of New South Wales in the Late Nineteenth Century". *Journal of Religious History* (June 1962) pp. 49–65.

"The Growth and Typology of the Wesleyan Methodist Church in New South Wales 1812–1901". *Journal of Religious History* (December 1971) pp. 331–47.

Weber, M. *The Sociology of Religion.* London: Methuen, 1965 (intro. T. Parsons).

White, C. A. *The Challenge of the Years. A History of the Presbyterian Church of Australia in the State of New South Wales.* Sydney: Angus and Robertson, 1951.

Wilson, B. R. *Religion in Secular Society. A Sociological Comment.* London: C. A. Watts and Co. Ltd., 1966.

Yinger, M. *Sociology Looks at Religion.* New York: Macmillan, 1966.

Index